Auto/biography in Canada
Critical Directions

Cultural Studies Series

Cultural Studies is the multi- and interdisciplinary study of culture, defined anthropologically as a "way of life," performatively as symbolic practice, and ideologically as the collective product of media and cultural industries.

The Cultural Studies series includes topics such as construction of identities; regionalism/nationalism; cultural citizenship; migration; popular culture; consumer cultures; media and film; the body; postcolonial criticism; cultural policy; sexualities; cultural theory; youth culture; class relations; and gender.

For further information, please contact the Series Editor:
Jodey Castricano
Department of English
Wilfrid Laurier University Press
75 University Avenue West
Waterloo, Ontario, Canada, N2L 3C5

Life Writing Series

In the Life Writing Series, Wilfrid Laurier University Press publishes life writing and new life-writing criticism in order to promote autobiographical accounts, diaries, letters, and testimonials written and/or told by women and men whose political, literary, or philosophical purposes are central to their lives. Life Writing will also publish original theoretical investigations about life writing, as long as they are not limited to one author or text.

Series Editor
Marlene Kadar
Humanities Division, York University

Manuscripts to be sent to
Brian Henderson, Director
Wilfrid Laurier University Press
75 University Avenue West
Waterloo, Ontario, Canada N2L 3C5

JULIE RAK, editor

Auto/biography in Canada
Critical Directions

Wilfrid Laurier University Press

WLU

This book has been published with the help of a grant from the Canadian Federation for the Humanities and Social Sciences, through the Aid to Scholarly Publications Programme, using funds provided by the Social Sciences and Humanities Research Council of Canada. We acknowledge the financial support of the Government of Canada through the Book Publishing Industry Development Program for our publishing activities. We acknowledge the Government of Ontario through the Ontario Media Development Corporation's Ontario Book Initiative.

Library and Archives Canada Cataloguing in Publication

> Auto/biography in Canada : critical directions / Julie Rak, editor.

(Life writing series)
(Cultural studies series)

Includes bibliographical references.
ISBN 0-88920-478-0

> 1. Canada — Biography — History and criticism. 2. Biography as a literary form. 3. Autobiography. I. Rak, Julie, 1966–   II. Series. III. Series: Cultural studies series (Waterloo, Ont.).

PS8119.A87 2005   920'.00971   C2005-902600-6

© 2005 Wilfrid Laurier University Press
Waterloo, Ontario, Canada
www.wlupress.wlu.ca

Cover image: Michael Snow, *Authorization* (detail), 1969. Instant silver prints (Polaroid 55) and adhesive tape on mirror in metal frame. 55.6 × 44.4 × 1.4 cm with integral frame. © National Gallery of Canada. Image used with permission of the artist. Cover and interior design by P.J. Woodland.

Every reasonable effort has been made to acquire permission for copyright material used in this text, and to acknowledge all such indebtedness accurately. Any errors and omissions called to the publisher's attention will be corrected in future printings.

Printed in Canada

This collection is dedicated to the memory of Gabriele Helms (1966–2004). Her strong support of auto/biographical studies in Canada and around the world endures in her work and in the memories of her colleagues, students, and friends.

Contents 🪶

Contents

JULIE RAK 🍃

Introduction— Widening the Field: Auto/biography Theory and Criticism in Canada

IN THE FIFTEEN YEARS SINCE THE FIRST book collection specifically dealing with autobiography and Canada was published, both the study of autobiography and the study of Canada have changed dramatically. When K.P. Stich wrote the introduction to *Reflections: Autobiography and Canadian Literature* in 1998, international autobiography studies was caught up in debates between humanists and poststructuralists about the referentiality of the subject in autobiography. Only a handful of feminist studies about autobiography had been published. Biography itself, as an area of study, was mostly confined to criticism about an author's life. In Canada, as Shirley Neuman has said, the study of autobiography consisted of taxonomies such as those in *The Literary History of Canada* (1963–), while critical works focused more on autobiography as part of a national project than on the international developments in the field. Neuman describes this as a divorce between nationalist and generic approaches. Furthermore, only two Canadian critics, Susanna Egan and Neuman herself, were working in the area of autobiography poetics during the 1980s, and neither of them was working on Canadian material at the time (1996).

In 2003, the situation in autobiography and biography theory and criticism is quite different. There have been hundreds of books and thousands of articles published in many countries about autobiography, biography, life writing, and other terms that have been coined to describe the representation of identity in non-fiction. This activity collectively has come to be called auto/biography studies.[1] Through the work of Sidonie Smith, Nancy K. Miller, and many others, feminist autobiography theory now constitutes a major contribution to the development of feminist theory and epistemology. Henry Louis Gates Jr, Joanna Braxton, William J. Andrews, and other scholars have made the study of auto/biography central to African-American studies.

Auto/biography studies has also grown as a field, and the International Association of Autobiography and Biography (IABS) was founded in 1999 to provide a regular international conference for the area. There are more than fifteen journals devoted to aspects of autobiography, biography, life writing, and diary writing in at least seven languages,[2] and there are now special series devoted to auto/biography and lifewriting at many academic presses. What Sidonie Smith said in 1987 still seems to be accurate: "Everyone in the universe of literary critics and theorists seems to be talking about auto-biography" (1987, 3).

In Canada, Shirley Neuman and Susanna Egan now have company. As a rough measure of the volume of scholarship now in print in literary studies, the Modern Language Association database currently has more than 350 references for the keywords "autobiography and Canadian" alone, more than twenty for "autobiography and Quebec," and another sixty-five for "life writing and Canadian." Scholars whose specialty is auto/biography in literary studies and the social sciences—including Helen Buss, Patricia Cormack, Valerie Raoul, Marlene Kadar, Patricia Smart, Ira Nadel, Barbara Havercroft, and Julie LeBlanc—have made contributions to the field in Canada and Quebec, as well as internationally.

Why has the field of auto/biography in Canada blossomed so in recent years? There are a number of answers to this question. For one thing, there is more to write about, as authors like Daphne Marlatt, Nicole Brossard, George Woodcock, Michael Ondaatje, and Fred Wah have specifically chosen to write experimental autobiography that, in turn, is receiving critical attention. The recently published *Vintage Book of Canadian Memoirs* includes autobiographical excerpts from more than twenty writers (2001). Clara Thomas's impassioned call for more Canadian literary biography (1976) has been answered by biographers including Sandra Djwa, Elspeth Cameron, James King, and Rosemary Sullivan. Auto/biographical scholarship has expanded well beyond literary studies to new areas such as cyberculture, ethnography, sociology, and history in Canada and internationally, and so now there are more texts and contexts to write about than ever before. This is, in part, because forms of biography and autobiography that are not necessarily literary have helped to make what Leigh Gilmore has called "a culture of confession" in the United States (2001, 2–3), where personal narratives and testimonials in the popular press or on television are to be found everywhere. In Canada, autobiographical and biographical production follows a similar pattern. Television shows such as the CBC's *Life and Times* series make popularized biographies of Canadians widely available in the same format as A&E's series *Biography* in the United States. Political memoirs sell well in Canada, as do memoirs by sports stars and entertainers—even a memoir by Canada's most famous hockey dad, Walter Gretzky, is a solid seller in Canada. As Susanna Egan and Gabriele Helms have recently pointed out, "we live in an auto/biographical age that uses the personal narrative as a lens onto history and the contemporary world" (2002). This in itself is a compelling reason to read, watch, and study developments in auto/biography theory and criticism in Canada, and it is a good reason to publish a collection like this one, since the collection itself shows how this field is developing in Canada.

The study of Canada itself since the early 1980s has been enriched by developments in a number of areas, including communications studies, cultural studies, women's studies, and Native studies. Developments in post-colonial theory, historiography, Quebec studies, Aboriginal studies, and cultural studies have led scholars to "trouble" the idea of Canada as a nation with an unproblematic history, and to foreground nationhood itself as a problem that preserves some forms of injustice. This has, in turn, led to a reconsideration of documents that have either been left out of the historical record because they are by people without power and influence, or that have been seen as unproblematic elements of the historical record. In areas such as women's studies and Aboriginal studies, decisions about what is studied and how scholarship takes place have become part of the deeply political questions that are being asked about the construction of knowledge, and who has access to it. In response, "life writing" in Canada has become a specifically feminist way to find and read texts, such as letters and diaries, as ways in which some women in Canada have expressed themselves (Kadar 1992). Testimonies and published autobiographies by First Nations people about residential school experiences are an important part of the 1996 *Royal Commission on Aboriginal Peoples*, not only as documentation but also in terms of what the rhetoric of these narratives communicates or refuses to communicate to its audiences.

Although Susanna Egan and Gabriele Helms have written several introductions to the area of auto/biography studies in Canada, they have focussed their discussions more on primary texts and auto/biographical practices than on the development of auto/biography theory and criticism, both in Canada and internationally. Since *Auto/biography in Canada* is meant to showcase recent developments in the field and to further the work of auto/biography studies in Canada, the next section will discuss what has happened in auto/biography theory and criticism about Canadian topics or texts since 1996.

Auto/biography in Canada since 1996

Shirley Neuman's introduction to the Winter 1996 special issue of *Essays on Canadian Writing*, "Reading Canadian Autobiography," represented a watershed in the study of autobiography in Canada. In it, she summarizes what kinds of scholarship had been done on autobiography to that point, and makes a strong call for new approaches that would take international developments in autobiography poetics into account (1996, 7). She also discusses the history of the entries for autobiography, biography, and life writing in various editions of *The Literary History of Canada*. For Neuman, these entries range from a consideration of autobiography as an artistic production to separate categories for biography and autobiography in the area of nonfiction. Neuman includes her own entry for volume 4 (1990), which discusses autobiography, biography, and what she called "life writing" to account for diaries and letters, or personal narratives produced by "ordinary" people (5).

Neuman's introduction clearly was written in the aftermath of the battles fought in the Canadian "theory wars," which consumed humanities departments during the 1980s and early 1990s, and summarizes the impact of two collections, published in 1988 and 1992 respectively, in light of these intellectual conflicts. K.P. Stich's collection *Autobiography and Canadian Literature*, which focussed on autobiography as literature and expressly did not call for international theoretical approaches, differed in approach from Marlene Kadar's *Life Writing: From Genre to Critical Practice*, which focussed more on poetics and on life writing as a feminist way of reading personal narrative. Kadar's collection also dealt with narratives that do not fit the category of formal biographies or autobiographies (1992, 152–53). Neuman saw Helen Buss's then recently published *Mapping Ourselves: Canadian Women's Autobiography*, a book that extensively refers to international scholarship in feminist autobiography studies, as an example of successful new work in the area. Buss uses the work of Sidonie Smith, Bella Brodzski and Celeste Schenk, Susan Friedman, and Shari Benstock to argue that the experience of women is excluded by the humanist approach to autobiography, which leaves women's experiences out. She also adds that the poststructuralist approach to autobiography does not take the position of women as othered within androcentric language seriously (1993, 4–5).

Many of the scholars in Neuman's collection also took international issues in auto/biography theory into account, and discussed texts and approaches that were non-canonical. The general challenges to the English-Canadian canon that were underway at the time are discussed here too, including new scholarly approaches such as postcolonial criticism, Native literary criticism, feminist postmodernism, new historicism, and queer criticism. Marlene Kadar's article on multicultural history (1996) and Roxanne Rimstead's article about oral history (1996) brought interdisciplinary approaches to the collection, and discussed non-canonical texts. But, Neuman acknowledges that there are gaps in the collection. She says that the original Call for Papers asked for contributions about media other than print, but the fact "that this call went largely unheard where art was concerned, and fell on completely deaf ears with respect to other media, points to a major and continuing gap in Canadian studies of autobiography" (1996, 7). The lack of response may have been due to a number of factors, but it does point out that, at the time, the study of autobiography in Canada was conceived primarily as part of literary studies.

In their introduction to a special issue on auto/biography for *Canadian Literature*, Susanna Egan and Gabriele Helms mention some additional highlights of auto/biographical theory and criticism in Canada and Quebec that include work about biography as well as autobiography and life writing (2002). They mention James Noonan's collection *Biography and Autobiography: Essays on Irish and Canadian History and Literature* (1993), which has essays about Irish settlers in Canada and problems in biography by Canadian historians and literary historians, and Valerie Raoul's *Distinctly Narcissistic* (1993), which deals with diaries and fictional diaries written by francophone Quebec women and represents the first book-length study of the diary form anywhere in Canada. Other studies of autobiography have dealt with francophone writers in Quebec. Julie LeBlanc and Barbara Havercroft have contributed to the study of autobiography by women in Quebec by editing a special issue of *voix et images* entitled "Effets autobiographiques au féminin" (1996), while the bilingual collection *La Création biographique/Biographical Creation*, edited by Marta Dvorak, contains a wide variety of articles about autobiography and biography by anglophone Canadian and francophone Quebec writers over several centuries (1997).

In both French and English, one of the most important new areas of auto/biographical study in Canada and Quebec has been the development of feminist autobiography criticism, with the study of women's autobiography and life writing by women. The growth of this area, in large part, is because of the early work on autobiography in Canada published in the landmark feminist collection *A Mazing Space: Writing Canadian Women Writing*, edited by Shirley Neuman and Smaro Kamboureli (1986). Many of the contributors, including Helen Buss, Kristjana Gunnars, and Bina Friewald, went on to write about autobiography by English Canadian and Quebecoise women in other contexts. The growth of feminist criticism in auto/biography studies internationally, especially in the United States, has also meant that there has been more theoretical work available to critics working in Canada as, in keeping with the American emphasis, feminist scholarship has focussed more on autobiography than biography. The type of work being done often shuttles between two poles which are more generally part of feminist literary criticism: theoretical work on language, genre, and identity, and the historical recovery of women's marginalized texts. There have been important contributions made by Helen Buss on women's memoir (2001), Jeanne Perreault on feminist "autography" (1995), Barbara Havercroft's extensive work on experimental autobiography and feminist discursive strategies by Quebecois women, and Patricia Cormack's work on activist Rosemary Brown and autobiography in a sociological context (1999). Other feminist work has focussed on recovering women's life writing from archives, including Helen Buss and Marlene Kadar's edited collection *Working In Women's Archives* (2001), which highlighted feminist methodological concerns in research. Recent examples of the recovery and publishing of women's life writing include Kathryn Carter's collection of women's diaries *The Small Details of Life* (2002), Ian MacLaren and Lisa LaFramboise's publication of Laura Vyvyan's 1926 travel journals (Vyvyan 1998), and J.I. Little's edition of Lucy Peel's Canadian journal of 1833–36 (2001). There has also been much feminist work about individual writers in the context of auto/biography studies, including Elly Danica, Daphne Marlatt, Nicole Brossard, Maria Campbell, Dionne Brand, Gabrielle Roy, Anne Hébert, Laura Salverson, Susanna Moodie, Catharine Parr Traill, and Emily Carr.

The growth of auto/biography studies in Canada since 1996 mirrors to some extent the international growth of auto/biography studies. Feminist approaches have dominated auto/biography studies in the international context as they have in Canada, so much so that development of auto/biography criticism and theory in other areas was slow to catch up to the variety and sophistication of feminist critiques. Scholars in other areas have now done so, and it means that in areas other than feminist auto/biography studies or the study of women's auto/biographical production, the field has become too wide to allow for a comprehensive overview of the kinds of scholarship now being done. However, I will provide a sketchy outline here of what I think are the more significant current trends in auto/biography studies in Canada.

One of the most important signs of the increase of interest in and sophistication of auto/biography scholarship has been in the work of Susanna Egan and Gabriele Helms, who have edited two special journal issues devoted to auto/biography. In 2001, Egan and Helms put together a special issue of *biography* devoted to papers from the International Association of Biography and Autobiography conference held at the University of British Columbia in 2000, a conference that helped to galvanize interest in auto/biography studies in Canada. While international in scope, the collection did contain some work on Canada and Quebec autobiography, although Egan and Helms say that they wish they had received more work on non-literary forms of autobiography (x) and note that there were few submissions about the Pacific Rim or First Nations issues (xiii). In their introduction to a special issue in *Canadian Literature* on autobiography (2002), Egan and Helms present a brief overview of auto/biography criticism in Canada, and include a detailed list of contemporary auto/biographical works and trends. They note that there has not been much international interest in Canadian auto/biography, with the exception of an extended discussion in Margaretta Jolly's recently published *Encyclopedia of Life Writing* (2001). They also feel that, while there have been extensive discussions of auto/biography poetics in Canada, much work needs to be done on specific texts, in part because the study of life narrative is closely connected to the cultural contexts in which auto/biography is made. To this end, the four articles and one interview (of Myrna Kostash) in that special issue cover different aspects of auto/biography and identity politics in specific texts across a wide variety of contexts. They include a discussion of autobigraphy in Quebec by Bina Freiwald; the questions of selfhood in Nega Mezlekia's *Notes from the Hyena's Belly*; and various issues surrounding collaboration in "twice-told" narratives about Aboriginal experience. That issue of *Canadian Literature* also answers Egan and Helms's concerns about the need to know about more Canadian texts and to discuss them within its extensive review section, which contains reviews of newly published autobiographies, biographies, memoirs, and works about auto/biography both in Canada and internationally.

Currently, auto/biography studies in Canada which is not overtly feminist in approach falls into two categories. The first is a cluster of studies on canonized texts by literary authors. The majority of published work focusses on Michael Ondaatje's memoir about his childhood in Sri Lanka, *Running in the Family*; Gabrielle Roy's *La Détress et l'énchantement* [*Enchantment and Sorrow*]; John Glassco's *Memoir of Montparnasse*; and Susanna Moodie's *Rough-*

ing It in the Bush. The second category takes a much wider approach, and explores issues that are connected to sets of texts in different areas. In literary studies of auto/biography, these kinds of studies often reflect trends in the study of literature, such as diaspora studies, postcolonial criticism, queer theory and criticism, or studies which highlight issues concerning people of colour. An important example of this tendency is the exploration of issues connected to collaboration and the idea of authenticity in texts by Aboriginal people, including Maria Campbell's *Halfbreed*, George Copway's memoirs, and Linda Griffith's book about her collaboration with Maria Campbell, *The Book of Jessica*. Newer work asks questions about Native auto/biographical production, which either engages or refuses non-Native tropes about the status of oral versus written knowledge and looks into how identity is understood by different interpretive communities (Cruikshank 1998; Wachowich et al. 1999; Ahenakew and Wolfart 1998; Beard 2000). This type of work is moving the consideration of auto/biography by and with Aboriginal people away from literary models which can reproduce non-Native assumptions about what a "good" life story is to an understanding about Aboriginal issues, which makes use of interdisciplinary paradigms about knowledge and cultural production developed in Native studies and in Aboriginal communities.

Another important text for the study of auto/biography in Canada is Susanna Egan's *Mirror Talk: Genres of Crisis in Contemporary Autobiography* (1999). Egan's study is part of the current tendency to consider auto/biography as a set of discourses, rather than as a genre with definable properties. *Mirror Talk* presents autobiography as a genre of crisis, where a crisis in the narrative of an autobiography must be enacted and then, in classic autobiographical accounts, resolved. Egan says that in many contemporary autobiographical texts, crises are invoked which cannot be resolved, which causes her to ask how autobiographical narratives of this kind engage with crisis and are remade by the autobiographer in need. Egan refers to the result as a dialogue that can occur between author and text, text and reader, and internal dialogue called "mirror talk," which is a performative moment that makes autobiography a discourse of self-presencing that can surface in any text, and can result in multiple subject positions (1999, 1–5). Egan includes some studies of texts by English Canadian authors, including Michael Ondaatje, the collaboration of Linda Griffiths and Maria Campbell, and Mary Meigs's *Lily Briscoe: A Self-Portrait*, and she includes the English Canadian film *The Company of Strangers* in her discussion of autobiography, ethnography, and the politics of interviewing.

The growing tendency to view the study of auto/biography as a set of cultural practices in Canada and elsewhere has meant that the field of auto-biography studies is beginning to recognize many types of writing and visual culture as auto/biographical. In turn, ways to study auto/biography which are not strictly literary are beginning to become part of auto/biography studies, and are changing it. One of the most significant book collections in Canada to reflect this trend is Marta Dvorak's La Création Biographique/Biographical Creation (1997), a collection based on a 1995 interdisciplinary, bilingual conference on biography held at the Centre d'Études Canadiennes in Rennes, France. As I mentioned previously, La Création Biographique/Biographical Creation is significant because it includes so much material about French Canadian and Quebecois writers, but it is important for other reasons too. The collection focuses on biographical production rather than on autobiography alone, and generally understands biography to be part of a continuum along which can be found different types of literary or historical biography, oral forms, and literary autobiography (1997, 17). Dvorak begins the collection as most auto/biography editors do, with a mention of the popularity of the genre of biography and discusses the complex relationship that biography has to the idea of truth telling. Dvorak also stresses the importance of biography to the social sciences, particularly in Quebec, with the reemergence of the popularity of historical biography and the study of life writing as part of Quebec's social milieu. As Dvorak says, "biography may thus be seen as an approach to cultural history" (22) but also as theory, which calls into question the stability of generic categories. The essays in La Création Biographique/Biographical Creation reflect this dual focus between cultural history and literary criticism, with its sections on "Theory" and "Literature" containing approaches to autobiography and biography studies found in the humanities; the section "Text and Culture," which combines studies of biography found in history and literary studies; and a section, "History and Society," which has studies of biography, oral history, and autobiography by historians and sociologists working on Quebec.

In anthropology, life history, an area that most commonly involves a combination of oral narrative and biography of subjects, has become part of auto/biography studies in Canada and elsewhere. Before the 1960s, anthropologists used the life history method to "collect" stories from native informants. Life history fell out of fashion in anthropology from the 1960s to the 1980s, when "scientism" discouraged the telling of individual stories and stressed the importance of other kinds of data collection (Reed-Danahay 1997). With the advent of postmodern anthropology and its stress on the self-reflexivity of anthropologists who write ethnography and its questioning of scientific objectivity, life history collection became important once again (Crapanzano 1984; Watson and Watson-Franke 1985; Blackman 1991). Feminist approaches to anthropological methodology also began to change what was thought to be "good" data from a stress on statistical gathering and structural analysis to subjective accounts and participant observation (Cole and Phillips 1995; Behar 1995). One of the earlier studies to take this approach in Canada was Julie Cruikshank's landmark collaboration with Yukon Cree female elders Angela Sydney, Kitty Smith, and Annie Ned, called *Life Lived Like a Story* (1990). This volume connected Cruikshank's reflexivity as a non-Native anthropological researcher who had learned new methods of research from these elders, to methodology from the area of oral history.

New work in auto/biography studies in Canada also includes interdisciplinary scholarship in medicine and literary studies. The upcoming publication of papers from the 2001 Peter Wall Conference at the University of British Columbia, called Refitting the Frame: Narratives of Disease, Disability and Trauma, will bring together considerations of life history, autobiography, and other types of personal narrative from the perspectives of scholars working in literary auto/biography studies, disability studies, and medicine. The papers are about such areas as trauma and narrative, narratives about death and dying, narratives about disability, and the uses (and abuses) of case studies in medical research and treatment.

In Canada, auto/biography studies is not currently a part of sociology, except for isolated studies such as Patricia Cormack's. At least, not yet. In Britain, feminist and materialist studies of auto/biography that include the self-reflexive positions of the researcher are an important part of cultural studies methodology, particularly due to the pioneering work of Carolyn Steedman on women and class, which includes her own experience (1986). Studies by Liz Stanley about feminist epistemology and autobiography that critique postmodernist feminism (1994) are also important, as are the recent essay collections *Feminism and Autobiography* (Cosslett et al. 2000) and *Women's Lives into Print: The Theory, Practice and Writing of Feminist Autobiography* (Polkey 1999), which highlight the material production of narratives by women. In the United States, the cross-disciplinary collection *Haunting Violations: Feminist Criticism and the Crisis of the "Real"* (Hesford and Kozol 2001) seeks to push feminist auto/biography studies away from considerations of genre and takes up paradigms from cultural studies in order to talk about subjectivity, history, and trauma in light of atrocities committed around the world. This collection is significant because it also seeks to move beyond the impasse between much feminist thinking about postmodern critiques of history and experience, and feminist theory which says that experience and history are essential to the political struggles of women (2001, 6–7). As cultural studies develops in a Canadian context, so could auto/biography studies move in this direction, as some of the essays in Auto/biography in Canada indicate is already beginning to happen in the area of social work and which I will discuss later.

Beyond Nationalism: The "Biography" of the Nation

If auto/biography studies in Canada has done what Shirley Neuman thought it should do and become more open to international developments in theory and criticism, why do a national collection at all? There is much that would seem to make the idea of a nationally based collection look a bit quaint. Current trends in the humanities and the social sciences in Canada and Quebec include post-colonial theory and its critique of nationhood as well as diaspora studies, with its emphasis on the permeability of borders that challenge national hegemony. The new field of globalization studies examines the international flow of capital, labour, refugees, and ideas, and looks at how the growth of multinational corporate power has the ability to transcend national borders and to eclipse the power of nation-states, including Canada's. At the same time, Aboriginal intellectuals in Canada and the United States have pointed out that, for many of them, national borders represent impositions on their cultures and histories and that, in effect, Canada is not post-colonial because, for them, colonization has not ended (Weaver 2000). The idea of Canada as a nation has been a difficult one for people living in Canada to work through for a number of reasons. These include both Quebec's difficult position within Canada and Canada's history as a part of the British Empire, a situation that has helped to foster ambivalence about what "Canada" is and what it means to be Canadian. This ambivalence, as Imre Szeman has recently pointed out, plays out in terms of questions about national and cultural authenticity in comparision to other nations who seem to be more authentic, such as Britain or the United States (2000). If the idea of Canadian identity itself were self evident, then I would not be wondering whether to do a nationally focussed essay collection at all.

This is where discourses of auto/biography that are closely connected to the promise of authenticity are, in fact, connected to the idea of nation as a fiction about origins. At the end of Imagined Communities, Benedict Anderson equates the narrating of national origins to the narrating of autobiography and biography because both tend to begin with what cannot be remembered. Since we cannot remember the circumstances of our birth and baby-hood but so many biographies and autobiographies start precisely with this, identity itself "because it cannot be 'remembered,' must be narrated" and be supported by many types of documentary evidence. The "need" for identity, and the subsequent need for biography and autobiography, is like the need for a nation to anchor itself in the fiction of continuous time against the ruptures and social dislocations of modernity itself, and to construct for itself an origin in serial time which gestures toward the future (1991, 204–205).

Therefore, the question of what "Canadian" auto/biography might look like as opposed to what auto/biography looks like in other countries is in fact a fictional question, a gesture to a mythic origin for national character which cannot ever be completed. But the study of auto/biography in Canada high-lights that auto/biography does not need to be read as a type of documen-tary evidence for the growth and development of Canadian literature, culture, or history. The proliferation of auto/biographical narratives may well be what Anderson thinks: part of the so-called "evidence" that bolsters the fic-tion of a continuous national history. Not everyone, however, "in" Canada is "of" Canada, or would consider himself or herself part of a Canadian national project. Rather, "Canada" is both a physical place where auto/biog-raphy is made and a discursive construct supported and at times critiqued by the production of different kinds of auto/biographical works. Therefore, it is important to study how autobiography, biography, life writing, and other types of life narrative are made in Canada without resorting to a nation-alist framework to do so. It is also important to highlight what texts and con-texts do exist in Canada, because, despite the growing presence of other scholars, international developments in auto/biography studies have been largely American, French, and British. Although there are comparativist studies of autobiography, these tend to be produced in countries that were formerly in the British empire, such as Australia and Canada (Dalziell 2002; Egan 2000; Whitlock 2000).

Finally, it is important to do a collection of auto/biography studies in Canada because, despite the growth in research, the area is still seen as marginal to other areas of study. In literary studies, for example, "litera-ture" usually means fiction or poetry. The contributors to an issue of *Essays on Canadian Writing* in 2000 about the future of Canadian literature dis-cussed, without exception, literature as fiction or poetry. In Canadian uni-versities, the novel is the most popular form of fiction studied, to such an extent that I must agree with Smith and Watson that in the classroom, stu-dents "typically... call autobiographical texts 'novels' though they rarely call novels 'autobiographies'" (2001, 7). Although hundreds of reviews appear each year for biographies and memoirs in the popular press, and the Canadian Governor General's Awards have categories for non-fiction, post-secondary Canadian literature courses do not tend to include non-fiction unless it is in the form of travel narrative or is Susanna Moodie's *Roughing It in the Bush*. The term "non-fiction" itself has meaning only as "fiction's" lack, which keeps fiction in a primary position even when non-fiction is discussed. The general tendency in literary studies to look at works by historical period or national grouping means that genre theory, which is central to auto/biography studies, is rarely taken as a primary focus unless the topic is women's or children's literature. Although I have discussed an example from literary studies, auto/biography is also marginal in other areas and disciplines, but for different reasons. In the study of Canadian history, for example, auto/biography is only now beginning to be considered critically, as the gulf between methods where the limits of genre are explored, and methods where biography seems to represent experience, appear in the collection *The La Création Biographique/Biographical Creation* (1997). As I have said, studies of auto/biography in English Canadian sociology are still relatively rare. And so, while Egan and Helms did observe in 2001 that auto/biography studies has come a long way in Canada since 1988, their caution that there is still much more work to be done also remains relevant. With a view to helping to make that new work happen and to contextualizing the work which appears in *Auto/biography in Canada*, the next section identifies some significant developments in the study of auto/biography internationally, and evaluates where auto/biography studies is heading now.

Auto/biography outside Canada: Current Trends in Theory and Criticism

The growth of auto/biography criticism and theory worldwide in the last fifteen years makes it impossible to provide an overview of everything that is happening in auto/biography studies. It is also not possible to enumerate the multitude of approaches currently being used in auto/biography studies since the "battle" Shirley Neuman saw in 1996 between theory and criticism and between postmodern feminist and liberal-humanist approaches ended. Now there are almost as many approaches as there are critics, particularly in literary studies, where auto/biography criticism is beginning to adopt critical approaches from other areas. Where conflict and development in auto/biography studies remains, however, is in the shifts and convergences taking place between disciplinary approaches. As Janice Dickin points out in her rather sardonic review of Buss and Kadar's collection, *Working in Women's Archives*, her point of view as a legal scholar and women's historian differs radically from Buss and Kadar's, even though they all work on collections of women's life writing, and that this difference affects the type of material collected and what is done critically with it (2002). Dickin's mixture of bemusement, interest, and dismay at what she is reviewing shows why it is important to identify some current trends in auto/biography studies not in terms of the critical approaches adopted, but in terms of the changes taking place in auto/biography studies as the result of disciplinary shifts. *Auto/biography in Canada* can and should be read as being in the midst of this changing context in auto/biography studies.

Feminism and Auto/biography by Women

It is not an exaggeration to say that feminist autobiography criticism has had the most impact on the study of auto/biography as a field. Early approaches to the study of autobiography in the United States and France during the 1970s sometimes mentioned texts by women, but as many feminist critics have pointed out, the discourse of representativeness in autobiography criticism was supported by androcentrism in the western world. This discourse meant that critics of autobiography tended to discount autobiographies by women, or they disregarded the importance of gender in the works by women which did get mentioned.[3] Early feminist scholarship sought to bring women's writing into the auto/biographical canon, and it developed what I call a paradigm of failure to account for why they thought so many women before the twentieth century treated their experiences as non-representative, or apologized for their stories and their lives (Jelinek 1980; Mason 1980; Nussbaum 1988; Heilbrun 1988). By the late 1980s, scholars were questioning the paradigm of failure and were beginning to develop a poetics of women's autobiography that principally saw women's auto/biographical writing as exempt from androcentric assumptions about the development of self in relation to an "other." Like scholars in other areas of women's studies, these critics connected androcentrism in culture to androcentrism in discourse, and used aspects of psychoanalysis to explain how women's rhetoric represents women as selves-in-community. By the 1990s, feminist critics of auto/biography had turned to other theories of subjectivity to talk about the politics of genre and gender to stress the importance of the experience of interrelated oppressions based on racial inequality, discrimination based on sexual orientation or, less frequently, discrimination connected to class inequality. These approaches tended to highlight the continuing importance of "experience" as a way to testify to atrocity, while they argued that the genre of autobiography itself was a way to resist oppression through the use of narratives about the self (Buss 1993; Perreault 1995; Neuman 1991; Smith and Watson 1992; Friedman 1988; Benstock 1988). Some feminists discussed gender in auto/biography as a performance in a poststructural sense that was not related directly to experience as a category of knowledge (Gilmore 1994; Bergland 1994; Smith 1995).

The growing concern that white, feminist critics had with other marginalized subjectivities, with their own possible complicity in their marginalization, led to their participation in what Laura Marcus has called "an autobiographical turn" in literary theory, particularly in philosophy and the social sciences. This became a way for feminists to avoid the pitfalls of making "grand narratives" about women's experience, while stressing the importance of local knowledge. Following Nancy K. Miller's call in *Getting Personal* for an autobiographical "personal criticism" to critique the fantasy of objectivity found in patriarchical scholarship (1994), Liz Stanley, in *The Auto/Biographical 'I'* (1992), among others, grounds her readings in what she calls an "accountable knowledge" that combines her own experiences as a working-class woman with her position as a feminist sociologist (210). Carolyn Steedman uses personal experiences to ground her analysis of working class women in a cultural studies context (1986). However, as the editors of *Haunting Violations* point out, the category of "experience," particulary in feminist work in the United States, is still undertheorized. Poststructural feminist approaches have had difficulty dealing with the problem of political agency when the force of narrative causes the "reality" of experience to be questioned, while materialist feminist approaches have not always been critical enough about what constitutes experience and evidence (Hesford and Kozol 2001). Therefore, feminist auto/biography studies is still dealing with the problems of its liberal ideological roots, especially in the United States, where the idea that the "real voices" of oppressed women can be heard and "recovered" for the benefit of those with more priviledge has not yet been critiqued in a rigorous way. Its dominance in auto/biography studies has also meant that other approaches have been slower to develop, with the notable exceptions being African-American studies of autobiography and slave narrative, and Chicano/a or Mexican-American approaches to auto-biography.

Terms and Definitions

One of the most salient features of auto/biography studies is the continuing debate about what autobiography and biography are and how they might be related to each other. While this originally occurred in studies of autobiography by critics like Karl Weintraub, Roy Pascal, and Wayne Shumaker, who were anxious to make the study of autobiography a "legitimate" area of literary study with a definable canon of texts, the debate about what autobiography actually is has marked the work of every theorist and critic who has done research in the area. The term "autobiography" literally means "self-life-writing" in Greek, and has been in use in English since the eighteenth century (Smith and Watson 2001, 1–2). But those three simple words are, as Smith and Watson point out in *Reading Autobiography*, anything but simple (1). Understanding what "self" and "life" mean can involve extensive work in psychology and philosophy, and since the advent of feminist and poststructural theory, which calls into question any easy connections between the act of writing and the representation of someone's self and life, even "writing" is no longer a given. In auto/biography studies, this has given rise to a host of more specialized terms for writing and representation that do not follow the so-called "classic" model of autobiography, which is thought to have evolved from Saint Augustine's *Confessions*, Jean Jacques Rousseau's *The Confessions*, and the autobiographies of other canonized writers such as Benjamin Franklin, Montaigne, and Goethe. I call these "terms of departure," because much auto/biography theory uses these terms to talk about what Caren Kaplan has called "outlaw genres": self-referential types of representation that do not adhere to the "laws" of genre which make the genre of autobiography seem definable and stable (1992). Some of these include memoir, which is understood as writing that combines public events with some private events in someone's life (Buss 2001); *testimonio*, which describes Latin American accounts of atrocity (Beverly 1992); African-American slave narrative; life writing, to describe diaries, letters, and other non-published documents (Neuman 1996) [or, as I have said, a feminist way to read unpublished documents when they are by women (Kadar 1992)]; psychobiography or therapeutic narrative; autogynography as a way to describe women's self-referential writing (Brée 1986); and *métissage* as a cultural braiding of different narrative styles (Lionnet 1989). There are also a host of other terms in other disciplines that describe what Smith and Watson term "life narrative" (2001), including life history and authoethnography in anthropology, oral history in history studies, and trauma narrative in Holocaust studies.

The most recent term to receive wide use is auto/biography, which in its use of a slash highlights the instability of autobiography as a genre, and expresses a continuum rather than an area of absolute difference between biography and autobiography (Egan and Helms 2001). In my use of the term, however, I also want to emphasize that as a genre or even as a discourse, "biography" has received short shrift in auto/biography studies. When biography is discussed, it is most often treated as a subset of autobiography (Smith and Watson 2001, 5–7), particularly when biographical and autobiographical discourse appear in a single work such as Carolyn Steedman's *Landscape for a Good Woman*. While there are book-length studies of biography criticism and theory (Gould and Staley 1998; Reid 1990; Batchelor 1995; Epstein 1991; Edel 1973), there are far more written on autobiography. The shift in the term "life writing" to mean a mixture or continuum of autobiography and biography (Couser 1997) also serves to elide what biography itself might be. Although I do not have space here to explain in detail why this has happened, I can suggest that the "disciplinary capture" of autobiography from history for literary studies facilitated by James Olney and the New Model theorists of autobiography in the 1970s and early 1980s meant that, until recently, biography and memoir were left behind in history studies as subgenres thought to be more about public events than the author's personality or experience (Olney 1980). Moreover, in literary studies, "biographical criticism" did not signify criticism about the writing of biography, but a kind of criticism which connected the events of an author's life to an author's work. In the wake of formalist criticism, biographical criticism went out of fashion. Theorists who have done cutting edge work in auto/biography studies have tended, as a result, to focus on autobiography, which has in turn encouraged the growth of scholarship in that area more than in any other. It is interesting, however, that in the generic classification systems used by bookstores and online bookstores such as amazon.com, "biography" is seen as the same search term as "autobiography" and either term yields up the same results. Since the term "biography" has, in fact, been around longer than the term "autobiography" (Smith and Watson 2001, 2), the priviledging of autobiography over biography in research seems to be more a function of critical preference than a reflection of contemporary practices in book production or even of its critical genealogy.

Auto/biography as Genre, Auto/biography as Discourse

What the proliferation of terms and definitions does say is that there has been a shift from considerations of autobiography and biography as genres with definable properties to an understanding of auto/biography as a discourse about identity and representation. In autobiography studies, there have been many attempts beyond those of Pascal and Shumaker to identify autobiography as a genre, culminating in structuralist studies of autobiography both as a type of performative speech act (Bruss

1976) and as a pact between reader and writer which depends on the text's ability to be non-fictional (LeJeune 1989a). However, almost since the beginning of contemporary studies in autobiography, these attempts have resulted in confusion, since autobiography seems to resist definitions that depend on truth claims, even as it requires them (Marcus 1994). What makes an autobiography truthful and not a fiction? Is it historical accuracy, the successful communicating of the writer's personality or experience, or the expectations of generic fidelity which make it part of a genre? Are genres of necessity closed systems which are always tested by limit cases, or are they really open systems that are able to change (Ongstad 2002)? These rather thorny questions are still part of auto/biography studies, but the urgency about definitions is changing to an understanding of auto/biography as an act (Smith 1995), a set of discourses about identity (Gilmore 1994; Bergland 1994; Marcus 1994), or as practices (Stanley 2000). The growing tendency to think of auto/biography as discursive means that the *genre* of autobiography is conditioned by expectations about the works and the identities of the people who make it. This is how autobiography became one of the institutions that helped to create ideas about the nature of individuality and personal agency in the western world. Thinking of auto/biography as discourse also helps theorists and critics to understand how auto/biography can work in non-literary forms in electronic media like photography, television, or the Internet, or in other forms where selves and lives are represented, such as resumes or court testimony (Stanley 2000).

Auto/biography and Interdisciplinarity

The study of auto/biography has always been interdisciplinary, although its popularity in some "home" disciplines has shifted at times. As I mentioned, autobiography studies in the United States developed intially as an attempt to make autobiography part of literary studies rather than part of history. While this has been partially successful, and has resulted in many studies of autobiography poetics and criticism that use literary models, auto/biography studies has—particularly in women's studies, African-American studies and in the study of diaries and letters—never been purely literary. Recent interdisciplinary approaches to scholarship in auto/biography studies in areas other than sociology include Genaro Padilla's use of auto/biography as part of Mexican-American social history in *My History, Not Yours* (1993); Philippe LeJeune's study of auto/biography and life writing as part of French social history (1989b); Timothy Dow Adams's study of auto/biography and photography (2000); Leigh Gilmore's use of auto/biography theory and legal theory (2003); and Nancy K. Miller's work on auto/ biography and feminist epistemology in philosophy (1994), to name a very few examples.

Auto/biography studies is also becoming part of other disciplines. Two examples are illustrative: the first is that of education, which is beginning to use biography and personal narratives as one of its research methodologies in the sociology of education (Erben 1998; Torres 1998; Hesford 1999). The second is that of anthropology, where approaches to auto/biography studies are experiencing a convergence. For example, Anne E. Goldman's *Take My Word: Autobiographical Innovations of Ethnic American Working Women* (1991) combines methods from autobiography theory and feminist anthropology to look at non-literary texts such as cookbooks. Katherine Reed-Danahay's collection *Auto/Ethnography: Rewriting the Self and the Social* groups personal narratives by the memoirs of ethnic minority groups, autobiography by ethnographers who come from the same group as the one studied, and self-reflexive ethnographic writing as "autoethnography" (1997, 2). Janet Hoskins's *Biographical Objects: How Things Tell the Stories of People's Lives* (1998) looks at how what she calls "personal narrative" in anthropological fieldwork does not necessarily result in "person-centred ethnography," but in stories where objects can be used as metaphors to help give an indirect account of the life of a person or of a community. Both of these examples of convergence are echoed in some of the essays of *Auto/biography in Canada*, which discuss the growing role of auto/biography discourse in social work as a methodology, and as a way of analyzing how people with disabilities and what they know has been treated institutionally, and by able-bodied individuals.

Auto/biography and New Media

One of the newest areas of research in auto/biography studies concerns the representations of selfhood in electronic media. Jim Lane's study *The Autobiographical Documentary in America* (2002) brings together contemporary theory about documentary with auto/biography theory, an interesting move since auto/biography studies and recent documentary theory (Renov 1993; Nichols 1991) are both concerned with the connection of truth-claims and authenticity to the construction of narrative. A recent special issue in the journal *biography: an interdisciplinary quarterly*, edited by John Zuern (2003) and called "Online Lives," was devoted to considerations of various online auto/biographical forms, including the diary form in online weblogs (blogs), the representation of personal biographies on the World Wide Web, and personal home pages as autobiographical presentations. Sidonie Smith and Julia Watson's collection *Getting a Life: Everyday Uses of*

Autobiography (1996) contains some mention of autobiography and confessional discourse on television, but as of yet there as have been few studies of auto/ biography in the mass media. And, as Liz Stanley has pointed out, the introduction to Smith and Watson's collection did not address the politics of autobiographical representation in everyday life in a consistent or highly developed way (2000), although some of the articles in the collection did.

Auto/biography in Canada: The Contributors

The contributions to *Auto/biography in Canada* actively participate in the disciplinary shifts occuring more generally in auto/biography studies, and are part of the ongoing scholarship that is remaking ways to understand Canada. Susanna Egan and Gabriele Helms's "Generations of the Holocaust in Canadian Auto/biography" makes a contribution to Holocaust studies in its detailed study of Canadian-made narratives about the Holocaust that have not received much international critical attention. It also makes a case for considering these narratives as part of auto/biography studies, since a study of them allows the connections between testimony, memory, and narrative to be critically explored. Albert Braz's "The Modern Hiawatha: Grey Owl's Construction of His Aboriginal Self" is concerned with another connection between history, identity, and authenticity in autobiographical narrative. Braz examines Grey Owl's discussions of his identity in his autobiographical writing, and finds that Grey Owl should not be accused of fabricating a Native identity for himself, since his identity claims are often circumspect. Braz suggests that Grey Owl's writings represent an early environmentalism that deserves to be critically read, and that the debates about whether he appropriated an Anishnabe identity revolve around an idea of "pure" Native identity which Native critics and artists themselves do not support.

Sally Chivers's "'This is my memory, a fact': The Many Mediations of *Mothertalk: Life Stories of Mary Kiyoshi Kiyooka*" looks at the complex collaborative circumstances of this text, which was originally compiled by Roy Kiyooka from conversations with his mother, Mary, and then edited after his death by Daphne Marlatt. Chivers sees these collaborations as "mediations" that occur because Mary Kiyoshi Kiyooka is an elderly woman whose stories can be appropriated and manipulated. Deena Rymhs's "Auto/biographical Jurisdictions: Collaboration, Self-Representation, and the Law in *Stolen Life: The Journey of a Cree Woman*" is another examination of the politics of collaborative narrative. Rymhs looks at Yvonne Johnson and Rudy Wiebe's text in the context of legal theory about jurisdiction and testimony. She considers the effect that Johnson's imprisonment had on the type of narrative that resulted in *Stolen Life*, and concludes that the differing narrative modes do not "mask" the truth of Johnson's story even though she worked with a non-Native male writer to tell it. *Stolen Life* represents a "limit case" in Leigh Gilmore's sense (2001), a text that highlights the complexities of voice, authorship, and storymaking when they combine under considerable material and cultural constraints.

The next three essays in the collection indicate that there is a developing convergence between auto/biography studies and social work, although each essay differs in its approach. Ann Fudge Schorman's "Biographical Versus Biological Lives: Auto/biography and Non-Speaking Persons Labelled Intellectually Dis/Abled" looks at what is at stake politically and theoretically in collecting and presenting the life stories of people who cannot make use of conventional ways to communicate. Fudge Schorman asks whether those people, who are often the subjects of certain kinds of therapeutic knowledge as well as the objects of research, can be considered as "knowers" themselves, and be understood on their own communicative terms. In "A Transfer Boy: About Himself" Ljiljana Vuletic and Michel Ferrari discuss a study which is demonstrative of what Fudge Schorman suggests should happen. Instead of using medical models to discuss the background of a boy with autism, they present the autobiographical narratives that the boy tells about himself as a collector of public transit transfer slips. They compare these narratives to the narratives of a friend of the boy's, who is not autistic. Vuletic and Ferrari conclude that these autobiographical accounts show how people with autism do have self-knowledge, and that the medical understanding of autism through such paradigms as "Theory of Mind" is limited. Si Transken's "Creativity, Cultural Studies, and Potentially Fun Ways to Design and Produce Autobiographical Material from Subalterns' Locations" is both an essay about the political empowerment that can come when people who have experienced oppression self-publish accounts of their oppression in a writing collective, and about the part that cultural studies theory and methodology play in Transken's rationale for writing and publishing collectively. Within the area of social work, Transken sees the activity of self-publishing as therapeutic and as a catalyst for political change.

In keeping with the current trend in auto/biography studies to move away from considering auto/biography as generic to auto/biography as discursive, Andrew Lesk writes about the complexities of queer identity in a different register of auto/biographical publishing. By examining the popular memoirs of two Canadian celebrities, the figure skater Toller Cranston and the singer/songwriter Carole Pope in "Camp, Kitsch, Queer: Carole Pope and

Toller Cranston Perform on the Page," Lesk argues that these texts are performances rather than instances of auto/biography as confessional. They were written to reaffirm the status of each performer as a cultural icon, and so their camp and kitsch images serve to create a public politics about celebrity rather than probe their inner lives and motivations. This is true particularly in the case of Cranston, whose references to his sexual orientation are almost wilfully muted in his narrative. Laurie McNeill's "Writing Lives in Death: Canadian Death Notices as Auto/biography" is part of a very recent shift in auto/biography studies towards treating auto/biography as a discourse which surfaces in non-literary texts that are part of popular culture. McNeill sees death notices in mainstream newspapers as instances of community auto/biography that situate their subjects as "simultaneously individual and representative" in everyday life.

The next three essays are concerned with different aspects of auto/biographical writing by women in Canada and Quebec. Barbara Havercroft's "(Un)tying the Knot of Patriarchy: Agency and Subjectivity in the Autobiographical Writings of France Théoret and Nelly Arcan" adds to the scholarship about feminist experimental auto/biography in Quebec with an examination of the diary-fiction of France Théoret and the autofiction of Nelly Arcan. Havercroft also identifies a recurring theme in these works, which she says "haunts" Quebec feminists even after the political gains for women of the 1970s and 1980s were made: the quest for female subjectivity and agency. Yuko Yamade discusses the work of another Quebecois writer of autofiction, Régine Robin, in "Auto/Bio/Fiction in Migrant Woman's Writings in Québec: Régine Robin's La Québécoite and L'immense fatigue des pierres." Yamade discusses Robin as an immigrant writer in Quebec society who writes about her experiences of hybridity in what she terms a new genre, "bio-fiction," and about an identity she invents, "cyber-soi," which locates her as a hybrid subject simultaneously inside and outside Quebec culture. Wendy Roy's "'The ensign of the mop and the dustbin': The Maternal and the Material in Autobiographical Writings by Laura Goodman Salverson and Nellie McClung" looks at Laura Salverson's text as an account which deserves to be better known than it is for its feminist discussions of poverty and class division in Canada. Roy contrasts the discussions of immigrant poverty in Salverson's autobiography to the autobiography of her friend and mentor, Nellie McClung, whose discussion of similar issues is marked by her middle-class background, and concludes that Salverson's text "continues to undermine her purported adherence to literary conventions, and assert instead her awakening to political consciousness."

Polemical Conclusion: Where Will Auto/biography Studies Head Now?

The essays in *Auto/biography in Canada* demonstrate that current scholarship in auto/biography studies has been marked by international theoretical concerns in areas inside and outside the field, and that scholarly work in Canada on classic texts and on auto/biographical discourse in a number of forms has developed far beyond what Shirley Neuman called the "scant previous work in Canadian autobiography" in 1996. No collection can be definitive, and so there are many areas, including art history and electronic media, that are not represented here. But *Auto/biography in Canada* is meant to be a continuance of what earlier collections have begun, and so it does contain sophisticated multidisciplinary work from many perspectives about the theory, criticism, and practice of self, community, and representation in Canada that widens the field of auto/biography studies in this country, and internationally.

However, there are some directions where I think that auto/biography scholarship in Canada will head, and there some places where I hope that auto/biography scholarship does not go. In the 1990s, auto/biography scholarship in Britain and the United States was characterized by something that I do not want it to lose. The area had many theorists who discussed auto/biography as a way to work through the impasse between political agency and poststructuralist approaches to subjectivity and language. Many of these theorists were North American feminists who were passionate about making work by women, especially women of colour, well known, and who saw their work as part of the broader political work in women's studies. Auto/biography studies seemed to be a place where "life writing," as Marlene Kadar hoped, could be a critical strategy for reading as well as a generic marker for discredited texts. In literary studies now, however, auto/biography theory is all too often treated as if it were "finished," so that debates about subjectivity and politics are not mentioned in criticism all that often, and auto/biographical texts are treated as something which can simply be close-read. The politics of many auto/biographical works becomes blunted when auto/biography is treated as a genre with definable properties, and not as a dynamic field of production which has much to say about what selfhood is, and how the world works. Today, I see the same energy and commitment of those earlier feminists and cultural critics in the work of Pauline Polkey, Liz Stanley, and other working class feminists in England who are interested in talking about auto/biography as a political strategy which informs their research methodologies. I also see it in cultural studies, in work on trauma and culture, which moves discussions away from classic autobiographical texts and into non-literary areas, like the collection *Haunting Violations* (Hesford and Kozol 2001), Leigh Gilmore's work on auto/biography and trauma (2000), or Cynthia Franklin's and Laura Lyon's special issue of *biography* on life writing and testimony (2004). These efforts bring together ideas about the ethics of self-representation and the politics of the "real" example or "experience" in ethically aware ways. As the study of non-fiction discourse, auto/biography studies can be an effective way to engage with ideas about truth, representation and power in a broader social sense. Examinations of non-literary forms of auto/biography as well as auto/biography in its mass marketed form could be examined as part of popular culture and cultural studies and not just mentioned in critical introductions. Finally, as an interdisciplinary area of study, I hope that auto/biography studies retains the productive tension it has fostered between different approaches to the study of identity, the politics of methodology and the politics of truth claims in a genre. The practice of auto/biography is something that shapes how people see themselves as they help to shape it. In the best of all possible worlds, the theory and criticism of auto/biography will remain responsive to auto/biography in all its complexity.

Notes

1 "Auto/biography" as a term expresses several things at once. It is a way to talk about biography and autobiography as interrelated genres (Smith and Watson 2001, 184–85). It also expresses the idea that the generic lines between autobiography and biography are often blurry in practice, and that in fact the generic distinctions are more properly expressed as discursive currents (Marcus 1994; Stanley 2000). There are other ways to describe autobiography and biography together; I will discuss them later on this introduction.

2 See the website *autopacte* by Philippe LeJeune < http://www.autopacte.org > and The Center for Biographical Research at the University of Hawai'i, Manoa < http://www.hawaii.edu /biograph/ >, for a listing of resources in auto/biography studies.

3 For a discussion of androcentrism and autobiography criticism, see Smith (1987); Brodski and Schenk (1988); Marcus (1994).

References

Adams, T. Dow. 2000. *Light writing and life writing: Photography in autobiography.* Chapel Hill: North Carolina Univ. Press.

Ahenakew, F., and H.C. Wolfhart, eds. and trans. 1998. *Kôhkominawak otâcimowiniwâwa/Our grandmothers' lives as told in their own words.* Regina, SK: Canadian Plains Research Centre, Univ. of Regina.

Anderson, B. 1991. *Imagined communities: Reflections on the origin and spread of nationalism.* Revised edition. London, UK: Verso.

Batchelor, J., ed. 1995. *The art of literary biography.* New York: Oxford Univ. Press.

Beard, L. 2000. Giving voice: Autobiographical/testimonial literature by first nations women of British Columbia. *Studies in American Indian Literatures* 12 (Fall): 64–83.

Behar, R. Introduction: Out of exile. In *Women writing culture*, ed. Ruth Behar and Deborah Gordon, 1–32. Berkeley and Los Angeles: Univ. of California Press, 1995.

Benstock, S. 1988. Authorizing the autobiographical. In *The private self: Theory and practice of women's autobiographical writings*, ed. Shari Benstock, 10–33. Chapel Hill: Univ. of North Carolina Press.

Bergland, B. 1994. Postmodernism and the autobiographical subject: Reconstructing the "Other." In *Autobiography and post-modernism*, ed. Kathleen Ashley, Leigh Gilmore, and Gerald Peters, 130–66. Amherst: Univ. of Massachussetts Press.

Beverly, J. 1992. The margin at the center: On *testimonio* (testimonial narrative). In *De/colonizing the subject: The politics of gender in women's autobiography*, ed. Sidonie Smith and Julia Watson, 91–114. Minneapolis: Minnesota Univ. Press.

Blackman, M.B. 1991. The individual and beyond: Reflections of the life history process. *Anthropology and Humanism Quarterly* 16(2): 56–62.

Breé, G. 1986. Autogynography. *Southern Review* 22(2): 223–45.

Brodzki, Bella, and Celeste Schenk. 1988. Intro. to *Life/Lines: Theorizing women's autobiography*, ed. Bella Brodzki and Celeste Schenck. Ithaca, NY: Cornell Univ. Press.

Bruss, E.W. 1976. *Autobiographical acts: The changing situation of a literary genre.* Baltimore: Johns Hopkins Univ. Press.

Buss, H.M. 1993. *Mapping ourselves: Canadian women's autobiography.* Montreal and Kingston: McGill-Queen's Univ. Press.

———. 2002. *Repossessing the world: Reading memoirs by contemporary women.* Waterloo, ON: Wilfrid Laurier Univ. Press.

Buss, H.M., and M. Kadar, eds. 2001. *Working in women's archives: Researching women's private literature and archival documents.* Waterloo, ON: Wilfrid Laurier Univ. Press.

Carter, K., ed. 2002. *The Small details of life: Twenty diaries by women in Canada, 1830–1996.* Toronto: Univ. of Toronto Press.

Cole, S., and L. Phillips, eds. 1995. *Ethnographic feminisms: Essays in anthropology.* Ottawa: Carleton Univ. Press.

Crapanzano, V. 1984. Life-Histories. *American Anthropologist* 86: 953–60.

Cormack, P. 1999. Making the sociological promise: A case study of Rosemary Brown's autobiography. *Canadian Review of Sociology and Anthropology* 26(3): 355–69.

Cosslett, T. et al., eds. 2000. *Feminism and autobiography: Texts, theories, methods.* London and New York: Routledge.

Couser, G.T. 1997. *Recovering Bodies: Illness, Disability, and Life-Writing.* Wisconsin studies in American autobiography. Madison: Univ. of Wisconsin Press.

Cruikshank, J. et al. 1990. *Life lived like a story: Life stories of three Yukon native elders.* Lincoln: Univ. of Nebraska Press.

Cruikshank, J. 1998. *The social life of stories: Narrative and knowledge in the Yukon Territory.* Vancouver: Univ. of British Columbia Press.

Danahay-Reed, D. 1997. Intro. To *Auto/ethnography: Rewriting the self and the social,* ed. Deborah Danahay-Reed. New York: Berg.

Dalziell, R. 2002. Intro. to *Selves crossing cultures: Autobiography and globalization,* ed. Rosemary Dalziell. Melbourne: Australia Scholarly Publishing.

Dickin, J. 2002. Review of *Working in women's archives: Researching women's private literature and archival documents,* ed. H.M. Buss and M. Kadar. In *biography: an interdisciplinary quarterly* 25 (Summer): n.p.

Dvorak, M., ed. 1997. *La creation biographique/Biographical creation.* Rennes, FR: Presses universitaires de Rennes.

Edel, L. 1973. *Literary biography.* Bloomington: Indiana Univ. Press.

Egan, S. 1999. *Mirror talk: Genres of crisis in contemporary autobiography.* Chapel Hill: Univ. of North Carolina Press.

Egan, S., and G. Helms. 2001. Introduction, in Autobiography and changing identities, ed. Susanna Egan and Gabrielle Helms. Special issue, *biography: an interdisciplinary quarterly* 24 (Winter): ix–xx.

———. 2002. Introduction in Auto/biography? Yes. But Canadian? ed. Susanna Egan and Gabrielle Helms. Special issue, *Canadian Literature* 172 (Spring): 5–16.

Epstein, W.H., ed. 1991. *Contesting the subject: Essays in the postmodern theory and practice of biography and biographical criticism.* West Lafayette, IN: Purdue Univ. Press.

Erben, M., ed. 1998. *Biography and education: A reader.* London, Bristol, PA: Falmer.

Fetherling, G., ed. 2001. *The Vintage book of Canadian memoirs.* Toronto: Vintage Canada.

Franklin, Cynthia, and Laura E. Lyons. 2004: Personal effects: The testimonial uses of life writing. Special issue, *biography: an interdisciplinary quarterly* 27 (Winter): v–xxii.

Friedman, S.S. 1988. Women's autobiographical selves: Theory and practice. In *The private self: Theory and practice of women's autobiographical writings,* ed. Shari Benstock, 34–62. Chapel Hill: Univ. of North Carolina Press.

Gilmore, L. 1994. *Autobiographics: A feminist theory of women's self-representation.* Ithaca, NY: Cornell Univ. Press.

———. 2001. *The limits of autobiography: Trauma and testimony.* Ithaca, NY: Cornell Univ. Press.

———. 2003. Jurisdictions: I, Rigoberta Menchú, The Kiss, and scandalous self-representation in the age of memoir and trauma. *Signs: Journal of Women in Culture & Society* 28 (Winter): 695–719.

Goldman, A.E. 1996. *Take my word: Autobiographical innovations of ethnic American working women.* Berkeley and Los Angeles: Univ. of California Press.

Gould, W., and T. Staley, eds. 1998. *Writing the lives of writers.* Houndmills, UK: Macmillan.

Havercroft, B., and J. LeBlanc, eds. 1996. Effets autobiographiques au féminin. *Voix et Images* 22: 1–64.

Hesford, W. 1999. *Framing identity: Autobiography and the politics of pedagogy.* Minneapolis: Univ. of Minnesota Press.

Hesford, W., and W. Kozol. 2001. *Haunting violations: Feminist criticism and the crisis of the "real."* Urbana and Chicago: Univ. of Illinois Press.

Jelinek, E., ed. 1980. *Women's autobiography: Essays in criticism.* Bloomington: Indiana Univ. Press.

Jolly, M., ed. 2001. *Encyclopedia of life writing: Autobiographical and biographical forms.* Chicago: Fitzroy Dearborn.

Kadar, M. 1992. Whose life is it anyway? Out of the bathtub and into the narrative. In *Essays on life writing: From genre to critical practice.* Toronto: Univ. of Toronto Press: 152–61.

———. 1996. The discourse of ordinariness and "multicultural history." *Essays on Canadian Writing* 60 (Winter): 119–38.

Kaplan, C. 1992. Resisting autobiography: Out-law genres and transnational feminist subjects. In *De/colonizing the subject: The politics of gender in women's autobiography,* ed. Sidonie Smith and Julia Watson, 115–38. Minneapolis: Minnesota Univ. Press.

LeJeune, P. 1989a. The autobiographical pact. In *On autobiography,* ed. Paul John Eakin. Trans. Katherine Leary, 119–37. Minneapolis: Univ. of Minnesota Press.

———. 1989b. The autobiography of those who do not write. In *On autobiography.* ed. Paul John Eakin. Trans. Katherine Leary, 185–215. Minneapolis: Univ. of Minnesota Press.

Lane, J. 2002. *The autobiographical documentary in America.* Madison: Univ. of Wisconsin Press.

Lionnet, F. 1989. *Autobiographical voices: Race, gender, self-portraiture.* Ithaca, NY: Cornell Univ. Press.

Little, J.I., ed. 2001. *Love strong as death: Lucy Peel's Canadian journal, 1833–1836.* Waterloo, ON: Wilfrid Laurier Univ. Press.

MacLaren, I.S., and L. LaFramboise, eds. 1998. *The ladies, the Gwich'in, and the rat: Travels on the Athabasca, Mackenzie, Rat, Porcupine, and Yukon Rivers in 1926.* Edmonton: Univ. of Alberta Press.

Marcus, L. 1994. *Auto/biographical discourses: Theory, criticism, practice.* Manchester, UK: Manchester Univ. Press.

———. 1995. Autobiography and the politics of identity. *Current Sociology* 43(2–3): 41–52.

Mason, Mary G. 1980. The other voice: Autobiographies of women writers. In *Autobiography: Essays theoretical and critical,* ed. James Olney, 207–35. Princeton, NJ: Princeton Univ. Press.

Miller, N.K. 1994. Representing others: Gender and the subject of autobiography. *Differences: A Journal of Feminist Cultural Studies* 6(1): 1–27.

Neuman, S., and S. Kamboureli, eds. 1986. *A mazing space: Writing Canadian women writing.* Edmonton, AB: Longspoon.

Neuman, S. 1991. Autobiography and questions of gender: An introduction. In *Autobiography and questions of gender*. 1–11. London, UK: Frank Cass.

———. 1996. Introduction: Reading Canadian autobiography. In Reading Canadian Autobiography. Special issue, *Essays on Canadian Writing* 60 (Winter): 1–13.

Nichols, B., ed. 1991. *Representing reality*. Bloomington: Indiana Univ. Press.

Noonan, J., ed. 1993. *Biography and autobiography: Essays on Irish and Canadian history and literature*. Ottawa: Carleton Univ. Press.

Nussbaum, Felicity. 1988. Eighteenth-century women's autobiographical commonplaces. In *The private self: Theory and practice of women's autobiographical writings*, ed. Shari Benstock, 147–71. Chapel Hill: Univ. of North Carolina Press.

Olney, J. 1980. Intro. to *Autobiography: Essays theoretical and critical*, ed. James Olney. Princeton, NJ: Princeton Univ. Press.

Ongstad, S. 2002. Genres: From static, closed, extrinsic, verbal dyads to dynamic, open, intrinsic, semiotic triads. In *The rhetoric and ideology of genre: Strategies for stability and change*, ed. Richard Coe, Lorelei Lingard, and Tatiana Teslenko, 297–320. Cresskill, NJ: Hampton Press.

Padilla, G. 1993. *My history, not yours: The formation of Mexican American autobiography*. Milwaukee: Univ. of Wisconsin Press.

Perreault, J. 1995. *Writing selves: Contemporary feminist autography*. Minneapolis: Univ. of Minnesota Press.

Polkey, P., ed. 1999. *Women's lives into print: The theory, practice and writing of feminist auto/biography*. New York: Palgrave.

Raoul, V. 1993. *Distinctly narcissistic: Diary fiction in Quebec*. Toronto: Univ. of Toronto Press.

Raoul, V. et al., eds. *Refitting the frame: Narratives of disease, disability and trauma*. Forthcoming.

Reid, B.L. 1990. *Necessary lives: Biographical reflections*. Columbia: Univ. of Missouri.

Renov, M., ed. 1993. *Theorizing documentary*. New York and London: Routledge.

Rimstead, R. 1996. Mediated lives: Oral histories and cultural memory. In Reading Canadian Autobiography. Special issue, *Essays on Canadian Writing* 60 (Winter): 139–65.

Smith, S. 1987. *A poetics of women's autobiography: Marginality and the fictions of self-representation*. Bloomington: Indiana Univ. Press.

———. 1995. Performativity, autobiographical practice, resistance. *a/b: Auto/Biography Studies* 10 (Spring): 17–33.

Smith, S., and J. Watson. 1992. Introd. to *De/colonizing the subject: The politics of gender in women's autobiography*, ed. Sidonie Smith and Julia Watson, xiii–xxxi. Minneapolis: Univ. of Minnesota Press.

———. 1996. Introd. to *Getting a life: Everyday uses of autobiography*, ed. Sidonie Smith and Julia Watson. Minneapolis: Univ. of Minnesota Press.

———. 2001. *Reading autobiography: A guide for interpeting life narratives*. Minneapolis: Univ. of Minnesota Press.

Stanley, L. 1992. *The Auto/biographical "I": The theory and practice of feminist auto/biography*. Manchester, UK: Manchester Univ. Press.

———. 1994. The knowing because experiencing subject: Narratives, lives and autobiography. In *Knowing the difference: Feminist perspectives in epistemology*, ed. Kathleen Lennon and Margaret Whitford, 132–48. London: Routledge.

———. 2000. From "self-made women" to "women's made-selves"? Audit selves, simulation and surveillance in the rise of public woman. In *Feminism and autobiography: Texts, theories methods*, ed. Tess Cosslett, Celia Lury, and Penny Summerfield, 40–60. London and New York: Routledge.

Steedman, C. 1986. *Landscape for a good woman: A story of two lives*. New Brunswick, NJ: Rutgers Univ. Press.

Stich, K.P. 1988. Introduction. In *Reflections: Autobiography and Canadian literature*. Ottawa: Univ. of Ottawa Press: ix–xii.

Szeman, I. 2000. Belated or isochronic? Canadian writing, time and globalization. *Essays on Canadian Writing* 71: 186–94.

Thomas, C. 1976. Biography. *The literary history of Canada: Canadian literature in English*, ed. Carl F. Klinck et al. 2nd ed., vol. 3. Toronto: Univ. of Toronto Press.

Torres, C.A., ed. 1998. *Education, power and personal biography: Dialogues with critical educators*. London and New York: Routledge.

Wasowich, N., with Apphia Agalakti Awa, Rhoda Kaukjak Katsak, and Sandra Pikujak Katsak. 1999. *Saqiyuk: Stories from the lives of three Inuit women*. Montreal and Kingston: McGill-Queen's Univ. Press.

Watson, L.C., and M. Watson-Franke. 1985. *Interpreting life histories: An anthropological inquiry*. New Brunswick, NJ: Rutgers Univ. Press.

Weaver, J. 2000. Indigenousness and indigeneity. In *A companion to postcolonial studies*, ed. Henry Schwarz and Sangeeta Ray, 221–35. Malden, MA: Blackwell.

Whitlock, G. 2000. *The intimate empire: Reading women's autobiography*. New York: Cassell.

Zuern, J. 2003. Introduction to online lives. *biography: an interdisciplinary quarterly* 26 (Spring): 1–21.

SUSANNA EGAN 🪶
and GABRIELE HELMS

Generations of the Holocaust in Canadian Auto/biography[1]

I am their priceless heirloom
Hidden from murderers
Where it could not be found.
I am their surviving words.
—*Endre Farkas*

WRITING ABOUT AUSCHWITZ IN HIS BOOK *Bialystok to Birkenau*, Michel Mielnicki thinks it "safe to assume the reader will have already a sufficient idea of its location, physical layout, the nature of the ss régime, etc." (2000, 142). Auto/biographers who write of Holocaust experiences enter a rich literature and suffer from a curious tension. On the one hand, stories like their own already exist and are well known; they even build on information in other stories. Anita Mayer in *One Who Came Back* (1981), for example, writes of sharing a bunk with Margot and Anne Frank, and of depending on the kindness of Mrs. Frank. On the other hand, each personal story memorializes very particular people and works through very personal trauma. John Munro, who worked closely with Michel Mielnicki, acknowledges this memorial quality in his epilogue to *Bialystok to Birkenau*, when he refers to Mielnicki's lost family as a way to explain the energy and ambition with which Mielnicki began life again after the war: "He was, after all, the son of Chaim Mielnicki" (228). With reference to Mielnicki's profound depression and to the nightmares from which they both suffered while working on this project, Munro adds, "Fortunately, I do not ever have to do another Holocaust story. Michel, on the other hand, will never escape from the one recorded in these pages" (233–34). Given that the ss intended neither Jews nor Jewish stories to survive,[2] every narrative provides remarkable witness and contributes to whatever can be understood of the whole experience. Each story also bears witness to the courage involved in survival and narration, the appalling difficulty being all too apparent in the number of suicides by those who told their stories, like Jean Améry, Tadeusz Borowski, and Primo Levi, to name just a few well-known instances.

Our questions begin here. As we approach the sixtieth anniversary of the end of the Second World War, we reflect on the changes in public memory of the Holocaust. The urgent collection of survivors' stories and the public memorials and exhibitions, both religious and secular, occur in a wide range of media. Archive building, conferences, and projects such as the Yale and Spielberg video projects ensure that materials are available and that the community has access to them. Television documentaries, popular films, and the media attention frequently paid to individuals (survivors, righteous Gentiles, Holocaust deniers, and those accused of war crimes) develop public memory, and ensure a Holocaust-conscious culture for the beginning of the twenty-first century.[3] Despite Theodor Adorno's famous statement, originally made in 1951, "nach Auschwitz ein Gedicht zu schreiben, ist barbarisch" [To write poetry after Auschwitz is barbaric] (1977, 30), many and varied forms of witness and response continue to figure prominently in public memory, including novels, fictional autobiography, poetry, and drama. However, auto/biographical genres in particular provide the primary narratives for those who survived and those who did not, and affect the narratives of those who came after. Given the risk that stories will be lost as survivors become old and die, we wonder about the role that auto/biography plays in how people today (should) come to know about the Holocaust.

For several reasons, we will confine our analyses to Canadian auto/biographies available in English.[4] First, we are concerned with inserting Canadian auto/biographies into a discussion of Holocaust writing that is, inevitably, international, but in which the specifically Canadian component tends to be lost. We also seek to open discussion within Canada on the nature and role of specifically Canadian memoirs; whereas much has been written on Jewish Canadian writing, its distinctive Jewishness, its relations with the Holocaust, and its significant value to Canadian literature (see, for example, Michael Greenstein [1989], Alexander Hart [1996], and Norman Ravvin [1997]), very little has been done with the auto/biographical materials themselves beyond the massive and ongoing task of assembling and publishing them. Within our exclusively Canadian focus, we recognize that immigrants frequently stayed in other countries before coming to Canada, or came to Canada entirely by chance. We do not, therefore, assume that immigrants deliberately chose Canada, which Eva Hoffman in *Lost in Translation* (1989), for example, found bleak and soulless, but rather that their stories over the past few decades have been important for shaping Canadian understanding of the Holocaust. The displacements of Europe's surviving Jews were so arbitrary that their auto/biographies necessarily contribute to a literature that is international in character. Further, as Marlene Kadar reminds us, "it is hard to separate out the writing according to the country that hosted the survivor—much about 'Canada' would really be about 'Hungary,' for example."[5] Nonetheless, a focus on Canada may enable us to consider, first, whether Jewish refugees faced particular conditions in Canada that affected their writing about the Holocaust and, second, what impact generations of Holocaust writing have had on Canadian literature, culture, and public memory.[6]

Given their moral weight, Holocaust auto/biographies have long been read as "non-literature," as psychological and/or historical documents; in fact, such witness testimony was considered "a new sacred text" in the 1960s and 1970s when it began to emerge (Berger 1990, 98). The content of Holocaust auto/biographies seemed to foreclose critical analysis; their importance lay in their proximity to historical writing, for their writers could claim authenticity and legitimacy. Lawrence Langer's *The Holocaust and the Literary Imagination* was one of the first major studies to examine the literature of the Holocaust critically, and to explore what he called in his study of fiction and poetry "the literature of atrocity" (1975, 1). Alvin Rosenfeld's *A Double Dying: Reflections on Holocaust Literature* (1980) and David Roskies's *Against the Apocalypse: Responses to Catastrophe in Modern Jewish Culture* (1984) shifted focus further by examining the textual strategies of survivor narratives. Both Sara Horowitz's *Voicing the Void: Muteness and Memory in Holocaust Fiction* (1997) and Sue Vice's *Holocaust Fiction* (2000) analyze narrative techniques and tropes to challenge what they perceive as a false binary between historical and literary discourse, especially fictional writing.[7] These critical studies in no way suggest that writers and readers no longer experience discomfort with literary representations of the Holocaust; in fact, "conflicting loyalties" between questions of morality and literary analysis remain foregrounded in these investigations (Horowitz 1997, 25). However, while many may question the legitimacy of fictional representations of the Holocaust, auto/biographies rest their necessary use of fictive form on their personal claim to experiential legitimacy. Certainly, few survivors enjoy the literary talents of an Elie Wiesel or a Primo Levi, and many have required extensive help with the writing process since only a small number of them have been professional writers. Their writing may not, therefore, sustain or reward literary analysis, but their sheer number, and the socio-historical contexts that have made these publications possible, warrant critical analysis. As Langer has speculated, it may be decades "before art will be able to displace memory as the measure of literary success" (1990, 123). As we join scholars who have begun to read Holocaust auto/biographies as more than evidence, we are careful in our critical examination not to trivialize the stories they tell.

Following the work of James Young (1987, 1988), Daniel R. Schwarz (1999), and Andrea Reiter (2000), we suggest that the critical analysis of auto/biographies of the Holocaust can teach us about the narrativization of experience, "the conceptual presuppositions through which the narrator has apprehended experience" (Young 1987, 420). We suggest, accordingly, that the question of where to place or how to read survivors' narratives belongs precisely in auto/biography studies (Egan 1999, 159–94). In the *Encyclopedia of Literature in Canada*, Marlene Kadar mentions a number of Holocaust auto/biographies in her essay "Life Writing," noting "the recent abundance of Canadian Holocaust survivor narratives" (2002, 665),[8] whereas the essay on "Jewish Canadian Writing" in the same volume contains no such discussion. Auto/biography both requires and receives a reading quite distinct from that of other types of literature. The conflation in the first person of author, narrator, and protagonist (even when the duties of author are shared, or when the first person speaks from somewhere along a spectrum of assumed names and identities) refers the narrative back to the life discussed, and values that life above the aesthetic value of its story.

Reading Holocaust auto/biographies within auto/biography studies allows us to recognize the importance of their referentiality, and to explore at the same time the strategies used to access archives of memory, to perform rhetorical acts, and to establish processes of exchange and understanding between writers and readers. Our current historical moment adds urgency to such an undertaking. If narrative strategies and styles of survivor narrative shape not only their own experience but also their readers' understanding of events, then we should compare their testimony to new writing about the Holocaust that emerges from the second and third generations. We can read these for different representations of the Holocaust experience, which result from other kinds of memory, but which may also be enabled by narrative strategies unavailable to survivors.

The Canadian Context

Survivors who published their Holocaust experiences in Europe have documented the apathy or incredulity with which they were initially received.[9]

All Europeans had been through a war and were anxious to rebuild their lives; few had the psychological energy to attend to the traumas of others. Nor was anti-Semitism finished with the Third Reich; the pogroms that followed the war as survivors tried to return home extended the effects of the death camps. As the new state of Israel fought for its toehold in an Arab context, survivors were called on to fight, not to mourn. By contrast, Canada had resisted pre-war immigration of Jews and was peaceful, undamaged, wealthy, and under-populated. However, Canada did not welcome Jewish immigration.

The "delayed impact" of the Holocaust, to use Franklin Bialystok's title (2000), began in the 1930s, as European Jews foresaw disaster and tried to escape, and continued through to the time of the over-crowded transit camps in Europe after the war was over. Irving Abella and Harold Troper have detailed the intransigence of the Mackenzie King government on the matter of Jewish immigration. Their dramatic title *None Is Too Many* (1982), apparently the words of a senior Canadian official on the subject of Jewish immigration, sums up the situation. Of more than eight hundred thousand Jews seeking refuge from the Third Reich during the 1930s, Canada accepted less than five thousand. For English-speaking countries alone, this Canadian record does not bear comparison with the fifteen thousand accepted in Australia, the seventy thousand accepted in Great Britain or the one hundred twenty-five thousand accepted by the United States (Abella and Troper **2000**, xxii). When Britain and the United States decided to discuss the refugee problem in 1943, Canada refused to host what became the Bermuda Conference in Ottawa, fearing that attention would be brought to its "extremely restrictive refugee policy" (Marrus 1985, 284).

In *Delayed Impact* (2000), Bialystok suggests that the Holocaust did not effectively become a part of Canadian culture until the decade between 1973 and 1985, a period that also saw a significant number of Holocaust memoirs published. One explanation is the political priority of the establishment of Israel as a Jewish state in 1948 and its survival thereafter. This priority, along with Canada's early and extended refusal of Jewish immigration, acceptance of Nazi war criminals, and frequently systemic homegrown anti-Semitism helped to shape the context for auto/biographical works about the Holocaust. Only when Holocaust survivors themselves became a force in the country did the political climate change and the Holocaust begin to be a focus for ethnic identification. Slow and difficult as the migration of Jews to Canada was, Bialystok points to the significant lobby that began to emerge over the space of a few decades. His statistics show the proportion of Jews to the Canadian population as relatively static from the

1920s to the time of the war, at about 1.5 percent. However, by the late 1950s, 13–15 percent of the Jewish population in Canada was immigrant survivors of the Holocaust (1996–97, 2). The activism of survivors within this number, and their adoption of the term "survivor" as an expression of pride, transformed the role of the Holocaust for Canadian Jewry and for Canadians in general, implicating both fellow Jews and the non-Jewish community as responsible for the Holocaust experience.

Survivor Witness

Reviewing Bialystok's *Delayed Impact* for the *National Post*, Ruth R. Wisse takes issue with his use of the Holocaust as a lens for study of Canadian Jewry, identifying the intensity of Jewish life and literature in Canada as restorative in ways that political lobbying could not be. If the Jewish community represents itself both outwards and internally through the lens of the Holocaust, the victim identity, she suggests, must divert and distort the real strengths of Jewish culture. However, survivor witness in Canada, while effectively demonstrating Wisse's point about the value of Jewish cultural life, engages with the politics of Bialystok's thesis. Resisting victim identity, survivors tie their personal experiences into their need to implicate both individuals and whole systems in their trauma—to describe, to accuse, and to resist their experiences of oppression. Attending neither to the energy of religious revival nor to the potential moral force of literature to which Wisse draws attention, many auto/biographical texts include not only the devastation of families and communities, the ordeals of physical survival, and the surreal brutalities to which writers were witness, but also, very frequently, their own tough resistance to oppression by the Nazis and others.[10] Significant numbers of Canadian auto/biographers explicitly privilege action. Rudolf Vrba, for example, in *I cannot forgive* (1964), tells of his escape from Auschwitz in 1944 and his broadcasting of the situation in the camps. Leon Kahn in *No Time to Mourn* (1978) and Faye Schulman in *A Partisan's Memoir* (1995) write about their time as Jewish Partisans and the high risks Jews faced even among the Partisans. Jack Kuper, in his first book, *Child of the Holocaust* (1967), recalls his desperate struggle for survival as a small child after the elimination of his community. Helene Moszkiewiez (*Inside the Gestapo*, 1985) worked with the Belgian resistance—inside the Gestapo Headquarters in Brussels. For each auto/biographer, resistance, endurance, and survival were of a piece. For each one, too, the story is complicated by their identification as Jews, which put them at risk among other inmates in the camps and among Gentiles outside the camps. The resistance they describe is driven, accordingly, not only by a sense of justice, or desperation, but also by hostile stereotyping. Produced, for the most part, with significant help, these texts do not doubt the transparency and reliability of language; they treat language quite simply as if it could approximate fact. They tend not to use the rhetorical strategies of narrative (such as characterization, nuancing of relationship, or dialogue) very effectively; in fact, nothing in these texts is as important as the chronicling of events and the claim to personal experience of them. As personal records, these works and others like them serve personal needs and political agendas, and make for powerful reading.

Chava Kwinta (*I'm Still Living*, 1974) associates her decision to go to Palestine after the war with the continuous small resistances she had enacted as a young girl in the ghetto of Sosnowiec and in labour camps. She also associates it with the other urgent need that all Holocaust auto/biographies document—the need to educate subsequent generations: "They will know that the Jews of Europe went to their deaths without resistance because they were broken, and not because they did not have the courage to fight for their lives" (140). Vrba describes peering through the slats of the transport train, trying to memorize the way back so that his break, when it came, could be effective. Fully aware of the odds, he was determined to survive and to tell others about the atrocities he had experienced and witnessed. Kwinta's whole project is to "explain to the young Jewish people of today why we did not rebel en masse" (1974, 15). Kwinta cites the religious faith of many of the older generation, as well as the respect and affection with which many had held German friends, making them both seriously doubt the rumours they were hearing and be too trusting of assurances they received from the Gestapo. She cites the very sudden and stunning irruptions of extreme violence, and the subjugation of Jewish communities at the hands of the *Judenrat* that had to answer for the Jewish community to the Gestapo. She cites acts of treachery within the civilian population that led to the rapid elimination of organized resisters. Repeated anticipation of the charge of helplessness and the determination to respond to it are distinctive of Canadian Holocaust auto/biography; Kwinta is most likely affected by her time in Tel Aviv, but Kahn, Moszkiewiez, Schulman, and Vrba seem to share her sense that their narratives of resistance fulfil what could be called "a sacred purpose" (15).[11]

This educational purpose, which takes so many survivors out into schools and community centres, whether they have written auto/biographies or not, is also driven in Canada by resistance to Holocaust denial and its potential impact on the next generation.[12] Further, Abella and Bialystok describe

Canada as "a haven for some of the world's leading hatemongers.... The exact number is not known, but a recent government commission found evidence that in 1985 there were several hundred potential war criminals worthy of further investigation" (1996, 764–65). Through the early 1980s, Ernst Zündel was a prime source of neo-Nazi materials for Western Germany. Meanwhile, James Keegstra and Malcolm Ross in Eckville, Alberta, and Moncton, New Brunswick, respectively, were teaching denial of the Holocaust in high-school classrooms.[13] Anti-Semitic thinking is, of course, international,[14] with the Internet providing a powerful tool in the circulation of hate speech and the coordination of international activities (Matas 2000).[15]

Where B'nai Brith and other Jewish organizations have been active in lobbying for legislation against hate literature and in seeking prosecution of the war criminals admitted to Canada while Holocaust survivors were unable to immigrate, survivor stories have been explicitly educational in purpose. Eva Brewster, for example, writes in response to Keegstra and Zündel, but also to those who, without such evident hate, think the Holocaust should be relegated to the past. She concludes her 1994 edition of *Progeny of Light* by expressing her delight that her memoirs are included in many social studies curricula. Similarly, to give an example from the large area of children's literature on the Holocaust, Lillian Boraks-Nemetz in *The Old Brown Suitcase* (1994) introduces what she calls her "documentary fiction" by inviting young readers to listen attentively to the stories of those who flee persecution. Dan Sonnenschein, too, presents writing by and about his mother in *Victory over Nazism* (2003) precisely because of her energetic role in educating schoolchildren about the Holocaust.

Because survivors feel so responsible for transmitting their memories, they focus quite specifically on their time in Europe, relegating their post-Holocaust lives to a private, non-narrative space. At most, they gesture to a future that is safer than the past. Sometimes they acknowledge such a future for themselves by expressing their gratitude to Canada and Canadians, as do Kuper (1967, dedication) and Raab (1997, 159); Grossman, on the other hand, focuses her hope for the future on her grandchildren's generation (1990, 146). Despite the personal nature of their trauma, however, they present the Holocaust as a public event to be retained in public knowledge and memory. Ensuring that both Jews and Gentiles know, understand, and remember, survivors ground their stories in their old communities, religious and secular, urban and rural, prosperous and poor. The reader is invited to recognize the shocking violence with which these private lives were disrupted; the suffering that followed was once beyond the imagination of the narrator as it may be now of the reader. Survivors use photo-

graphs of themselves and of family members who did not survive (see Grossman 1990, Mielnicki 2000, Raab 1997); these are both poignant and authen-
ticating. While some of the photographs of objects that survived Raab's
imprisonment ordeal (such as a recipe book and a comb) emphasize the
personal nature of her narrative and the preciousness of these items, Mielnicki's images of sites in Birkenau (such as the grounds, the crematorium,
or a mass grave), which readers may know from history books, have the
opposite effect; even if they are familiar images, these pictures may startle
and shock unsuspecting readers as they place Mielnicki's personal story in
the historical context of the larger collective experience. Focussing on knowledge and evidence, Vrba (1964) includes maps and diagrams of the layout
at Auschwitz and Birkenau and the original report that he prepared with
Alfred Wexler after they escaped from Auschwitz in April 1944. Raab pref-
aces her story with a map of her movements across Europe (1997, viii). In
keeping with their unadorned narrative and restraint in describing their
personal trauma, these texts use contextual information so that readers can
refer the narrative back to specific events in specific times and places.

Remarkably, perhaps, most survivor stories are framed by their anglophone co-writer, editor, or recipient. Such framing tends to do more than
clarify the allophone need for editorial assistance; it tends also to support
and authenticate the text. What is foreign here, or incomprehensible, becomes regrounded in the culture for which the story is produced. Whereas
the purpose in all cases is to honour the dead and take warning from history,
survivors are either too courteous or too careful about their audience to
point to Canada's complicity in the horrors they recount. However, the very
act of writing becomes in both contexts an act of resistance.

Generations of the Holocaust

> The only way writing after Auschwitz, poetry or prose, could proceed was
> by becoming memory and preventing the past from coming to an end.
> —Günter Grass

Whereas Holocaust education has been the central responsibility of survivors the world over, the Canadian context has provided intense and specific prompts that also implicate succeeding generations. It is often those
of the second generation who, in the last few decades, have inherited the project of collecting and publishing survivor stories, and of organizing activities at education centres which bring survivors into classrooms to keep the

memory of the Holocaust alive. Sometimes child survivors, born during the war, will refer to themselves as second generation, but most often the term maps the generation of the children of survivors.[16] They are the "first and the last," the first to be born after the Holocaust and the last to have a direct link with those who died and those who survived.[17] While they cannot rely on their own memories about the Holocaust, others' memories and stories about a time before they were born permeate and have an impact upon their lives. They have what Marianne Hirsch calls a "postmemory," "distinguished from memory by generational distance and from history by deep personal connection" (1997, 22). Their own stories are stories of absence. No longer eye-witnesses themselves, they can only witness through the imagination and bear witness to the witnesses. As a transitional generation, this second generation may experience most acutely the burden of memory, and with it the tensions between the need to remember and the need to forget, an insecurity about one's own self-worth that is possibly informed by what Eva Hoffman has called "envy of significance" (2002), and the difficult struggle of defining one's own identity as relational to families and communities traumatized by the Holocaust.

The second generation serves the important and difficult function of a bridge between a world almost gone and one shaping its own response to the Holocaust (Berger 1997, 186). Survivors themselves recognize the importance of the generations that come after them. Bronia Sonnenschein, in her prologue to the second edition of *Victory over Nazism* (2002), writes: "I am getting older while wanting to do so much. And that is why I'd like to tell the readers about two of my grandchildren, Emily, 24, and Claire, 22, who have risen to the challenge to speak and reflect when the occasion presents itself.... They have become my living legacy. They, together with my children, Vivian and Dan (who by the way encouraged me again to write for a second edition), will preserve the memory of the Holocaust" (n.p.). And Eva Brewster reflects on the experiences of her own children in the epilogue to *Progeny of Light/Vanished in Darkness*, and wonders "Why had it taken me so many years to realize that the only hope for a change in human attitudes rests with our very young people?" (266). Until very recently, efforts have focused on archiving and making accessible the auto/biographies of survivors. Now the Holocaust Education Centre in Vancouver, for example, is beginning to train members of the second generation as speakers in public venues. In part, of course, the age of survivors makes it necessary for our attention to shift to the next generations, but the belatedness of a (self-)critical Canadian response to the Holocaust may also explain why written and/or creative reflection by the second generation is only beginning.[18] Given the boom in auto/biographical production in Canada over the last decade, which now includes a well-established tradition of narratives of immigration and trauma, Canadians may be increasingly ready to write about their inheritance of this experience, and to hear from those who have come after.

Lisa Appignanesi's family memoir *Losing the Dead*, published in 1999, is one of the first auto/biographies by a member of the second generation in Canada.[19] Unlike most Canadian survivors, she already had a well-established career as a writer and academic when *Losing the Dead* was published.[20] The same is true for Elaine Kalman Naves (1996), Irena F. Karafilly (1998), and Eva Hoffman (1989). Hoffman, for example, was a journalist with the *New York Times* (1979–90) when she published *Lost in Translation* (1989). For these children of survivors, it cannot be their own experience of the Holocaust that led them to writing; they are writers who use their writing skills to explore how their parents' wartime lives shaped their own life trajectories and sense of self. While Hoffman is not actually a Canadian writer, with only the middle section of her auto/biography focusing on Canada as her first destination in this double-emigration narrative,[21] and since Naves's *Journey to Vaja* and Karafilly's *Ashes and Miracles* are primarily travel narratives, we have chosen Appignanesi's *Losing the Dead* for a closer analysis of the kinds of issues we see as characteristic and most challenging in these second-generation auto/biographies. Her narrative begins where many survivor accounts end—with the immigration of her family to Canada. While the post-war years are often "judged to be unremarkable" by survivors, as Mervin Butovsky and Kurt Jonassohn have pointed out in their work on unpublished memoirs by Canadian survivors (1996–97, 149), they are the only years Appignanesi herself has witnessed and can speak of from firsthand experience.

Born in 1946, Appignanesi tries to understand how her parents' wartime experiences in Poland shaped both her brother's life and her own, especially their experience of growing up in Canada where the family immigrated in 1951. She describes the effects of the Holocaust on her life as a "transgenerational haunting" (1999, 8), what passed between the generations as "ghost language" (221), and the war itself as a "ghost" in her family (217), but the book is not so much about exorcizing the ghost and the hauntings as it is about understanding them (8, 218). The list of behavioural patterns that she attributes to her parents' legacy includes a fascination/obsession with duplicity and appearances, family closeness and loyalty, fatalism, equanimity, general anxiety (at borders, about waiting, etc.), and ambivalence about her Jewishness, as well as feelings of shame, self-hatred, and guilt. Her experience combines what is often described as the two extremes encountered by the children of survivors. On one hand, her father is largely silent with his children about his war experiences; his personal history remains suppressed and becomes visible only in his anger and fear. Appignanesi's mother, on the other hand, tells many stories about her heroic adventures, her ability to pass as a Gentile, and her powerful charms. Her parents' new friends in Canada, survivors themselves, add their own reminiscences about the war to the family stories. Either shut out or bombarded with stories, Appignanesi remembers a childhood permeated by experiences that were not her own. The exasperation and rebellion of her youth resulted in the kind of necessary "amnesia" that made it possible for her generation "to become functioning New-World beings" (87). However, when her father's long-silenced memories of ss camps resurface in his delirious state before his death in 1981 and she sees her mother's memories fade with Alzheimer's, Appignanesi begins to see her personal story as part of a much larger collective history. Wanting to be able to answer her children's questions about their family, Appignanesi recognizes that hers is "the last generation for whom the war is still a living tissue of memory rather than a dusty and barbaric history of facts and statistics" (5–6): that her generation is, in fact, "the first and the last."[22] On a more personal level, Appignanesi's writing becomes a way to assuage her feelings of guilt for being "a bad daughter" (7, 79, 80); her book thus contributes to her own self-healing, a function of auto/biographical writing that Suzette Henke has called "scriptotherapy" (1998). Such self-healing, however, can only happen in the context of her family history, for her life is, in John Eakin's words, a "relational life," based on an identity developed collaboratively with others, especially family members (1999, 57). As such, Losing the Dead bridges the generational gap between survivors and their children.

Appignanesi appears to be most troubled by the parallel she sees between the confusion and lack of coherence in her mother's stories on one hand, which result from her Alzheimer's, and the confusion, the blanks, and disorder of the war experience she tries to retrace on the other. Unlike the first generation of immigrants, whose stories move with energy but are rarely self-reflexive or able to represent emotion or relationship, Appignanesi foregrounds her own processes of making sense of both kinds of confusion in a highly fragmented narrative. Each story, Appignanesi notes, is a fragment in itself, informed by her own perspective. Her own version of her family's past is exactly that, a version, and Appignanesi insists on its limitations by using expressions of modality (adverbs such as "perhaps," "probably," and "maybe," as well as modal verbs); introducing her stories by pointing out her lack of knowledge or remembering ("I don't know," "I don't remember," "All I remember"); or by highlighting the retrospective nature of her narrative by distancing her narrating self from the experiencing self she describes ("I didn't realize then," "It was only retrospectively that I understood," "I can now understand"). Appignanesi can witness her parents' struggle, but she cannot claim to have been an eye-witness. However, she is not satisfied to accept this absence of memory even though her self-consciousness supports the fact that "the past is a 'trace' in the present that haunts the second generation with the presence of the absent memory, an amnesia in which the only memory is of not remembering anything" (Sicher 1998, 30). Time, distance, and changing needs mark the second generation as more literary than the first. The nature of their own personal experience values exploration, analysis, and understanding over testimony. They are also, we speculate, less likely to write about their family's Holocaust experience unless they are already writers.

Versed in postmodernism and its representatives (1999, 100, 201), Appignanesi examines critically what it means today to speak of truth, history, and memory. *Losing the Dead* is a family history, but it is also an attempt to wrestle with (and possibly reconcile) the testimonial endeavour paramount in Holocaust writing and the realization that we can only access past events through language and memory, which are always already informed by subjective experience. Documentary genres (for example, birth and death certificates, letters, identity cards, and her mother's Survivor Interview) are integral to her search for her parents' history, and so are the photographs she finds and takes on her trips.[23] While Appignanesi does not include actual photos or maps and drawings, however, as many survivors do, she mentions their existence and the important role they play in her research. In fact, since she cannot herself rely on her own memories of wartime events and places, she repeatedly refers to history books, interviews, archives, and such organizations as the Red Cross and Yad Vashem. We have already noted the value of such documents to survivor testimony, grounding—even justifying—personal memory in historical evidence. These sources are what connect Appignanesi's parents' memory with her own postmemory. They confirm the past's existence, as Hirsch points out, at the same time as "they signal its unbridgeable distance" (1997, 23). The paradox of the documents and sources is thus placed side by side with, and framed by, the telling of stories: stories told by her parents, her relatives, and herself.

Appignanesi describes *Losing the Dead* metaphorically as "a journey into [her] parents' past" (1999, 8), but traveling itself takes on an important role in her researching and writing of the family history. Unlike survivors, such as Grossman (1990) and Raab (1997), who explore the ambivalence of returning to their homelands, and to the places of their imprisonment, which had been certain to bring their death, Appignanesi travels to Poland, trying to make her parents' past present. She becomes one of many whose pilgrimages to their parents' birthplaces and to death camps as well as to Israel serve as "physical markers of second-generation Holocaust remembrance" (Berger 1997, 3).[24] Even though Appignanesi's goal, "to give [her] mother's past back to her, intact, clear, with all its births and deaths and missing persons in place" (8), remains impossible, she initiates a new remembering, carefully conveyed through the literal and metaphorical journey of the text. This remembering can turn the statement "The dead are lost" (8) into the process of "losing the dead" (200). While nothing can return her uncle Adek to her mother, nor any of the other Jews who died in the Holocaust, she insists that there is a "proper" way of losing the dead (8), of mourning them (223). If that proper way is to remember the dead and to learn as much about them as possible, then that is exactly what Appiganesi and the second generation can do for the survivors and the generations to come.

As Appignanesi gathers information about her parents' wartime experience and the fate of other family members, she invites readers to witness her struggle between the (post-)memory of her own generation and her parents' memory. That she resorts to a fragmented narrative and self-reflexively foregrounds her own role in the process of making sense of the stories and documents negates neither the project of narrativization nor the value of testimony and history. In fact, Losing the Dead throws into sharp relief the different strategies available in writing family histories, which gives us, as readers, a chance to examine their effectiveness and limitations. Having examined second-generation auto/biographical narratives in relation to survivor auto/biographies, we would like to revise Lawrence Langer's observation that it may be decades "before art will be able to displace memory as the measure of literary success" (1990, 123). There is no doubt that second-generation narratives are more self-reflexive literary productions than survivor narratives: more open-ended, less authoritative. They require more of the reader in terms of engaging with the auto/biographer's activities of discovery and interpretation. However, the difference between memory and postmemory is the relatively uncomplicated burden of the former. As the Holocaust recedes into the history of the last century, we suspect that no literature, however fine, will displace the imperatives that drive survivor texts, their unique contributions to public memory, or their role in educating successive generations. To find respectful ways of analyzing auto/biographical writing about the Holocaust does not mean that art has displaced memory; instead, it allows us to recognize both. While the academy may need to acknowledge the value of survivor's nonliterary auto/biographies in the curriculum in order to enhance Canadian cultural memory, we suspect that the work of "the second generation" will need to include acknowledging Canada's complicity in the suffering and deaths their parents memorialize.

Notes

A number of people have been kind and helpful consultants for this paper. We are grateful to Scott Anderson, Mervin Butovsky and Kurt Jonassohn, Marlene Kadar, Roberta Kremer, Seymour Levitan, Elizabeth Maurer, Richard Menkis, and Norman Ravvin. A shorter version of this paper was presented at the Giessen Graduate School for the Humanities, Justus Liebig University, in Germany, on June 18, 2003. Gabriele would like to thank Ansgar Nünning for the invitation and her audience for the lively discussion.

1 The term "Holocaust" is, of course, problematic, with its connotation of religious sacrifice and its focus on victim rather than perpetrator of genocide. An alternative term, Shoah, refers in Hebrew to a great catastrophe. Nonetheless, we are using Holocaust because it is the most commonly recognized term for the Nazi genocide. Despite its much wider implications, the Holocaust in this paper refers to the experience of European Jewry. We use the virgule in auto/biography to acknowledge the overlap in much contemporary writing between biography (writing the life of another) and autobiography (writing a life of oneself), an overlap that is particularly pertinent for Holocaust memoirs, which are often communal productions and contribute to a communal history.

2 In his famous speech at the ss Group Leader Meeting in Posen, 4 October 1943, Heinrich Himmler said of the "extermination" of the Jews: "This is an honor roll in our history which has never been and never will be put in writing."

3 Butovsky and Jonassohn identify the popularity of *Schindler's List*, indicating "broad public acceptance of Holocaust settings" (2003, 3) as one motivation for survivors to write belated memoirs.

4 We are not including the extensive archives of oral narration in this paper. For an extraordinary record of individual voices, see Jack Kugelmas and Jonathan Boyarin (1998). For archival holdings of unpublished diaries and memoirs, see Butovsky and Jonassohn (1996–97); for more information about the publishing of many of these texts in copy print format and on the Internet, see Butovsky and Jonassohn (2003) and their project website < http://migs.concordia.ca/survivor.html >. See also Janice Rosen in the issue of *Canadian Jewish Studies* dedicated to Holocaust studies, and the bibliography in CJS 1999–2000. We are also aware of the urgent need to translate memoirs written in French and, also, in Yiddish. Seymour Levitan, for example, is currently working on translation of two works by Rachel Auerbach. Such translation into English, and Levitan is not alone, speaks to the destroyed world of Yiddish while also extending possible readership beyond Yiddish-speaking Jewish communities, and therefore also extending Canadian cultural responsibility for this history. Where unpublished materials form a valuable archive, they also point to the very personal nature of stories intended for families alone, to the linguistic or narrative limitations of writers with stories to tell, and to the trauma of working with editorial help.

5 Marlene Kadar, email correspondence, 10 May 2003.

6 Finally, for our own part, as two Canadian academics, both immigrants from Europe, we recognize some of the complex ways in which readers need and associate with these

materials. As a German, born long after the war, Gabriele's sense of Canadian culture was permeated by an experience with which her growing up and education in Germany were suffused but on which her grandparents were silent. As a granddaughter of an American WASP, Susanna discovered only as an adult that her other grandparents were Jewish and that one had died at Mauthausen. While neither of us claims personal affiliation with the Holocaust experience, both of us recognize profound personal reasons for contributing to its place in public memory.

7 Special attention has been paid to the treatment of the Holocaust in children's literature. See, for instance, Adrienne Kertzer (2002) and issue 95 of *Canadian Children's Literature*, "Children of the Shoah: Holocaust Literature and Education," which is devoted to the subject.

8 Similarly, our overview chapter of life writing in Canada for *The Cambridge Companion to Canadian Literature* includes a section on Holocaust writing. See Egan and Helms (2004).

9 In "A Self-Interview: Afterwords to *If This Is a Man* (1976)," Levi wrote about the speed with which he wrote his memoirs of Auschwitz and the response he received: "The manuscript was turned down by a number of important publishers; it was accepted in 1947 by a small publisher who printed only 2,500 copies and then folded. So, this first book of mine fell into oblivion for many years; perhaps also because in all of Europe those were difficult times of mourning and reconstruction and the public did not want to return in memory to the painful years of the war that had just ended" (Belpoliti and Gordon 2001, 185). See also Butovsky and Jonassohn (2003): "Too often the survivors were met with incredulity when they told their stories. And when disbelief was mixed with indifference survivors recoiled in anguish and pain" (3). On Canadian reactions, see Bialystok: "Not a single article on the survivors' experience, as expressed by themselves, appeared in 1948 ... no apparent interest was expressed in discovering who these immigrants were, what they had lost, how they had survived, and what obstacles the had faced" (2000, 65). Note, however, that Barbara Schober's analysis of Holocaust Commemoration in Vancouver indicates that local experience was significantly more varied than the official information of the national Jewish leadership would suggest, with gatherings for mourning and protest occurring as early as 1933 (2001, 20).

10 When we speak of the auto/biographers' resistance, we refer to both their actions during the Holocaust and their subsequent writing about these experiences. See Barbara Harlow (1987), whose treatment of literary resistance to colonizing powers identifies the value of rhetorical skills in combination with force, and the need for the speaker to be thoroughly implicated in resistance. She describes resistance literature as "call[ing] attention to itself, and to literature in general, as a political and politicized activity" (28).

11 Richard Menkis suggests considering the issue of armed resistance in relation to Zionist attitudes to the Holocaust and the shifting attachment of Canadian Jewry to Zionism.

12 Jerry Grafstein's collection of personal reflections by Jewish Canadians in *Beyond Imagination* was similarly inspired by "a fulsome interview of Canada's most notorious Holocaust revisionist" as part of a major North American news program (1995, vii). He sought contributions from an eclectic mix of Canadian writers, historians, and journalists to record "the Holocaust's impact on Canadians of [his] generation who bore witness so far and so safely removed from the threat" (viii). Karen R. Mock (2000) discusses the need for anti-racist education against the background of Holocaust denial in Canada; she focuses on the Holocaust and Hope program initiated by the League for Human Rights of B'nai Brith Canada in 1985.

13 In private conversation with Susanna Egan, Helene Moszkiewiez said she did not dare to use a current photograph for her book or the married name by which she was known in

Canada. Six thousand miles away from Brussels and thirty-five years after the end of the war, she feared reprisals if she were identified with the actions described in her book.

14 For example, David McCalden from Northern Ireland, known as Lewis Brandon in the United States, was present for the trials of both Keegstra and Zündel in Canada, and David Irving from England provided witness for Ernst Zündel at his second trial.

15 Given the particular responsibilities inherent in Holocaust writing, we suspect that recent events, such as increased attacks on synagogues after the terrorist attacks on the United States on September 11, 2001, or David Ahenakew's (former chief of the Assembly of First Nations) appreciation of Hitler's "frying" of six million Jews, may well generate further writing by survivors or their children. For more information on Ahenakew, see < http:// www.globeandmail.com/servlet/ArticleNews/front/RTGAM/20021217/wxnati1217/Front/h omeBN/breakingnews >.

16 Sometimes the term second generation is also used to describe, more broadly, all those who were not there and who came after the Holocaust, extending George Steiner's self-definition as "a kind of survivor," someone who "happened not to be there when the names were called out" (1967, 164). In order to distinguish between the writing of those who have an immediate family connection with the survivors themselves and those who do not, we reserve the term second generation for children of survivors. However, we recognize the validity of Efraim Sicher's observation that "adopted children, children of refugees, or the generation contemporaneous with children of survivors…may share many of their psychological, ideological, and theological concerns," which challenges our narrow definition (1998, 7). This is not the place to review the extensive literature on the second generation, but we note that analysis rarely focuses on the specific situation of children of survivors in Canada.

17 Alan Berger quotes Menachem Rosensaft's description of the second generation: "the first to be born after the Holocaust and the last to have a direct link with that Eastern European Jewish existence that was so brutally annihilated" (1990, 99).

18 Loren Lerner's *Afterimage* (2002) is the first book to discuss the impact of the Holocaust on Canadian culture by examining specific examples from literature and the fine arts.

19 Given the scope of this paper, we are unable to examine fictionalized accounts of the Holocaust in contemporary Canadian literature, but they certainly exist. Anne Michaels's *Fugitive Pieces* (1996), for instance, would be an excellent novel for a comparative analysis.

20 By 1999, Appignanesi had published a number of critical works, such as *Femininity & the Creative Imagination: A Study of Henry James, Robert Musil & Marcel Proust* (1973), *Simone de Beauvoir* (1988), and *Freud's Women* (1992) with John Forrester; she had also edited collections of papers based on conferences on postmodernism, French theory, Rushdie, and the sciences at the Institute of Contemporary Arts, where she had been director. Her first novel, *Memory and Desire*, appeared in 1993, followed by *Dreams of Innocence* (1994), *A Good Woman* (1999), *The Dead of Winter* (1999), *Paris Requiem* (2001), and *Sanctuary* (2001).

21 See Sarah Phillips Casteel's (2001) perceptive analysis of Hoffman's treatment of Canada and the place of traumatic memory in the middle section of *Lost in Translation*.

22 In an interview that also involves her daughter Jessica, Naves comments on the challenges of how to pass on narratives about the Holocaust. Rather than insisting on one right way to do so, she explains that "the problem here is that there is no kind of hidden access route to the truth of the Holocaust…. There is no way of teaching it that is going to be okay, because it is not okay" (Robertson and Keon 1999, 43).

23 Hirsch's (1997) analysis of family photographs as means of self-representation and Timothy Dow Adams's (2000) discussion of photography in auto/biographical genres invite a more extensive discussion of Appignanesi's mention of photographs and other documents in comparison with the direct use that survivors make of such documents.

24 See also Norman Ravvin's (2002) critical reflection on the popularity of Jewish travel to Eastern Europe and his own trip to Poland. For other examples, see Karafilly (1998), Naves (1996), and Swartz (1998). For an interesting comparison, consider Mary Lagerwey's (1998) analysis of Holocaust auto/biographies, which weaves reflections on her own travels as a non-Jew to Auschwitz, into her critical discussions of survivor memoirs.

References

Abella, Irving, and Harold Troper. 1988. 'The line must be drawn somewhere': Canada and Jewish Refugees, 1933-1939. In *A Nation of Immigrants: Women, Workers, and Communities in Canadian History, 1840s-1960s*, 412-45. Toronto: Univ. of Toronto Press.

———. 1982. *None is too many: Canada and the Jews of Europe 1933–1948*. Toronto: Lester and Orpen Dennys.

Abella, Irving, and Franklin Bialystok. 1996. Canada. In *The world reacts to the Holocaust*, ed. David S. Wyman, 749-81. Baltimore: Johns Hopkins Univ. Press.

Adams, Timothy Dow. 2000. *Light writing & life writing: Photography in autobiography*. Chapel Hill: Univ. of North Carolina Press.

Adorno, Theodor W. 1977. Kulturkritik und Gesellschaft. In *Kulturkritik und Gesellschaft I*. Vol. 10.1 of *Gesammelte Schriften*, 1-30. Frankfurt: Suhrkamp.

Appignanesi, Lisa. 1999. *Losing the dead: A family memoir*. Toronto: McArthur.

Belpoliti, Marco, and Robert Gordon, eds. 2001. *The voice of memory: Primo Levi interviews, 1961–1987*. Trans. Robert Gordon. New York: New Press.

Berger, Alan L. 1997. *Children of Job: American second-generation witnesses to the Holocaust*. New York: State Univ. of New York Press.

———. 1990. Ashes and hope: The Holocaust in second generation American literature. In *Reflections of the Holocaust in art and literature*, ed. Randolph L. Braham, 97-116. New York: Columbia Univ. Press.

Bialystok, Franklin. 2000. *Delayed Impact: The Holocaust and the Canadian Jewish community*. Montreal and Kingston: McGill-Queen's Univ. Press.

———. 1996-1997. Neo-Nazis in Toronto: The Allan Gardens riot. In *New perspectives on Canada: The Holocaust and survivors/Nouvelles perspectives sur le Canada: La Shoah et les survivants*, ed. Paula J. Draper and Richard Menkis. *Canadian Jewish Studies/Études Juives Canadienne* 4-5: 1-38.

Boraks-Nemetz, Lillian. 1994. *The old brown suitcase*. Brentwood Bay, BC: Ben-Simon.

Brewster, Eva. 1994. *Progeny of light/Vanished in darkness*. Edmonton, AB: NeWest.

Butovsky, Mervin, and Kurt Jonassohn. 2003. From victim to witness: The publication of unpublished Holocaust survivor memoirs. Address to Fifth Biennial Conference of the International Association of Genocide Scholars, June 7-10, Galway, Ireland.

———. 1996-97. An exploratory study of unpublished memoirs by Canadian Holocaust survivors. *Canadian Jewish Studies/Études Juives Canadienne* 4-5: 147-61.

Eakin, Paul John. 1999. *How our lives become stories*. Ithaca, NY: Cornell Univ. Press.

Egan, Susanna. 1999. *Mirror talk: Genres of crisis in contemporary autobiography*. Chapel Hill: Univ. of North Carolina Press.

Egan, Susanna, and Gabriele Helms. 2004. Life writing. *The Cambridge companion to Canadian literature*, ed. Eva-Marie Kröller. Cambridge: Cambridge Univ. Press.

Farkas, Endre. 1999. "Heirloom." In *So others will remember*, ed. Ronald Headland, 142–44. Montreal: Véhicule.

Gerber, Jean Miriam. 1989. Immigration and integration in post-war Canada: A case study of Holocaust survivors in Vancouver 1947–1970. Master's thesis, Univ. of British Columbia.

Goldberg, Abraham. 2002. *A long way home*. Israel: Kotarot.

Grafstein, Jerry S., ed. 1995. *Beyond imagination: Canadians write about the Holocaust*. Toronto: McClelland and Stewart.

Grass, Günter. 1999. To be continued... Nobel Prize Lecture, 7 November 1999. Trans. Michael Henry Helm [cited 9 July 2003]. Available at < http://www .nobel.se/lit erature/layreates/1999g/lecture-e.html >.

Greenstein, Michael. 1989. *Third solitudes: Tradition and discontinuity in Jewish-Canadian literature*. Montreal and Kingston: McGill-Queen's Univ. Press.

Grossman, Ibolya (Szalai). 1990. *An ordinary woman in extraordinary times*. Toronto: Multicultural History Society of Ontario.

Harlow, Barbara. 1987. *Resistance literature*. New York: Methuen.

Hart, Alexander. 1996. Writing the diaspora: A bibliography and critical commentaryon post-Shoah English-language Jewish fiction in Australia, South Africa, and Canada. Ph.D. diss., Univ. of British Columbia.

Headland, Ronald, ed. 1999. *So others will remember*. Montreal: Véhicule.

Henke, Suzette. 1998. *Shattered subjects: Trauma and testimony in women's life writing*. New York: St Martin's.

Himmler, Heinrich. 1943. Posen Speech, 4 October 1943 [cited 9 July 2003]. Available at < http://www.nizkor.org/hweb/people/h/himmler-heinrich/posen /oct-04-43/ >.

Hirsch, Marianne. 1997. *Family frames: Photography, narrative and postmemory*. Cambridge, MA: Harvard University Press.

Hoffman, Eva. 1989. *Lost in translation: A life in a new language*. New York: Penguin.

———. 2002. After such knowledge: The meaning of the second-generation experience. Keynote Address at the Annual Commemorative Program, November 10. Beth Israel Synagogue, Vancouver.

Horowitz, Sara R. 1997. *Voicing the void: Muteness and memory in Holocaust fiction*. New York: State Univ. of New York Press.

Kadar, Marlene. 2002. Life writing. In *Encyclopedia of literature in Canada*, ed. W.H. New, 660–66. Toronto: Univ. of Toronto Press.

Kahn, Leon. 1978. *No time to mourn: A true story of a Jewish partisan fighter*. Vancouver: Laurelton.

Karafilly, Irena F. 1998. *Ashes and miracles: A Polish journey*. Toronto: Malcolm Lester.

Kertzer, Adrienne. 2002. *My mother's voice: Children, literature, and the Holocaust*. Peterborough, ON: Broadview.

Koerner, Loren, ed. 2002. *Afterimage: Evocations of the Holocaust in contemporary arts and literature*. Montreal: The Concordia Univ. Institute for Canadian Jewish Studies.

Kugelmass, Jack, and Jonathan Boyarin, eds. and trans. 1998. *From a ruined garden: The memorial books of Polish Jewry*, 2nd ed. Washington, DC: United States Holocaust Memorial Museum and Bloomington: Indiana Univ. Press.

Kuper, Jack. 1967. *Child of the Holocaust*. New York: American Library.

———. 1994. *After the smoke cleared*. Toronto: Stoddard.

Kwinta, Chava. 1974. *I'm still living*. Toronto: Simon and Pierre.

Lagerwey, Mary D. 1998. *Reading Auschwitz*. Walnut Creek, CA: Altamira.

Langer, Lawrence L. 1975. *The Holocaust and the literary imagination*. New Haven: Yale Univ. Press.

———. 1990. Fictional facts and factual fictions: History in Holocaust literature. In *Reflections of the Holocaust in art and literature*, ed. Randolph L. Braham, 117–30. New York: Columbia Univ. Press.

Lerner, Loren. 2002. *Afterimage: Evocations of the Holocaust in contemporary Canadian arts and literature*. Montreal: Concordia Univ. Press.

Marrus, Michael R. 1985. *The unwanted: European refugees in the twentieth century*. New York: Oxford Univ. Press.

Matas, David. 2000. Countering hate on the Internet: Recommendations for action. In *The Holocaust's ghost: Writings on art, politics, law and education*, ed. F.C. Decoste and Bernard Schwartz, 483–95. Edmonton: Univ. of Alberta Press.

Mayer, Anita. 1981. *One who came back*. Ottawa: Oberon.

Michaels, Anne. 1996. *Fugitive pieces*. Toronto: McClelland and Stewart.

Mielnicki, Michel. 2000. *Bialystok to Birkenau: The Holocaust journey of Michel Mielnicki as told to John Munro*. Vancouver: Ronsdale Press and Vancouver Holocaust Education Centre.

Mock, Karen R. 2000. Holocaust and hope: Holocaust education in the context of anti-racist education in Canada. In *The Holocaust's ghost: Writings on art, politics, law and education*, ed. F.C. Decoste and Bernard Schwartz, 465–82. Edmonton: Univ. of Alberta Press.

Moszkiewiez, Helene. 1985. *Inside the Gestapo: A Jewish woman's secret war*. Toronto: Macmillan.

Naves, Elaine Kalman. 1996. *Journey to Vaja: Reconstructing the world of a Hungarian-Jewish family*. Montreal and Kingston: McGill-Queen's Univ. Press.

Phillips Casteel, Sarah. 2001. Eva Hoffman's double emigration: Canada as the site of exile in *Lost in Translation*. *biography* 21(4): 288–301.

Raab, Elisabeth M. 1997. *And peace never came*. Waterloo, ON: Wilfrid Laurier Univ. Press.

Ravvin, Norman. 1997. *A house of words: Jewish writing, identity, and memory*. Montreal and Kingston: McGill-Queen's Univ. Press.

———. 2002. Tragic tourism and North American identity: Investigating a Radzanow Street, a mlawa apple and an unbuilt museum. *Canadian Literature* 174: 13–28.

Reiter, Andrea. 2000. *Narrating the Holocaust*. 1995. Trans. Patrick Camiller. London, UK: Continuum.

Robertson, Judith P., and Nadene Keon. 1999. "The Question Child" and passing on intergenerational tales of trauma: A conversation with Elaine Kalman Naves. *Canadian Children's Literature* 25(3): 29–49.

Rosen, Janice. 1996–1997. Holocaust testimonies and related resources in Canadian archival repositories. *Canadian Jewish Studies/Études Juives Canadienne* 4–5: 163–75.

Rosenfeld, Alvin. 1980. *A double dying: Reflections on Holocaust literature*. Bloomington: Indiana Univ. Press.

Roskies, David G. 1984. *Against the apocalypse: Responses to catastrophe in modern Jewish culture*. Cambridge, MA: Harvard Univ. Press.

Schober, Barbara. 2001. Holocaust commemoration in Vancouver, BC, 1943–1975. Master's thesis, Univ. of British Columbia.

Schulman, Faye. 1995. *A Partisan's memoir: Woman of the Holocaust*. With the assistance of Sarah Silberstein Swartz. Toronto: Second Story.

Schwarz, Daniel R. 1999. *Imagining the Holocaust*. New York: St Martin's.

Sicher, Efraim, ed. 1998. *Breaking crystal: Writing and memory after Auschwitz*. Urbana: Univ. of Illinois Press.

Sonnenschein, Bronia. 2003. *Victory over Nazism: The journey of a Holocaust survivor*, ed. Dan Sonnenschein. Vancouver: Memory.

Steiner, George. 1967. A kind of survivor. 1965. In *Language and silence: Essays, 1958–1966*, 164–79. London: Faber and Faber.

Swartz, Sarah Silberstein. 1998. Return to Poland: In search of my parents' memories. In *From memory to transformation: Jewish women's voices*, ed. Sarah Silberstein Swartz and Margie Wolfe, 72–89. Toronto: Second Story.

Vice, Sue. 2000. *Holocaust fiction*. London and New York: Routledge.

Vrba, Rudolf, with Alan Bestic. 1964. *I cannot forgive*. Vancouver: Regent College.

Wisse, Ruth R. 2000. Beyond the Holocaust. Review of *Delayed Impact*, by Franklin Bialystok. *National Post* 30 September: E8.

Young, James. 1987. Interpreting literary testimony: A preface to rereading Holocaust diaries and memoirs. *New Literary History* 18(2): 403–23.

———. 1988. *Writing and rewriting the Holocaust: Narrative and the consequences of interpretation*. Bloomington: Univ. of Indiana Press.

ALBERT BRAZ 🍃

The Modern Hiawatha:
Grey Owl's Construction
of His Aboriginal Self

We are what we imagine. Our very existence consists in
our imagination of ourselves. Our best destiny is to imagine, at least, completely, who and what, and *that* we are.
—*N. Scott Momaday*

THE DEATH OF GREY OWL ON APRIL 13,
1938, at the age of forty-nine, marked not only the end of a life but also of
a reputation. Following the revelations that he was an Englishman and not
an "Apache halfbreed," as he had sometimes claimed, he was posthumously
transformed from a renowned conservationist and nature writer into a fraud
or fake—a racial impostor. We live in a time when identity is often perceived
as contingent, when self-made consensual theories of group identity purportedly have displaced ancestral or hereditary ones. Yet, to this day, discussions of Grey Owl and his writings are invariably accompanied by a profound
sense of outrage at his deception, which indicates the general discomfort still
felt about the idea of a white man pretending to be a Native North American. As the Anishinabe playwright Drew Hayden Taylor says of the so-called
prophet of the wilderness, he is "a wanton cultural appropriator" (1999,
120)—the founder of "the Spirit-On-Ice Syndrome" (1996, 97). Grey Owl's
story, though, does not merely bring to the fore questions of biocultural
authenticity and voice appropriation; it also underscores the degree to which
people's lives may be improvised. The popular image of Grey Owl is that of
a long-haired man clad in moccasins and buckskins; that is, the popular
image of a real "Red Indian." However, in his own writings, Grey Owl can
be rather circumspect about his ethnocultural identity. In the late 1920s, he

had a natural epiphany. After years of trapping beaver for a living, he became aware of the possible extinction of the animal, and had "a sudden feeling of regret, something of that vacant feeling of bereavement that comes upon us on the disappearance of a familiar landmark, or on the decease of some spirited, well-respected enemy." Yet, even after Grey Owl metamorphosed himself from a trapper into a naturalist, he seldom described himself as Aboriginal. As such, my essay will have a dual focus. First, it will argue that when it comes to Grey Owl's self-construction in his writings, there tends to be less outright duplicity than strategic evasion. Second, it will attempt to show that, even in these postmodern times in which the writer is supposed to be dead, or at most a discursive construct, we often do not read texts but authors.

It is not that surprising that Grey Owl's admirers were shocked when they learned that their hero was not Aboriginal but a "full-blooded white man"[1] named Archibald Stansfeld Belaney (Smith 1991, 210). Belaney had been born in 1888 into a middle-class family in Hastings, England. After migrating to Canada at the age of seventeen, he moved to Northern Ontario and gradually turned himself into Grey Owl/Wa-Sha-Quon-Asin, or He Who Walks By Night.[2] Nevertheless, one cannot help but be somewhat perplexed by the level of vitriol that Grey Owl's "masquerade" still attracts. For some critics, he is not merely a "fake Indian" (Chapin 2000, 98) but "a pervert," who became famous because "he wore a disguise and grew his hair long" (Ross 1979, 79). This unequivocal, and highly self-righteous, condemnation of Grey Owl's actions is problematic because it seems wilfully naive. The very idea of imposture is conceivable only in relation to some fully transparent subject, a state that has become increasingly untenable as a theoretical concept in the last few decades, particularly for scholars working in areas such as life writing. Paul John Eakin, for instance, is so convinced of the centrality of fictions in the construction of any life story that he considers it wise to speak, not of the individual self, but of "*selves*" (1999, x). Moreover, the focus on Grey Owl's imposture has been so unrelenting that it has overshadowed every other aspect of his life, including the audacity of his disguise. One of the principal tenets of social identity is that, whatever else one may do, one cannot change one's biological ancestors. As the philosopher Horace Kallen puts it in a celebrated (if androcentric) phrase, "Men may change their clothes, their politics, their wives, their religions, their philosophies, to a greater or less extent: they cannot change their grandfathers" (1924, 122). This assumption has recently been questioned by advocates of theories of consensual affiliation or postethnicity, who challenge "the right of one's grandfather or grandmother to determine [one's] primary identity." Yet even such scholars stress that an individual does not usually choose to be, say, "a Japanese American in the absence of an element of Japanese ancestry to begin with" (Hollinger 1995, 116–17). However, this is precisely what Grey Owl did. In his attempt to construct his ideal self-identity, he jettisoned his whole biological family and embraced a new one to which he had no genetic connection whatsoever.

The most unfortunate consequence of the obsession with Grey Owl's imposture has been that it has completely obscured his achievement as an environmentalist and nature writer. In the 1930s Grey Owl emerged as one of the pre-eminent conservationists in the world. Modelling himself on Longfellow's "noble Hiawatha," who learns the "language" of every bird and every beast (Longfellow 1983, 255, 193),[3] he established himself as the champion of Canada's nature and wildlife. In particular, Grey Owl became the great protector of "our national animal," the beaver (1972, 153). As his biographer Donald B. Smith states, "He was one of the few individuals in Canada" at the time who "had awakened to the fact" that the nation's natural resources "have a limit to them" (1991, 104). Grey Owl owed his public image and credibility to two different factors—his writings and his lectures. In just over five years, he published four best-selling books: The Men of the Last Frontier (1931), a collection of essays about the Canadian (Northern Ontario) wilderness; Pilgrims of the Wild (1935), a much fictionalized memoir; The Adventures of Sajo and Her Beaver People (1936), a book for children, published in North America as Sajo and the Beaver People; and Tales of an Empty Cabin (1936), another collection of essays about the Canadian wilderness. In addition to his books, Grey Owl promoted what he termed his "insidious propaganda in favour of conservation and consideration for the weaker brethren" (1938b, 58) through a series of lecture tours of Canada, the United States, and—especially—Great Britain. At such events, he was usually dressed in moccasins, "with a single feather in his hair." Sometimes, he also wore on one shoulder "a maple leaf embroidered in shiny beads, the symbol of his adopted country," and on the other shoulder, "a beaver, the symbol of his crusade to preserve the North's forests, lakes, and its wildlife" (Smith 1991, 1, 2).

The fact that Grey Owl normally addressed his audiences wearing Aboriginal regalia leaves little doubt as to the identity he wished to project, something he reinforced when he described himself as a "North American Indian" and his compatriots as "our Indian people" (1938a, 103, 108).[4] Curiously, in his writings, he is much more judicious about specifying his ethnonational background. Indeed, in The Men of the Last Frontier he often appears to construct himself as a white man. Grey Owl's first book tends to be considered inferior to the subsequent Pilgrims of the Wild, whose focus on the author's "individual soul" makes it more amenable to critics (Deacon 1935, 158; Dickson 1975, 222; Smith 1991, 78). Yet, in many ways, The Men of the Last Frontier is his pivotal work. Grey Owl submitted it, under the title The Vanishing Frontier, to his London publisher, Country Life, the owners of the magazine of the same name in which his essays first appeared. When Country Life changed the manuscript's title without consulting him, he "disowned" the publisher (Smith 1991, 115)[5] and initiated a fateful relationship with Lovat Dickson, a Canadian who had recently opened a publishing house in London and who would become not only Grey Owl's English publisher but also his lecture-tour organizer, biographer, and main promoter. No less significant, since it is not easily apparent whether the "I" in the text is Aboriginal or white, the book vividly illustrates the tentative nature of Grey Owl's construction of his identity.

The Men of the Last Frontier is a meditation on the fast-vanishing Canadian wilderness, and with it its flora and fauna. However, one of the surprising elements in the work is that it is a paean not only to the wilderness but also to its apparent nemesis, the trapper. "Trapping," writes Grey Owl, "is, after all, a gamble on a large scale, the trapper's life and outfit against the strength of the wilderness and its presiding genii, to win a living" (1972, 20). Here he justifies the trapper's lifestyle in a statement that seriously undercuts his image as a sentimental lover of all things natural:

> Nature is cruel, and the flesh-eating animals and birds kill their prey in the most bloodthirsty manner, tearing off and eating portions of meat before the unfortunate animal is dead. The thought of this considerably lessens the compunction one might feel in trapping carnivorous animals, as they are only getting a dose of their own medicine and do not undergo a tithe of the sufferings they inflict on their victims, often hastening their own end by paroxysms of fury. (41)

He claims there is no reason for trappers to feel defensive about their means of earning a living, for nature itself countenances their profession:

> Man is not the only trapper in the wilderness. There are insects that dig holes into which their prey falls and is captured before he can get out. Water spiders set nets shaped like saxophones, the large end facing upstream, to catch anything floating down, and round the curve, in the small end, waits the spider. Wolves divide their forces to capture deer, and I saw one of them drive a deer across a stream, whilst another waited in the brush on the other side for him to land. (40)

It is true that, after Grey Owl's conversion from trapper to conservationist, he does come to perceive the landscape around him as a "place of peace and clean content," where he is "the only profane thing, an ogre lurking to destroy" (142). Still, even then, there is little idealization of nature, or the romanticization of the woods that purportedly made his work so appealing to "Canadian ladies" (Ross 1979, 79, 82). In his rather problematic words, "Civilization will not let you starve; the wilderness will, and glad of the opportunity" (83).

Excluding that which exists between animals and humans, the central binary opposition in *The Men of the Last Frontier* is not between Natives and non-Natives, but between full-time or professional trappers and amateur ones. For Grey Owl, the crucial difference between the two groups is that "real" trappers have a "proprietary feeling" toward the wilderness, which impels them to protect their "stamping grounds" (1972, 8, 179). This is the case for both Natives and non-Natives. In fact, he makes no discernible ethical difference between Native and non-Native trappers. When Grey Owl concludes that the only way to prevent the extinction of the beaver is by severely reducing the number of trappers, he targets only recent arrivals from the south. The solution to the problem, he says, is "the removal from the woods of all white trappers except those who could prove that they had no alternative occupation, [and] had followed trapping for a livelihood previous to 1914." That is, he wishes to banish just "the draft evaders and others who hid in the woods during the war" (151). However, Grey Owl's partiality toward "the resident white trappers" may not be due solely to his considering them "genuine woodsmen" (150), and as ecologically responsible as their Aboriginal counterparts. It may also reflect the fact he is likely one of them.

The ethnonational identity of the "I" in the text is largely indeterminate and, during Grey Owl's life, there was only one critic who questioned the author's purported Aboriginality—or at least the ability of someone with Native blood to be a writer. After arguing that there was no way that a formally uneducated "half-breed trapper" could have developed such "an elegant style," the University of Manitoba English professor W.T. Allison postulated that *The Men of the Last Frontier* revealed the hidden "hand of the editor" or some other literary "ghost" (qtd. in Smith 1991, 106).[6] Yet, in retrospect, there are several indications in the text that the speaker, Grey Owl, is not Aboriginal but white, and probably of British stock. For instance, his antagonism toward part-time white trappers derives not only from the fact they are "get-rich-quick vandals" who do not care for the welfare of the forest (1972, 150) but also that they are primarily Eastern European immigrants. According to Grey Owl, the reason "noble forests" have been "reduced in a few hours to arid deserts" is that the "'Bohunk' or 'Bolshie' is seldom seen without a home-made cigarette, hanging from his lower lip" (174, 175). These "South-eastern European" interlopers are guilty of other sins, too. They "work for less wages than the 'white' races," like "the English-speaking and French-Canadian nationalities," and, as a result, have "to a very large extent supplanted the old-time, happy-go-lucky lumberjack of song and story" (175). In short, Grey Owl cannot fathom why the Canadian government is allowing this "alien race," this "clamouring multitude of undesirables" (177, 178), to drive bona fide Canadians, those of British and French ancestry, out of the woods.

Grey Owl's whiteness or Britishness is also evident in his descriptions of the beaver. For him, Canadians should make a concerted effort to preserve the beloved rodent because it is the most intelligent of all the wild denizens of the forest. Therefore, "to inflict such torture on this almost human animal is a revolting crime which few regular white hunters and no Indian will stoop to." But there is another fundamental reason why Canadians ought to ensure the beaver does not become extinct, and that it does not go "the way of the buffalo" (1972, 148, 149). In addition to its natural acumen, and its iconographic value, it possesses identifiably Victorian qualities. As Grey Owl elaborates,

> This little worker of the wild has been much honoured. He ranks with the maple leaf as representative of the Dominion, and has won a place as one of Canada's national emblems, by the example he gives to industry, adaptability, and dogged perseverance; attributes well worthy of emulation by those who undertake to wrest a living from the untamed soil of a new country. He is the Imperialist of the animal world. He maintains a home and hearth, and from it he sends out every year a pair of emigrants who search far and wide for new fields to conquer; who explore, discover, occupy, and improve, to the benefit of all concerned. (154)

Elsewhere in the text, Grey Owl makes similar imperialist pronouncements. Thus, he praises professional white trappers and other wily pioneers as "the people who are actually laying the foundation of an Empire overseas," the pro-nature "Empire-building" of which he approves (85, 87). Yet given that he also writes that the "passage of the paleface through his ancestral territories is, to the Indian, in effect, what the arrival of the German Army would have been to a conquered England" (214–15), those very statements cannot help but call into question the probability that he is Aboriginal.[7]

The most compelling reason for suspecting that Grey Owl is not Aboriginal, however, is the way he usually presents the First Nations. Grey Owl tells us that he was "accustomed to hunting on the plains" before he moved to Northern Ontario (1972, 101), where he casts his "lot" with the Anishinabe, who eventually adopt him as "a blood-brother" (225, 244). Tellingly, he does not claim he is Aboriginal, only that he is embraced by the Anishinabe. More significantly, he tends to refer to the First Nations not only as "they" but also in the past tense, as if he believes they are destined to vanish from the face of the earth. For instance, he asserts that one of the consequences of the deforestation of Canada is the disappearance of the white trapper, but adds that "with him will go his friend the Indian to be a memory of days and a life that are past beyond recall" (1931, 26). Similarly, he says that the Anishinabe are "a fading people. Not long from now will come one sunset, their last; far from the graves of their fathers they are awaiting with stolid calm what, to them, is the inevitable" (226–27). So convinced is he of the fate progress has in store for the First Nations that he suggests it is preferable that they disappear with a flourish, before their situation deteriorates even further:

> It is better that [the Indian] should follow where the adventurer and the free trapper already point the way, to where the receding, ever shrinking line of the Last Frontier is fading into the dimness of the past. Better thus, than that he should be thrown into the grinding wheels of the mill of modernity, to be spewed out a nondescript, undistinguishable from the mediocrity that surrounds him, a reproach to the memory of a noble race. Better to leave him, for the short time that remains to him, to his recollections, his animals, and his elfin-haunted groves, and when the end comes, his race will meet it as a people, with the same stoic calm with which they met it individually when defeated in war in former times. (221)

But come the end will, and before long. As his Anishinabe mentor declares, "Soon another sun will set for the Indian; and it will be forever" (246). In any case, what becomes rather apparent is that the "I" in *The Men of the Last Frontier* usually does not portray himself as being genetically part of the people amongst whom he lives.

Grey Owl is more forthright about his (ostensibly) Aboriginal identity in his second book. *Pilgrims of the Wild*, his autobiography, documents his transformation from a killer of wild animals to their passionate protector. His natural conversion is precipitated primarily by Gertrude Bernard or Anahareo, the fourth of his five wives or common-law partners, also known by her nickname of Pony. An assimilated Mohawk who ironically attempts to indigenize herself through the man she calls her own "Jesse James, that mad, dashing, and romantic Robin Hood of America" (1988, 2), Anahareo plays a critical role in Grey Owl's life. It is thanks to his "strictly modern" wife, he professes, that he becomes aware that his is a "bloody occupation" (1935b, 16, 24). After meeting Anahareo, Grey Owl for the first time begins to see wildlife not just as part of the forest, but as the forest itself. As he says of the beaver, they "stood for something vital, something essential in this wilderness, were a component part of it; they *were* the wilderness. With them gone it would be empty; without them it would be not a wilderness but a waste" (48). He claims that a "feeling of kinship for all the wild that had been growing on me for years, at this time seemed to have reached its culmination" (139). But it is in response to Anahareo's revulsion to trapping that he comes to sense that animals such as the beaver "were more fun alive than dead, and [that] perhaps if I could write about them they would provide many times over the value of their miserable little hides, beaver included, and still be there as good friends as ever" (141). Consequently, instead of killing those creatures for a living, he decides to help preserve them through his writings and the creation of nature reserves.

Still, even in *Pilgrims of the Wild*, Grey Owl is quite reticent about his origins. He writes in the preface that while his and Anahareo's is "not altogether an Indian story, it has an Indian background" (1935b, xiii). Later, he adds that "we are Indian, and have perhaps some queer ideas" and also that they are "representatives of two tribes who, above all others, had each in their day made the war-trail a thing of horror" (163, 38). Yet, in his case, he never specifies what is that tribe. As in *The Men of the Last Frontier*, the "I" in the text is again a man close to the land, someone who boasts that he has "lived with Nature all my life" (203). Nevertheless, his ethnonational affiliation remains elusive. The most significant comment he makes about it occurs early in the narrative. He asserts that even prior to his epiphany, he was already "not without a certain sense of justice which, though not recognized as such at the time, evinced itself in strange ways" (24–25). To him, this early identification with wild animals means that a "primitive and imaginative ancestry had not been without its influence" (25). However, perhaps the word he truly intended to use was not "imaginative" but "imaginary" ancestry.

In his last book, *Tales of an Empty Cabin*, Grey Owl refers only once to himself and his kin as people "who are part Indian and part White" (1999, 152), again underscoring the fact that he almost never unequivocally identifies his ethnonational affiliation in his writings. He does so only in the numerous interviews he gave promoting his books or lectures tours—in which he usually declares that he was born in Hermosillo, Mexico, to an Apache mother and a Scots father (Smith 1991, 206, 122–23)—and in his correspondence with his admirers and associates. For example, in a 1935 letter to his British and Canadian publishers, in which he describes himself as "a modern Hiawatha and perhaps an interpreter of the spirit of the wild," Grey Owl writes: "Do not bill me as a full-blooded Indian; let it be known that I am of mixed parentage. I favour the Indian in build, action, mentality, and to a large extent facially, but am not very dark skinned, about a rather light bronze, have blue eyes and black hair, worn in braids" (1938b, 68–69). Then, in a postscript to the letter, he urges his interlocutors not to introduce him to the British public "as specifically Scotch and Apache." As he elaborates, "Half-breed trapper I am, and far more closely identified with the Ojibway Indians than any other people. I want the Ojibways to get their share of any credit that may accrue. I am their man. They taught me much" (71). Incidentally, this is a debt he often acknowledges elsewhere, notably in *The Men of the Last Frontier*, where he candidly admits that he owes his knowledge of nature to the Anishinabe (1972, 225–27).

In two separate letters to the influential Canadian literary critic William Arthur Deacon, written that same year, Grey Owl presents a somewhat different version of his past. In the first letter he claims he was born, not in Mexico, but in "the United States, which country I respect & admire (less the emasculate gigolo element we hear in the monkey band over the radio)." He adds that he arrived in Canada in 1905 and was later "made a Canadian citizen," his "status as a native-born [having] been conceded by the Native Sons of Canada" (1935b, 161). Grey Owl's second letter was triggered by a note from Deacon informing him that "an acquaintance of yours from the woods" has charged that "you are all Scotch without a drop of Indian blood in you" and that "you assume the Red Brother for artistic effect" (Deacon 1935, 162). An outraged Grey Owl first tries to discredit his alleged friend, stating that "no one living in this country knows anything of my antecedents except what I have chosen to tell them." Yet, after declaring that "I have not analysed my blood mixture quite as minutely as some would wish," he proceeds to describe its "component parts" (1935b, 162–63) in considerable detail:

> Mother— ½ Scotch (American)
> ½ Indian
> Father— Full White, American
> reputed Scotch descendent. (163)

That is, as he underlines, he is "a quarter Indian, a quarter Scotch & the rest reputed Scotch, tho unproven." He further states that, even though he is technically a halfbreed, "my whole life-training, my mentality, methods, & whole attitude is undeniably Indian." He insists that the only reason he told his editor he was "a bushwacker, a man of Indian blood," was that "I was tarred with the brush, & felt I was admitting something" (1935a, 163).

Needless to say, what becomes conspicuously evident in Grey Owl's writings is that there is an appreciable degree of improvisation in his construction of his Aboriginal self. The Anishinabe poet Armand Garnet Ruffo captures beautifully the provisional nature of the subject's identity in his long poem about the Englishman-turned-trapper-turned-Indian:

> I begin by signing my name Grey Owl,
> and saying I was adopted by the Ojibway,
> and that for 15 years I spoke nothing but Indian;
> then, before I know it, I have Apache blood.
> Finally I'm calling myself an Indian writer.
> Fast, it all happens so fast. (1996, 71–72)

Given the apparent tentativeness of Grey Owl's self-construction, one cannot help but agree with him that he probably was not quite prepared for his literary success and "never figured on all this racial stuff" (Grey Owl 1935b, 164).[8]

Still, whether or not Grey Owl should have anticipated the repercussions of presenting himself as Aboriginal, the fact remains that the matter of his ethnoracial identity has come to eclipse virtually every other aspect of his life and career. This incessant focus on his impersonation raises a series of questions. First, as Grey Owl's critics concentrate on his identity, they tend to simplify what may not be simple at all. That is, they create the impression that fictionality does not normally play a central role in the construction of the self. But, as we have seen at least since the advent of poststructuralism, one of the challenges in the study of life writing is that "we cannot say for sure where the 'I' begins and ends" (Eakin 1999, 181). Grey Owl's critics also seem too certain of the conservationist's psychological motivation, usually depicting him as a member of the "Wannabee" tribe, one of those "Indian poseurs" whose role playing is supposedly a form of cultural "'genocide'" (Green 1988, 44, 31). However, there are some writers who have perceived him differently. The poet Gwendolyn MacEwen, for instance, suggests there is nothing necessarily nefarious about Grey Owl attempting to "turn himself into an Indian," since his journeys through the

Canadian wilderness are really "in search of himself, in search of Archie Belaney" (1987, 72). Similarly, the novelist Howard O'Hagan writes that the most significant factor about April 13, 1938, is that it marked the passing of a "man...who had never, in fact, been born" (1993, 99). Arguably the most perceptive commentator on Grey Owl, O'Hagan contends that the champion of the beaver was not merely playing a role but "living it." He was "neither red nor white. He was Grey Owl, Archie Belaney's imaginary man." Furthermore, the British-born conservationist had not merely "created a character to suit the part. He had even created a country for him. The term 'Grey Owl country,' a nebulous region of forest and stream in the Canadian hinterland, was already in common use" (1993, 117). In other words, for O'Hagan, the creation of Grey Owl is a considerable achievement, one that is likely to endure for some time to come.

Grey Owl's detractors also are wont to claim that his "masquerade...was only successful with tourists and newcomers" (Chapin 2000, 95). However, there is at least one Aboriginal person that they conveniently ignore, the individual ostensibly responsible for his becoming not only an environmentalist but also a writer: Anahareo (Anahareo 1988, 101).[9] Since she was Grey Owl's romantic partner for several years, and produced one daughter with him, it is fair to deduce that Anahareo must have been somewhat intimate with the man she always called Archie (Anahareo 1940, 6). Yet even after he dies and she learns of his English past, she continues to insist that "to me he was an Indian, as I was" (1940, 7). More significantly, she maintains that during their whole life together, "Never once did I suspect that Archie was anything but what he said he was, Scotch and Indian, born in Mexico" (1988, 180). In light of Anahareo's response, one should thus at least consider the possibility that Grey Owl's transformation must not have been as transparent as some people insinuate. Moreover, even if one were to accept that Grey Owl is guilty of Aboriginal impersonation, his transgression may not be that uncommon. According to the historian Philip Deloria, "Playing Indian is a persistent tradition in American culture, stretching from the very instant of the national big bang into an ever-expanding present and future." Because non-Natives had no "natural affinity with the continent," they reasoned that they could only acquire it by mimicking Aboriginal people, which they supposedly have been doing almost since the very first contact between the two cultures (1998, 7, 5). Of course, if the phenomenon is as widespread as Deloria implies, then perhaps the hostility toward Grey Owl by some critics may simply reveal their fear of their own complicity in the process: the suspicion that they themselves are playing Indian.

Another troubling aspect of the fixation with Grey Owl's imposture is that it seems to discount the possibility of acculturation. This is particularly curious given the work of such Aboriginal writers as Ruffo and N. Scott Momaday. In his seminal essay "The Man Made of Words," part of which serves as the epigraph to my paper, Momaday not only writes "We are what we imagine" but also that "an Indian is an idea which a given man has of himself" (1970, 55, 49). That is, Momaday appears to sanction the notion of self-construction, something that becomes even more evident when he states that he believes "fiction is a superior kind of reality. What we imagine... that's the best of us" (qtd. in Schubnell 1985, 47).[10] A similar position is embraced by Ruffo. In his aforementioned long poem, he appears determined to prove that Grey Owl underwent an ethnonational transformation upon arriving in the New World. Throughout the text, Ruffo shows the Anishinabe teaching the newcomer not only their language but also how to canoe and trap. As Ruffo writes, Grey Owl is "Ojibway taught." Or, as the poet adds, "Indian can't say he is / Can't say he isn't. Speaks the language though" (1996, 31, 66). Actually, it is Grey Owl's apparent adoption of Anishinabe culture that leads Gary Potts to assert that what disturbs the white critics of Grey Owl is not that he is a perpetrator of voice appropriation but that he goes Native. The ex-chief of the Bear Island Anishinabe, among whom Grey Owl lived when he arrived in Canada, argues that white people do not seem overly concerned when Native people become assimilated into the dominant culture. But the idea that one of their own would prefer Native ways to European ones "troubles" them to no end (qtd. in Braz 2001–2002, 182). In short, for Potts, the crux of the matter is not Grey Owl's ethics but his ethnocultural apostasy.

Needless to say, there are contradictions in Grey Owl's self-construction. This is especially true in light of his frequent (but unannounced) departures into what he calls the "treacherous field of poetic licence" (1977, xv) and, above all, of his ambivalent relationship to the First Nations. Grey Owl clearly is not very confident that Aboriginal people have much of a future, at least those who derive their sustenance from the wilderness. Yet, at the same time that he believes in the imminent disappearance of the First Nations, he is also their great champion. He is someone who invariably asserts their "inalienable and perpetual" right to the be the wardens of Canada's forests (1972, 151). Even some of Grey Owl's most unforgiving critics, who claim that he "exploited non-Indian stereotypes of Indianness," concede that he "consistently advocated better treatment of Native people in Canada" (Chapin 2000, 104). In fact, it is precisely because of Grey Owl's forceful defence of Aboriginal causes that someone like Ruffo is so intent on incorporating him into the Aboriginal world (Ruffo 1996, 173–74).[11]

As I have suggested throughout this essay, though, the main reason the obsession with Grey Owl's identity is so problematic is that it has led critics to ignore his writings. While categorical, the condemnation of Grey Owl's impersonation is based on a self-portrait that seldom appears in his writings. Indeed, the structure of his texts, particularly *The Men of the Last Frontier*, seems to have been largely determined by the author's desire not to draw attention to himself and his life story. During his quarrel with Country Life over the publishing house's decision to unilaterally change the title of his first book from *The Vanishing Frontier* to *The Men of the Last Frontier*, Grey Owl complains that, as the text stands, "I have written a book about myself, a thing I studiously avoided" (qtd. in Dickson 1975, 214). As he expounds,

> The original title has a greater appeal, it has the lure of the vast, though disappearing frontier, which in the nature of such a work as I tried to produce, dwarfs and belittles that of mere diminutive, short-lived man. That you changed the title shows that you, at least, missed the entire point of the book. You still believe that man as such is preeminent, governs the powers of Nature. So he does, to a large extent, in civilization, but not on the Frontier, until that Frontier has been removed. He then moves forward, if you get me. I speak of Nature, not men; they are incidental, used to illustrate a point only. (Qtd. in Dickson 1975, 215)

Grey Owl's strategy to focus on the wilderness, as opposed to his own self, probably has less to do with any innate diffidence than with his awareness of his unstable biography. As Lovat Dickson points out, "It was not modesty which hamstrung him, but the difficulty of combining the marvelous truth of what he observed with the un-truth about himself which he had established: his Indian birth and upbringing" (Dickson 1975, 193). Of course, in order to become aware of such nuances, one must be familiar Grey Owl's writings. Aritha van Herk has stated that "to judge *authors* living or dead, under real or assumed names, not texts, hah, that would demand the act of *reading*" (1991, 68).[12] However, this very basic step is one that the controversy over the would-be modern Hiawatha has not yet taken. After all, it would necessitate that we read Grey Owl's books, not Grey Owl.

Notes

1 That was the expression used by the North Bay *Nugget* of 13 April 1938 in the article that first revealed Grey Owl's British background. The Northern Ontario newspaper quotes the conservationist's former Anishinabe wife Angele Egwuna as saying that "Grey Owl ... is not an Indian but a full-blooded white man, probably of English descent" (qtd. in Smith 1991, 210).

2 Donald Smith's *From the Land of Shadows* is the definitive biography of Grey Owl, and much of the information in this essay about the subject's life is gleaned from it.

3 Grey Owl expresses his admiration for Hiawatha throughout his writings, but never more comprehensively than in chapter 9 of *Tales of an Empty Cabin*, which is entitled "The Mission of Hiawatha" (1999, 79–90).

4 Grey Owl makes those comments in his "Farewell" to the children of Great Britain, which he was scheduled to deliver on the British Broadcasting Corporation on December 20, 1937. However, the BBC cancelled the broadcast when Grey Owl refused to remove references to "fox-hunting" and other blood sports. See Grey Owl (1938a) and Dickson (1938, 22–23).

5 As late as 1935, in a letter to William Arthur Deacon, Grey Owl still refers to his first work as "the *Vanishing Frontier* book" (1935a, 161). Lovat Dickson also asserts that Grey Owl had asked him to become his publisher because "*Country Life* had decided to tidy up his English, and for this he would not and could not forgive them" (1963, 162). Thomas Raddall, in contrast, claims that the split between Grey Owl and Country Life was "a mutual affair," since "*Men of the Last Frontier* had only a modest sale in Britain" (1968, 132).

6 The accusation that he had a ghostwriter reportedly "made Grey Owl livid" (Smith 1991, 106), which may explain the effort that his Canadian editor Hugh Eayrs makes, in the preface to *Pilgrims of the Wild*, to prove that Grey Owl is the work's sole author. As Eayrs writes: "This is Grey Owl's book. It appears between these covers precisely as he wrote it. His publishers in Toronto, London and New York have suffered no hand to touch it. Written in the Wilderness (a capital W for you, Grey Owl!) he loves so well, in the time he could spare from his Little People and their care, it came, copied into typescript, to me" (1935, vii).

7 Admittedly, in the early decades of the twentieth century, British imperialism was not always anathema to Aboriginal people. The part-Mohawk poet Pauline Johnson, for instance, writes not only that Canadians "have one credential that entitles us to brag/ That we were born in Canada beneath the British flag" but also that the reason Canada has such prospects is that, while the "nation's wealth" lies below it, above flies the "Empire's pennant" (1972, 79, 142).

8 Anahareo, too, asserts that if "Archie [had] known how seriously people were going to take his ancestry," he would "have clamped down on that 'full-blooded Indian' stuff. But how was he to know that the more he wrote, the more Indian he became in the eyes of the public?" (1988, 138).

9 In *Pilgrims of the wild*, Grey Owl states that, when he first started to write his essays, Anahareo even provided him with the writing manuals (1935b, 199–200).

10 The ellipsis in the quotation is Schubnell's.

11 As I have argued elsewhere, there may be a personal explanation for Ruffo's rather sympathetic treatment of Grey Owl, since the family that introduced Grey Owl to Anishinabe culture was Ruffo's own, the Espaniels. See Braz 2001–2002, especially pages 182–83.

12 In a letter to *Maclean's*, following the release of Richard Attenborough's 1999 feature film about Grey Owl, Bill Plumstead charges that the reason "the custodians of CanLit" have not included Grey Owl's writings in recent anthologies is that they fail to realize that "literature is surely an appraisal of texts, not personalities" (1999, 4).

References

Anahareo. 1940. *My life with Grey Owl*. London: Peter Davies.

———. 1972. *Devil in deerskins: My life with Grey Owl*. Toronto: PaperJacks, 1988.

Braz, Albert. 2001-2002. The white Indian: Armand Garnet Ruffo's *Grey Owl* and the spectre of authenticity. *Journal of Canadian Studies* 36(4): 171–87.

Chapin, David. 2000. Gender and Indian masquerade in the life of Grey Owl. *American Indian Quarterly* 24(1): 91–109.

Deacon, William Arthur. 1935. Letters to Grey Owl. In Lennox and Lacombe 1988, 157–58, 162.

Deloria, Philip J. 1998. *Playing Indian*. New Haven, CT: Yale Univ. Press.

Dickson, Lovat, ed. 1938. *The green leaf: A tribute to Grey Owl*. London: Lovat Dickson.

———. 1963. *The house of words*. Toronto: Macmillan.

———. 1975. *Wilderness man: The strange story of Grey Owl*. Toronto: New American Library of Canada.

Eakin, Paul.1999. *How our lives become stories: Making selves*. Ithaca, NY: Cornell Univ. Press.

Eayrs, Hugh. 1935. Foreword. In Grey Owl 1935b, vii–xi.

Green, Rayna. 1988. The tribe called wannabee: Playing Indian in America and Europe. *Folklore* 99(1): 30–55.

Grey Owl. 1935a. Letters to William Arthur Deacon. In Lennox and Lacombe 1988, 160–66

———. 1935b. *Pilgrims of the wild*. London: Lovat Dickson and Thompson.

———. 1938a. Grey Owl's farewell. In Dickson 1938, 103–109.

———. 1938b. Grey Owl's letters. In Dickson 1938, 53–80.

———. 1972. *The men of the last frontier*. Toronto: Macmillan. (Orig. pub. 1931.)

———. 1977. *Sajo and the Beaver People*. Toronto: Macmillan. (Orig. pub. 1935.)

———. 1999. *Tales of an empty cabin*. Toronto: Stoddart. (Orig. pub. 1936.)

Hollinger, David A.1995. *Postethnic America*. New York: Basic.

Johnson, E. Pauline. 1917. *Flint and feather: The complete poems of E. Pauline Johnson (Tekahionwake)*. Toronto: Paperjacks, 1972.

Kallen, Horace M. 1924. Democracy versus the melting-pot. 1915. In *Culture and democracy in the United States*, 67–125. New York: Arno and the *New York Times*.

Lennox, John, and Michèle Lacombe, eds. 1988. *Dear Bill: The correspondence of William Arthur Deacon*. Toronto: Univ. of Toronto Press.

Longfellow, Henry Wadsworth. 1955. *The song of Hiawatha*. In *Poems*, ed. Thomas Byrom, 183–258. London: Everyman's Library.

MacEwen, Gwendolyn. 1987. Grey Owl's poem. In *Afterworlds*, 72. Toronto: McClelland and Stewart.

Momaday, N. Scott. 1970. The man made of words. In *Indian voices: The first convocation of American Indian scholars*, ed. Rupert Costo, 49–62. San Francisco: Indian Historian Press.

O'Hagan, Howard. 1993. Grey Owl. 1978. In *Trees are lonely company*, 99–120. Vancouver: Talonbooks.

Plumstead, Bill. 1999. Letter [on Grey Owl]. *Maclean's* 18 October: 4.

Raddall, Thomas. 1968. Grey Owl. In *Footsteps on old floors: True tales of mystery*, 95–156. Garden City, NJ: Doubleday.

Ross, Colin. 1979. The story of Grey Owl. *Compass: A Provincial Review* 5: 79–83.

Ruffo, Armand Garnet. 1996. *Grey Owl: The mystery of Archie Belaney*. Regina, SK: Coteau.

Schubnell, Matthias. 1995. *N. Scott Momaday: The cultural and literary background*. Norman: Univ. of Oklahoma Press.

Smith, Donald B. 1991. *From the land of the shadows: The making of Grey Owl*. Saskatoon, SK: Western Producer Prairie Books.

Taylor, Drew Hayden. 1996. Grey Owl is dead, but his spirit lives on. In *Funny, you don't look like one: Observations from a blue-eyed Ojibway*, 96–98. Penticton, BC: Theytus.

———. 1999. James Owl or Grey Bond. In *Further adventures of a blue-eyed Ojibway: Funny you don't look like one two*, 119–21. Penticton, BC: Theytus.

van Herk, Aritha. 1991. The fictioneer as ficto-critic: Footnotes on the edge of nowhere. In *Literary genres/les genres littéraires*, ed. I.S. MacLaren and Claudine Potvin, 63–72. Edmonton: Univ. of Alberta's Research Institute for Comparative Literature.

"This is my memory, a fact": The Many Mediations of *Mothertalk: Life Stories of Mary Kiyoshi Kiyooka*

"Redress," the word, functioned as a conceptual rupture that initiated as well as necessitated what was a massive subjective act of remembering to remember.

—Miki 1998, 196

M: Well, when do you know when a text is over with?
K: I abandon it. That's what I do, really.
M: You abandon it, then it's completed, well it's not completed, but it's over with.
K: Or it abandons me, either way.
M: That's an interesting notion of closure, abandonment.

—exchange between Roy Miki and Roy Kiyooka in Miki 1998, 75

THE DEDICATION TO *Mothertalk: Life Stories of Mary Kiyoshi Kiyooka* reads "To the Issei women of Mary Kiyooka's generation," but given the many mediations between Mary Kiyooka's words and the final text made by translators and editors, it is immediately difficult to ascertain who the author of that dedication is (Kiyooka 1997, dedication). The wording draws attention not only to Mary's historical situation as Susanna Egan and Gabriele Helms have argued (1999, 71) but also to her age, which final editor Daphne Marlatt draws upon to destabilize key aspects of the life stories. The collection fits—as do the more overtly fictional Hiromi Goto's *Chorus of Mushrooms* and Anita Rau Badami's *Tamarind Mem*—within a contemporary literary tradition wherein older bodies of women and men are considered primarily in terms of stories to be transcribed, and, accordingly, become potentially controllable markers of difference. In this essay, I address the significance of this remarkable text as the reproduction of the life stories of a very old woman whose "specific historical, economic and cultural circumstances" make her a noteworthy commentator not only about a shameful period of Canadian history but also about what it means to grow old in a world that does not adequately recognize that history.

In "The Many Tongues of Mothertalk: Life Stories of Mary Kiyoshi Kiyooka," literary scholars Susanna Egan and Gabriele Helms, while considering "the finished product as a work in progress" and trying to establish the "actual process of making Mothertalk," lay out the results of their archival research into the text—research that included extensive readings of all available manuscript versions and personal letters as well as conducting interviews with many collaborators (1999, 48). In the resulting essay, Egan and Helms answer several questions about the genesis of Mothertalk, and attempt to infer the intentions of the numerous interlocutors involved. Their early assertion that they hope to "raise questions, explicitly and implicitly, about authority and originality" (1999, 48), in combination with their conclusion that the work must be considered in terms of multiple authorship, invites future scholarship about the effects—on Japanese-Canadian historiography and on the place of elderly women within that record—of a text that defies generic description. In this essay, I rely on their excavation in order to make claims about the published version of Mothertalk; my title reflects a continuation from their work, shifting the focus from the "many tongues of Mothertalk" to its many and continuing mediations, and onto the place of Mary Kiyooka's voice within them. While Canadian literary scholars will continue to read this work in relation to Roy Kiyooka's ongoing commitment to experiments in language and form, I want to add an understanding of this text from the perspective of what Margaret Morganroth Gullette calls critical age autobiography, based on the assumption that "the narrativisation of your 'ageing'—always takes place in specific historical, economic and cultural circumstances: national, regional, gendered, racialised / ethnicised, classed, and, above all, linguistic/mythical/narrative" (2004, 67). As Sneja Gunew puts it in her combined review of Mothertalk and Roy Kiyooka's Pacific Windows (edited by Roy Miki), "In the case of Pacific Windows there is the expected mediation of a dedicated editor whose commitment is modestly expressed in an afterword; in the case of Mothertalk the mediation doubles and trebles" (1999, 184). I argue that the amplified mediation both reflects and comments upon Mary's advanced age and that, read in its social context, this amplification signifies the ambivalent value placed on older women's words. I want to raise questions not so much about the individual roles played by the editors of this manuscript—the term "age biotext" fits well into the trajectories of both Daphne Marlatt and Roy Kiyooka's literary production—but rather about the way that this process of publication comments on the socially embedded process of aging and, especially, on being old.

One productive way to think about the complexities of this mediation is to consider *Mothertalk* as a biotext. The term "biotext," coined by George Bowering in 1988, has become popular nomenclature recently because of Fred Wah's early use of the term for his first prose book, *Diamond Grill* (1996). As Joanne Saul explains it, "'Biotext' captures the tension at work between the thematic content and the linguistic and formal content of the texts, between the fragments of a life being lived, the 'bio' (with its emphasis on the self, family, origins, and genealogy), and the 'text,' the site where these various aspects are in the process of being articulated in writing" (2001, 260). In his answer during an interview to Ashok Mathur's question about how "biotext" differs from "autobiography" or "lifewriting," Wah explained that the term works for him as a "hedge" against restrictive generic expectations on the part of readers (Mathur 1997). It is precisely those generic expectations that scholars have struggled with to date in relation to *Mothertalk*, and I suspect that current scholarly attempts (like my own) to draw critically on the term "biotext" in order to explicate a slippery text are precisely what invited Wah's hedge in the first place. Wah admits that he had to "call the hedge a hedge," and so he chose to "[tint] it as biofiction": "*Diamond Grill* settles nothing (I hope)" (1997). I adopt the term "biotext" to describe *Mothertalk* for most of this essay not to impose a generic paradigm upon a text that defies such description and not to place the book within a new set of conventions, but rather to capture the sense of the "hedge" offered by Wah in combination with the tension described by Saul.

Like *Diamond Grill*, *Mothertalk* settles nothing about what kind of text it actually is, and it is unsettling not only in its refusal to allow comfortable reading strategies, but also in its corporate construction of an underrepresented voice. The book relies simultaneously on Mary Kiyooka's advanced age authorizing her as storyteller, and on Mary Kiyooka's elderly body because her age undermines her authority as a voice in the text. As a result, I add the adjective "age" before "biotext" to combine the instability of form with the instability of age identity implied in this narrative structure. As Gullette explains, "Age autobiography is a form we need to write in order to understand better the biased and backward age ideologies that do us harm, as creatures aged by the particular culture in which we chance to live" (2004, 67).

Rather than continuing the scholarly examination of the archival materials that culminate (at least for now) in the current edition of Mary Kiyooka's life stories, I want to explore Egan and Helms's questions about authority and originality through a discussion of the narrative appropriation manifest in the published version of *Mothertalk*, and to argue that this multivalent appropriation happens and is even celebrated in part because the subject whose voice is adapted is that of an elderly woman. Mary's advanced age makes her an authority through personal experience about the historical events that the editors want to frame. Both the assumption that her natural role is storyteller and the contradictory assertion that her stories are unreliable because of her age and presumed loss of memory allow a number of interlocutors to play at authority over this document, making this an intriguing commentary on the ambivalent value of old women in contemporary Canadian literary expression.

In *Woman, Native, Other*, Trinh T. Min-ha brings out the ambivalent investment family members have in an elderly woman's stories: "In this chain and continuum, I am but one link. The story is me, neither me nor mine. It does not really belong to me, and while I feel greatly responsible for it, I also enjoy the irresponsibility of the pleasure obtained through the process of transferring" (1989, 300).

In the case of a Canadian immigrant family, for example, a generational difference can also be cultural, and auto/biographers such as Roy Kiyooka appropriate a cultural heritage that is theirs and *not* theirs. The many ways in which *Mothertalk* is mediated through translators, family members, family friend Daphne Marlatt, and later reviewers and literary scholars, speak to the ways in which appropriation can be simultaneously productive and out of place. Mary Kiyooka escaped the official internment experienced by many of her peers but not the racism that dictated the policy, and her witness to events of the Second World War pushes her stories beyond the personal to a familial and political significance in which many people share. Not despite but through narrative appropriation, the fabrication of Mary Kiyooka's "life stories" continues in form and content the argument about internment and state-sanctioned racism of which Joy Kogawa's novel *Obasan* is the most famous literary document, as the text itself moves its readers towards a new argument about the accomplishments of the Japanese Canadian Redress Agreement (the Canadian government's official response to the internment). What Egan and Helms call "serial collaboration" (although their own intervention demonstrates and claims it is not sequential) creates a commemorative document that calls into question both the nature of memory and the perils of its preservation.

Making Mother Talk

Writers and readers continue to struggle to understand what this text's participation in genre codes might be began well before it was published, and each critical essay that has been written on the book (including Mothertalk's introduction) contains a section that explains the structure of the book to those readers not familiar with the process of its making. Mothertalk was Canadian artist and poet Roy Kiyooka's idea. He wanted to record his mother's stories, particularly of her life in Japan before immigrating to Canada, but did not feel his Japanese was sufficient to the task. Daphne Marlatt explains, "It was Roy, feeling the inadequacy of his own Japanese, who asked his friend, the translator Matsuki Masutani, to interview his mother at length in her mother-tongue and then transcribe and translate her stories into English" (Kiyooka 1997, 3). Roy then reworked the transcriptions: he changed the English into a colloquial language that he thought best reflected the dated, local dialect (Kochi-ben) spoken by his mother, whose Japanese had not changed much since the turn of the century. In keeping with his mother's mode of narration, he rejected chronology as an organizing principle, and instead juxtaposed sections to bring out repeated motifs.

Roy was intensely aware of his odd predicament when he set out to produce Mothertalk. As Marlatt explains, "Matsuki Masutani recalls Roy laughing about this process, 'I need a translator to listen to my own mother's story—what a funny situation I'm in.'"(personal letter, June 13, 1995) (Kiyooka 1997, 3). This linguistic gulf looms throughout the book, as Mary's voice comments on the irony and difficulty of the predicament she finds herself in. She says, "My kids will never know all that befell their Mom because she never learned to speak English well and they didn't learn enough Nihongo [Japanese]" (14–15). Roy's Japanese is as limited as his mother's English and so he refers to the resulting tongue as "inglish," of which Roy Miki says, "Kiyooka's 'inglish'... stands for his own transformation of anglocentric 'english' into a language that could articulate the networks of a subjectivity nurtured in another mother tongue, in his case the vernacular, childhood 'japanese' which he absorbed through his mother" (1998, 76 n. 2). This "inglish," for which Roy is well known and which appears throughout Mothertalk both in the life stories and in the interspersed poetry, enacts how slang attempts to fix in time expressions that exceed its attempts. Marlatt describes the language in which Roy tried to convey his mother's stories: "A plastic fusion of formality and distinctly colloquial words or phrases, many of them with an out-of-date whiff about them, this language is an English version of the Tosa dialect she acquired as a child at the turn of the century, a dialect arrested in time from the point of her emigration" (4). The most jarring example of this linguistic collision, particularly between anglicized expression and vernacular "japanese," occurs when Mary is purported to say, of her estranged daughter Mariko, "She said Kyoto was her true Bailiwick" (130). The conjunction of Kyoto with the Anglo-saxon term "Bailiwick" highlights the transformation to which Miki refers while the collision of the two languages marks the devastating dislocation that was forced upon Mary and her children by racialized governmental policy when they were made to separate. While Roy Kiyooka does seem to have wanted a sense of his mother's antiquated voice to be memorialized as much as her stories, he also manages to capture within her expression the tension of living between worlds that he experienced from, at times, an opposite perspective. This juxtaposition, evoked through language, continues the experiments in form, or "interfaces" as Kiyooka puts it, that occur throughout his visual and textual oeuvre.

Roy died in 1994, before his mother and before he could complete the project. At the request of his daughters, Roy's former companion, Canadian poet and novelist Daphne Marlatt, agreed to complete the editorial project as what she calls her "last gift to Roy" (qtd. in Egan and Helms 1999, 63). In seeing the book through to publication, Marlatt made difficult decisions to undo much of the work Roy had done. For example, she organized the stories into chronological order, believing that the new structure would make the book a better contribution to Canadian history. As Egan and Helms put it, "Marlatt also shared Masutani's interest in the Canadian stories but for a different reason from his. She felt very strongly that Mary's stories were important for Canadian history" (1999, 62). Her decision to set more of the book in Canada went along with her goal to not just enhance Canadian historiography but to do so within the same geographical confines that Mary herself faced during wartime. Consequently, the book is not set so much in Tosa, the "landscape-of-[her]-heart," as the manuscripts compiled by Roy would indicate (Kiyooka 1997, 160).

In an introduction largely at odds with the text that follows, Marlatt explains, "I opted for a more conservative approach and carefully unwove the stories he had rewoven, establishing when each occurred and what it stood in relation to" (Kiyooka 1997: 6). Roy's imprint remains on the manuscript that Marlatt changed considerably from his draft because she also chose to intersperse his poetry throughout the prose narrative meant to convey Mary Kiyooka's voice. This addition does reinsert his voice and a sense of disjunction into the process, but it also results in the voice of Mary

Kiyooka sharing space with his within the biotext. The further additions of "Papa's Version," a strikingly first person singular transcription of an interview with Mary's husband, Harry Kiyooka, and of two essays by Roy Kiyooka, detract further from the impact of Mary's voice. Despite these additions, for the life stories of a woman who lived through a number of wars and repeated violence to reach the age of one hundred, Mothertalk is a surprisingly thin book. What is more, Mary Kiyooka's always mediated words only comprise about 125 pages of the 190 page text. Even before she is granted the possibility of a unified, authoritative position, she must relinquish it, the interests of postmodern aesthetics, to the interests of family documentary, the interests of the linguistic majority, and the interests of contemporary notions of Canadian identity. Miki claims that

> language, the vehicle of power, is a contaminated site. Truth does not reveal itself in the voice of clarity and plenitude—so Asian Canadian and other minority writers, speaking out of the finitude of their subjectivities, have to be vigilant not simply to mime the given narrative, genre, and filmic forms through which dominant values are aestheticized. (1998, 117)

The vigilance in relation to subjectivities reveals itself throughout Mothertalk in how, with each mediation of Mary Kiyooka's life stories, another subject tries to impose a sense of order or its opposite on an impossibly slippery narrative. The painstaking and shifting layers, and the visible and intangible interactions among them, enact the impossibility of conventional narration (where the story has a beginning, middle, and end) in the face of racist policies and attitudes. That the text has no clear author symbolizes the attempted erasure by the Canadian government through devastating labels, such as "enemy alien," and demonstrates the strong collaborative response to such racism. The life stories, and particularly the ways in which they have been over-mediated, express the difficulties of living across cultures made enemies by war. However, in subverting the conventional notion of the author, the collaborative textual process of Mothertalk, including an oral narrator, a translator, and at least two editors, also calls into question the authority of an already under-authorized voice. As do other controversial "collaborative" auto/biographies such as Rudy Wiebe and Yvonne Johnson's Stolen Life (1998, Knopf Canada) and Nega Mezlekia's Notes from the Hyena's Belly: An Ethiopian Boyhood (1999, Penguin Canada), Mothertalk depends on the speaker's lack of social agency so that others—her editors, her translator, and the transcription itself—speak for her and through her.

The Aging "Facts" behind *Mothertalk*

The most recent contributions to scholarship on aging reject not only the automatic association of old age with deterioration (most evident in Margaret Morganroth Gullette's *Declining to Decline* [1997]) but also the limits of thinking about late life primarily as a time of grace and wisdom—most evident in Kathleen Woodward's essay "Against Wisdom." The challenge to emerging theories of old age is to avoid restricting the study of late life to increasing corporeal limits while not replicating a popular revulsion towards the aging body. This challenge is gendered since, as Susan Sontag has famously articulated, men may gain wisdom as they age whereas women "lose" beauty (1979). In a chapter especially salient to this essay, "Elderly Parents Seen through Middle-Aged Children's Eyes," literary gerontologist Barbara Frey Waxman suggests that increasing longevity has altered familial relationships with the negative ramifications of new attitudes towards elderly parents as dependent and "on the positive side, increased opportunities for elders to pass down their philosophical wisdom and spiritual advice to the younger generations, so that both groups may reconceptualize old age" (1997, 18). That Mary Kiyooka outlived her son indicates that the process of "passing down" stories is not necessarily linear—perhaps Mary should have sought to record Roy's experiences instead of the other way around. The central text of *Mothertalk* contributes to literary gerontology a narration of a life not limited to past youthful achievement but celebratory of the strengths and productivity of a late life lived well. However, the mediating introduction and the other ancillary materials challenge this contribution by, at times, playing into standard assumptions of old age as a time of deterioration and, especially, senility.

In conversation, Fred Wah has referred to *Mothertalk* as a "difficult biotext." The difficulty arises not only because Marlatt made considerable changes to Roy's draft but also because the editors both appropriate and celebrate the cultural and generational stories of an underrepresented subject position. As a result, the overly mediated structure, at times hidden and at others highlighted, asks that the reader of this shifty text re-evaluate the supposed authority of the auto/biographical voice and also that the reader reject the quest for a "true" story. However, there is a discomfort with overseeing the reliability of the story of an elderly Japanese-Canadian woman whose citizenship was called into question in her lifetime. Mary's age makes her vulnerable to assumptions about her supposed unreliability, especially to her readers. In her introduction to the biotext, Marlatt wants to highlight the inevitable shifts in memory that affect the accuracy of the information that reaches the reader (and, in this case, also the listener). She emphasizes that Mary Kiyooka's age makes her an unreliable arbiter of memory; "Even the original material, recorded when Mary was in her nineties, had already undergone subtle transformations of memory over time, altering from lived experience into a form of family legend" (1997, 7). Despite attempted disclaimers, Marlatt's initial emphasis on Mary's age presides over her rather diluted argument that all life stories are mediated.

While it is often the case that life writing is composed of many mediated genres, this text is an extreme example. Even more so than a solo-edited, translated transcription of an oral narration of a life, the source material of a text mediated so candidly will mutate through design *and* chance, so that Mary Kiyooka's words can only have suggested the final words on the page, and they are still always also in process. Marlatt, despite her own past publication success with feminist revisionism—especially in *Ana Historic* (1988) and *Taken* (1996)—points out which sections can accurately be read as factual. The final text goes so far as to include corrective footnotes that quote other family members who remember things differently than Mary did. Such footnotes could call the entire biotextual process into question merely by provoking curiosity about the possibility of other versions that could emerge from interviews with members of the Kiyooka family. However, Marlatt draws on them simply to contradict Mary's version of events, thus rendering her unreliable. For example, she includes Frank's, one of Mary's sons, amendment to Mary's description of her husband Harry's deathbed: "Frank: He had an unquenchable thirst, nothing pleased him more than to have a good last drink. But the story Mother tells is just not true" (1997, 155 n. 4).

To Marlatt, the strength of the book lies not in its authority, but in its expression of the emotional investment of the speaker, despite its deviation from "fact." As she explains, "What continues to remain 'true,' however, is the emotional weight of the story for the teller, and this is what comes through so clearly in the memories told and retold in *Mothertalk*" (1997, 7).

To Mary Kiyooka, her memories are themselves facts; as she puts it in an interview transcript excerpt not included in the published version of her lifestories, "This is my memory, a fact" (qtd. in Egan and Helms 1999, 59). Within *Mothertalk*, her voice expresses what her age means beyond the unreliability stressed in the introduction. For example, *Mothertalk* narrates a stereotypical Japanese folk tale of abandonment, wherein the elderly are taken to barren mountaintops to die. Mary's voice links this to the contemporary North American practice of placing the elderly in nursing homes: "The son doesn't have to bear his parent up a steep mountain any more because there's no such thing as scarcity of food. No, they load their parents and all their belongings into the station wagon and drive them to the nearest old-age home" (1997, 154). Her resistance to this practice emerges from the storytelling role into which the Mothertalk process casts her: "old people don't want to spend their last days with old people.... They want to see their reflections in the world they'll soon be leaving for good" (1997, 155). Refusing the automatic assumption that the present is so barren as to render old age a time enriched solely by memories, Mary's voice figures late life as a time when the desire to pass on memories becomes stronger because she feels she is unique in her experience of both Japan and Canada. It is not simply that an old woman can play no active role in the world and retreats to a rocking chair on the porch to tell stories. Rather, the linguistic gulf and its ironic place in her family life motivates her to tell stories that she feels her youngest children and her grandchildren ought to have in order to connect them to her homeland. It seems possible that the voice constructed for her might have chosen to dedicate the book to a different generation than that Marlatt chose in consultation with Miki (Egan and Helms 1999, 70–71).

Remembering Motherhood

The story that underlies Mothertalk is of war and forced familial separation. The Kiyookas were not interned since they were already in an area deemed acceptable for Japanese Canadians (beyond the Rockies from BC), but they were fingerprinted, and labeled "enemy aliens." They consequently lost their jobs and had to leave Calgary to farm in Northern Alberta. What haunts the published version of Mothertalk most, however, is the continued estrangement between Mary and her two eldest children, George and Mariko, who were the only offspring to share her mother tongue fluently and yet remained too resentful to discuss the past with her. According to the biotext, this estrangement is marked not just by Mary's memories but also by her relationship to memory.

Mothertalk hinges on memories, some of which did not concur. Its contribution to what Roy Miki has called the "post-redress horizon" sharpens the role of memory in relation to community identity (1998, 11). The text documents the unknowability and relativity of the "true" story. It is not just that Mary's age makes her one of the few remaining people who remember the experiences of that tumultuous decade. Mary's experience of immigration, forced relocation and imposed family separation commits her to memory. As her voice asks, "Who else lives in the house of memory but a once-immigrant mother?" (1997, 99). Of the nature of memory, Mary's voice laments, "What mothers remember in time is usually forgotten. That's why

I'm talking this way. Big steamer trunks with strong brass clasps don't mean much these days when everyone flies, but let me tell you, for an Issei big steamer trunks hold the heart's journeyings" (116–17). Her trunk symbolizes her connection to Japan and her disjunctions from her children. "I'm the sort who keeps everything of value stored in their memory—or else tucked away in my steamer trunk" (151). As the title indicates, Mary Kiyooka is primarily cast in a familial role, and the stories that relate to her maternal experience have been forced into a chronological structure to convey the ways in which her mothering was affected by national missteps.

According to *Mothertalk*, Mary immigrated to Canada in 1916 to marry Harry Kiyooka, whom she had met briefly in Japan. The couple participated in a large and vibrant Japanese Canadian community in British Columbia until Mary agreed to return to Japan with her eldest child, George, while pregnant with Mariko, who was then born in Kochi.[3] After living in Japan for two happy years, Mary returned to Canada to be with her husband. When she joined Harry in a prescient move from Victoria to Moose Jaw, enticed by promises of work, she left her two children behind in Tosa. As *Mothertalk* explains,

> I had been in Tosa for nearly two years when I reluctantly took leave of George and Mariko....They waved and waved and turning I waved back but I made sure they didn't see my tears. I had just taken George to Umagi to live with his grandparents, and now I was leaving Mariko in Kochi with mine. It was the promise of returning for the two of them that kept me going. (67–68)

Circumstances intervened, and Mary was not able to return to Japan to collect her children as planned. She describes the events: "First we had the Depression. Then in '39 the Germans invaded Czechoslovakia and ignited the Second World War. Then after Pearl Harbour we were uprooted fingerprinted and duly registered as 'enemy aliens.' All these horrible events overtook us and got in the way of Papa and I uniting the family" (94–95). By the time she was able to send for George and travel to retrieve Mariko, irrevocable damage to the filial bond interfered with any kind of joyous reunion.

George's resentment appears to have affected their relationship well into his seventies, demonstrating the agony imposed by wartime and nationalist racism. In *Mothertalk*, Mary expresses the gulf between her and her eldest son.

> Ah it's too bad but those ten years George spent in Umagi have turned out to be the very heart of our estrangement. From the very day George came to join us Papa and I had a hard time understanding him. George is seventy-

plus now but I still feel a coolness when I'm in his company. I know he can't help it and I can't do a thing to warm him up. We don't share a sense of humour and he hasn't any memory of how proud I was of my first-born son and all the hours we spent together in a long ago Victoria. (115)

The Canadian government imposed not just a physical, but a distinctly cultural gulf between the two Kiyookas. George is denied memories that his mother feels would have alleviated the estrangement.

A similar chasm exists between Mary and her eldest daughter Mariko, who refused to travel to Canada with her mother when eventually given the chance. Mary first attempted to convince her in 1938. As *Mothertalk* puts it, "My Kyoto aunt wrote to say it's time now to come and fetch your daughter. Mariko has finished high school and her time is ripe. Besides she's going around pretending she doesn't have a mother" (126). Mary traveled to Japan, and the visit was replete with the mixed emotions of dislocated motherhood:

> Now despite all the years we'd been parted I still felt I was her mother. After all who else worried themselves sick about her across an ocean. But as soon as we met it was clear to each of us we could never play the part of a respectable mother and a dutiful daughter. Still we made the most of it and I suppose you could say that as mother and daughter we got along. (128–29)

Despite an uneasy truce, Mariko stayed in Japan, and Mary once again had to return to Canada without her daughter.

Mothertalk's narrator simultaneously tries to normalize her experience and grieves the circumstances that caused her filial dislocation. She explains that "lots of Issei families went through the same kind of separations though they don't like to talk about it because it's still too painful to recall" (1997, 67-68). Despite this matter-of-factness, regret and self-blame seeps through each chapter of *Mothertalk* and infiltrates each mother-child bond described. The narrator implores other parents who may be reading (listening to) her stories, "O I tell you even if you don't have a cent to your name don't ask others even your kin to look after your kids because you'll pay for it like I have" (129-30). Though the emotional gap between Mariko and Mary never closed, she and her eldest daughter do, unlike Mary with her younger children, share a language and a knowledge of the Japan in which she herself grew up. Ironically, the two children who could "read and write Japanese…don't want to be reminded of their Tosa years" (63). Without the intervention of *Mothertalk*, as the narrator puts it, "Now it turns out that Mariko's the only one I can talk with in 'Kochi-ben' about our uncommonly common past" (95). Roy's attempt to intervene in the (mis)communication results in a document that, through the work of all collaborators, turns that filial dislocation into a comment on racial policies which can never be adequately compensated.

Commemoration in the "Post-Redress Horizon"

To set up Mary's role as mother, Mothertalk reproduces a narrative thread about her daughterhood and, accordingly, depicts Mary's own preoccupation with commemoration. Her mother is for the most part absent, but her father plays a large role both in justifying her sense of loyalty to her Japanese heritage and in justifying the practice of commemoration that Mothertalk itself tries to employ. An embedded narrative frame consists of the central speaker's preoccupation with the need to erect a stone memorial to her samurai father. Her plea to officials for "a piece of consecrated ground" gains weight from her reference to her impending death: "Please do everything you can to hasten the deed. I won't be around much longer and I would like to see that big stone hold its blunt head up to the sun" (1997, 19). Towards the final pages of the text ascribed to Mary, we learn that the "big stone still lies on its side in the temple grounds, its shoulders covered with dust" (163). Although the memorial exists, the appropriate site for it does not yet. Mary's desire for an officially sanctioned physical memorial to her father entails an insistence on a commemoration that "freezes ideas in space and time" (Osborne 2001: 56). But the stone "goes on gathering dust in the temple grounds," and therefore, as far as Mothertalk is concerned, risks being lost in retrospect (Egan and Helms reveal that the monument was erected "while Kiyooka was still alive and in Mary's very old age" [1999, 74 n. 15]).

The narrated struggle to erect the stone memorial comments on Mothertalk's own commemorative function. Roy Miki claims, speaking of Japanese-Canadian redress, "Despite that dazzling accomplishment by our community, the past still shimmers with the unknown. Our history still remains baffling as we continue to construct stories that evade completion" (1998, 15). The shameful legacy of the internment and forced relocation of Canadian citizens during and after World War II can never be erased or adequately commemorated. The treatment of Japanese Canadians during that period stands as a supposed anomaly in Canada's otherwise admirable attempts at multicultural inclusion, and the Japanese Canadian Redress Agreement symbolizes an apparent progress towards improved tolerance. The burden of proof post-war fell to Japanese-Canadian citizens, such as Muriel Kitigawa, Roy Miki, and Cassandra Kobayashi, who went to the archives to proclaim themselves innocent of the charges of "enemy alien" that had already indelibly circumscribed the Japanese-Canadian community. In the 1980s, the fight for Japanese-Canadian redress gained momentum from an apology and compensation package from the United States government to Americans of Japanese origin who had been forced to relocate. With the September 22, 1988 signing of the Japanese Canadian Redress Agreement, Prime Minister Brian Mulroney, if only symbolically, put to rest one locus of Canadian racism. The settlement included

> a government acknowledgement of the injustice done to Japanese Canadi-ans during the Second World War; a $21 000 payment to each survivor; $12 million to the Japanese Canadian community, to be administered by the NAJC, for education, social, and cultural activities and programs; and $24 million for a jointly funded Canadian Race Relations Foundation to foster racial harmony and help fight racism. (Otsaku 1992, 19–20)

In a moving account of the September 22, 1988 parliamentary announce-ment of the signing of the Redress Agreement, Miki tells of how Japanese-Canadian representatives were seated in the visitor's gallery and told by a government aide, "No matter what, remain seated in silence" (1998, 196). Silence overwhelms the narrativization of Japanese-Canadian history. The most renowned literary document of the Japanese-Canadian internment, Joy Kogawa's novel *Obasan*, is famous in part for its much discussed epigraph, "There is a silence that cannot speak, there is a silence that will not speak" (1981, n.p.). The multivalent silence thematized throughout *Obasan* makes any narration of internment a breaking of silence that may be "protective, stoic, and attentive" rather than merely powerless (Cheung 1993, 128). Roy Miki takes issue with this pervasive reading of culturally inflected voice-lessness, arguing, "While the narrative of self-imposed 'speechlessness' was evoked as an explanation for the lack of 'redress' in the past, it is equally the case that such a positioning was not 'called for' within the boundaries of an assimilated minority" (196). The story he tells of Japanese-Canadian witnesses to the redress announcement who stood and cheered despite admonitions to the contrary speaks volumes about the connection between speech and redress. *Mothertalk* is an example of what Cassandra Kobayashi and Roy Miki refer to when they say, "the silence broken by the Redress movement was transformed into the language of resolution and affirmation" (1989, 7).

In the post-redress publication of the narration of her life, Mary's voice argues that the accomplishment of the redress settlement is limited, in part by what is yet unexpressed, and in part by the broader strokes of Canadian racist policy:

Now given all the unspoken anger and all the heartache it's small comfort knowing that we're going to be compensated. I mean no amount of money can make up for an immigrant's dream gone awry. And if we're compensated will the federal government compensate the Chinese who had to pay such a humiliating head tax? Will they compensate all the Native People who have been treated much worse than us? (1997, 139–40)

This articulation matches the prevailing sentiment of her Issei generation that this gesture is too little, too late (Makabe 1998, 151). *Mothertalk* locates in Mary an awareness of the broader racist questions raised by this compensation and thereby puts the biotext into a broader political context than Japanese-Canadian historiography. The focus here on the most widely known aspect of the agreement, the individual compensation, seems to mistrust the apparent good intentions behind setting up a national entity aimed at eradicating racism. *Mothertalk*'s preoccupation is with the "immigrant dream," articulated as always out of reach. Mary's voice is resolute that money is not going to "make up for" what happened.

In *Against Race*, Paul Gilroy raises another danger of compensatory measures such as redress: "Official restitution promotes a sense of closure and may be welcomed as a sign that justice has been belatedly done, but it may also undercut the active capacity to remember and set the prophylactic powers of memory to work against future evils" (2000, 25). Literary documents, such as *Obasan*, played a pivotal role in achieving redress, and its achievement opens up the "post-redress horizon." But *Mothertalk* is a remarkable post-redress document of Japanese-Canadian history that came to be as the result of a set of active choices to remember. Its attempt at commemoration follows that of *Obasan*, and its narration is a vital commentary on the redress agreement. In keeping with Mary's own skepticism about what redress can actually accomplish, her life-stories deny the closure Gilroy links to such forms of restitution. The narrative of *Mothertalk* refuses fixity. This absolute refusal passes the mediation on to readers and, accordingly, the textual process can continue to change without risking iconoclasm. As a result, *Mothertalk* has to date invited a critical legacy of source-hunting which, though it diminishes attention to the effect of the published document, at least keeps scholars in the archives where alternate tellings of Japanese-Canadian history may also be found. However, this surrogate site does not invite the dust that covers the memorial stone, and instead contributes to an ongoing debate about the veracity of the details and the genesis of the reflexive form begun by Marlatt's introduction.

Documenting *Mothertalk*

Marlatt claims that certain reading strategies are inappropriate to *Mother-talk*. "It should be evident by now that *Mothertalk* cannot be read as documentary. It is a creative retelling that has been carefully worked, a blend of both mother's and son's vision and voices" (Kiyooka 1997, 7). Her attempt at self-effacement removes both credit and blame from her for the manipulations that follow. However, as Nicole Markotić argues in a review, "[*Mothertalk*] can *only* be read as such: this is the documentary of an extraordinary woman and the stories she both generates and that surround her" (1999, 160). Marlatt's effort to oppose creativity and accuracy does not protect readers from Mary Kiyooka's supposed fallibility, but instead repeats familiar, unimaginative relations between the "young" and supposedly aware and the "old" and therefore supposedly faulty. The standard notion of a documentary is that it ought to "[purport] to present factual information about the world outside" (Bordwell and Thompson 2001, 42), and Marlatt goes to great lengths to undermine the facticity of *Mothertalk*. However, John Grierson's 1926 philosophy of documentary film is much more in the spirit of the type of documentaries that might resemble *Mothertalk*'s contribution. As John Izod and Richard Kilborn explain it:

> The documentarist must deploy a whole range of creative skills to fashion the "fragments of reality" into an artefact that has a specific social impact: that is educationally instructive or, in some measure, culturally enlightening. This account must be, in Grierson's phrase, a "creative treatment of actuality," being aesthetically satisfying while also having a clearly defined social purpose. (1998, 427)

By her own terminology, Marlatt's coordination of this "creative retelling" makes her a documentarist who pulls together a miscellany of purported facts, in the form of memories, with the aim of representing one woman and one family's compelling experience of immigration, racism, and motherhood in Canada.

Conclusion

Whether labelled autobiography, memoir, biography, biotext, documentary, elegy, memorial, or a hybrid of these things, *Mothertalk* demands a reading that considers its place in the continually unfolding historiography of Japanese Canadians who faced institutionalized racism during World War II. *Mothertalk* expands Japanese-Canadian literary production geographically and temporally beyond the common focus on internment and Canadian citizenship, telling of how state-sanctioned racialized policies displace people both formally and informally. In appropriating the stories of an elderly Japanese-Canadian woman whose experience is marked by more than one war, Mothertalk contributes to a "post-redress horizon" in a manner that challenges any closure the Japanese Canadian Redress Agreement may have attempted to impose.

Marlatt rejects the term "documentary" for precisely the reason I (like Markotić) think that the term is apt. The slippery layers and opaque mediation of Mothertalk evoke the challenges to memory and especially commemoration faced by Mary Kiyooka, and others like her. The published version of Mothertalk likely fits the vision of Mary Kiyooka, the translator and her two editors to some degree, but most importantly it documents a period in Canadian history that defies typical reader expectations of authorship, it places the forced relocation of Canadian citizens in the broader context of lives that spanned continents, and, although it reduces the life of a one-hundred-year-old woman to 125 pages of a 191-page text, it does convey her yearning for a home she can never ultimately find. Ironically, in this deft manipulation of one woman's memories, the prevailing theme is her own preoccupation with memory. As Mary's constructed voice puts it, "It's odd what one remembers but in the end it's all one has" (1997, 41).

Notes

1 For clarity, I refer to Mary Kiyooka by her first name and her son, Roy Kiyooka, at times by the surname Kiyooka. Although it would be more equitable to refer to Roy by his first name only, I have periodically chosen his surname in order to avoid confusion with critic Roy Miki, whom I cite as Miki.

2 Roy Kiyooka's other writing, especially StoneDGloves, Transcanada Letters, and Pear Tree Pomes, demonstrate his affinity with mixed form and place Mothertalk in a trajectory of what Roy Miki calls "that paradoxical but generative situation of having to construct a subjectivity through what Kiyooka has deemed an 'inglish' inflected by the memory of speaking his mother tongue" (55).

3 According to Mothertalk, Mary Kiyooka returned to Japan because her father was ill. The date 1920 is added in square brackets, presumably by Marlatt. Mary says, "For two years I played the part of the dutiful daughter and a full-time mother and I enjoyed every moment of it" (64).

4 Guy Beauregard examines a similar tendency within Obasan criticism, pointing out that most scholarly work on that novel considers the racism behind internment an "aberration from an otherwise presumably tolerant Canadian norm"(2002, 224). Similarly, Heather Zwicker is critical of Multiculturalism Canada's tendency to emphasize a supposed progress from racism to inclusion that "whitewashes Canadian history" (2001, 147).

References

Beauregard, Guy. 2002. What is at stake in comparative analyses of Asian Canadian and Asian American literary studies? *Essays on Canadian Writing* 75: 217–39.

Bordwell, David, and Kristin Thompson. 2001. *Film art: An introduction.* 6th edition. New York: McGraw Hill.

Bowering, George. 1988. *Errata.* Red Deer, AB: Red Deer College Press.

Cheung, King-Kok. 1993. Attentive silence: *Obasan.* In *Articulate silences: Hisaye Yamamoto, Maxine Hong Kingston, Joy Kogawa,* 126–67. Ithaca, NY: Cornell Univ. Press.

Egan, Susanna, and Gabriele Helms. 1999. The many tongues of *Mothertalk: Life stories of Mary Kiyoshi Kiyooka. Canadian Literature* 163: 47–77.

Gilroy, Paul. 2000. *Against race: Imagining political culture beyond the color line.* Cambridge, MA: Harvard Univ. Press.

Gullette, Margaret Morganroth. 1997. *Declining to decline: Cultural combat and the politics of the midlife.* Charlottesville: Univ. Press of Virginia.

———. 2004. The Sartre-de Beauvoir "Conversations" of 1974: From life story-telling to age autobiography. In *Writing Old Age,* ed. Julia Johnson, 64–79. London: Centre for Policy on Ageing.

Gunew, Sneja. 1999. A mediated/meditatory/mediating life. *Canadian Literature* 163: 184–85.

Izod, John, and Richard Kilborn. 1998. The documentary. *The Oxford guide to film studies,* ed. John Hill and Pamela Church Gibson, 426–33. Oxford: Oxford Univ. Press.

Kiyooka, Roy. 1997. *Mothertalk: Life Stories of Mary Kiyoshi Kiyooka,* ed. Daphne Marlatt. Edmonton, AB: NeWest.

Kobayashi, Cassandra, and Roy Miki. 1989. *Spirit of redress: Japanese Canadians in conference.* Vancouver: JC Publications.

Kogawa, Joy. 1981. *Obasan.* Markham, ON: Penguin.

Makabe, Tomoko. 1998. *The Canadian Sansei.* Toronto: Univ. of Toronto Press.

Markotić, Nicole. 1999. Review. *Canadian Ethnic Studies* 31(2): 159–60.

Marlatt, Daphne. 1997. Introduction. In Kiyooka, 1–9.

Mathur, Ashok. 1997. "An interview with Fred Wah on *Diamond Grill.*" < http://www .eciad.bc.ca/~amathur/ > (last accessed June 29, 2003).

Miki, Roy. 1998. *Broken entries: Race, subjectivity, writing.* Toronto: Mercury.

Min-ha, Trinh T. 1989. *Woman, native, other: Writing postcoloniality and feminism.* Bloomington: Indiana Univ. Press.

Osborne, Brian A. 2001. Landscapes, memory, monuments, and commemoration: Putting identity in its place. *Canadian Ethnic Studies/Études Ethniques au Canada* 33(3): 39–75.

Otsaku, Maryka. 1992. *Bittersweet passage: Redress and the Japanese Canadian experience.* Toronto: Between the Lines.

Saul, Joanne. 2001. Displacement and self-representation: Theorizing contemporary Canadian biotexts." *Biography* 24(1): 259–72.

Sontag, Susan. 1979. The double standard of aging. *Psychology of women: Selected readings*, ed. Juanita H. Williams, 462–78. New York: Norton.

Wah, Fred. 1996. *Diamond Grill*. Edmonton, AB: NeWest.

————. May 25, 2001. Personal interview.

Waxman, Barbara Frey. 1997. *To live in the center of the moment: Literary autobiographies of aging*. Charlottesville: Univ. Press of Virginia.

Woodward, Kathleen. 2002. Against wisdom: The social politics of anger and aging. *Cultural Critique* 51: 186–218.

Zwicker, Heather. 2001. Multiculturalism: Pied piper of Canadian nationalism (and Joy Kogawa's ambivalent antiphony) *Ariel: A Review of International English Literature* 32(4): 47–75.

DEENA RYMHS 🌿

Auto/biographical Jurisdictions: Collaboration, Self-Representation, and the Law in *Stolen Life: The Journey of a Cree Woman*

YVONNE JOHNSON IS A CREE-MIXED BLOOD woman serving a twenty-five-year prison sentence in Canada. Convicted of first-degree murder in 1991 for the death of a Wetaskiwin man, Johnson has served time at the Kingston Prison for Women (P4W), the Okimaw Ohci Healing Lodge in Saskatchewan, and more recently, at the Edmonton Institute for Women. She was an inmate at P4W when she contacted Rudy Wiebe in 1992. Moved by his writing in *The Temptations of Big Bear* (1973)—Wiebe's historiographic work about the Plains Cree leader who Johnson claims is her great great-grandfather—she wrote a letter to the author revealing her genealogy, and asking him to share the knowledge he had gained from his vigorous research. Wiebe admitted his interest in "this self-aware, storytelling descendant of the historical Big Bear" (Wiebe and Johnson 1999, 14), and subsequently agreed to help Johnson write her story, undertaking a five-year collaboration that culminated in the publication of *Stolen Life* in 1998.

Johnson's imprisonment prompted her appeal to Wiebe to help her write her life story, while the process of writing it reflected the way in which the law continues to restrict her agency. The focuses of this discussion are on the limitations and restrictions which the law places upon Johnson as a testifying subject, and the sympathetic narrative context that *Stolen Life* creates to enable her to come forth with her account. As a convicted prisoner, Johnson writes from a position of assumed culpability; as an author of this text, she does not start off on neutral footing with the reader. Her enlisting of Wiebe's editorial assistance suggests the challenges for self-representation that exist for an author who has been publicly condemned, as Johnson was already writing before she met Wiebe, compiling the materials of her "life-story book" (40). Wiebe's presence in *Stolen Life* is not only as an editor and author but also as Johnson's "representative." His role moves from collaborator to advocate in the text, framing her account in a way that prepares the reader for a certain telling and, at times, doing the telling himself. In addition to examining the legalistic framework surrounding Johnson's testimony, then, I will also examine the effects of joint authorship on her self-representation. What narrative strategies does Wiebe deploy to generate reader confidence in Johnson's testimony? How is the reader called upon to adjudicate? My examination of the various discursive contexts in which Johnson testifies in *Stolen Life* will draw on a number of relevant concepts—collaboration, limit-cases, trauma, and witnessing—to explore their effect on the process of representation.

Yvonne Johnson did not testify at her trial for the murder of Leonard Charles Skwarok. Where her account might have been, or where it might have changed the court's presentation of her, there is a silence, a crucial void in the testimonies and proceedings that indict her for first-degree murder.[1] Johnson's absent testimony is significant for a number of reasons. Most obvious, perhaps, is that she leaves herself to be represented by others—by her attorney, by the prosecutor, and by other witnesses whose criminal sentences are reduced by their implication of her. Johnson maintains that she was represented before a word was spoken; before an all White, predominantly male jury, she saw her presence as reduced to "an Indian face to judge and sneer at" (318). But Johnson's forfeited testimony can also be seen as a refusal to "give voice" in this specific context. Her silence retains the possibility of setting the public record straight at some later point, of testifying in a different medium. *Stolen Life* enters where this silence leaves off, and fills in for the testimony not given in the courtroom.

Testimony is a term that has appeared with increasing frequency in recent literary discussions. What are the generic and discursive contours of testimony, and why, as Shoshana Felman asks, has it become "at once so central and so omnipresent in our recent cultural accounts of ourselves?" (1992, 6). Definitions of testimony centre around a constative process of verifying a statement or fact with written or spoken evidence. Among the definitions that appear in the *Oxford English Dictionary*, two usages are particularly evocative in understanding *Stolen Life's* function as testimony. The first usage is defined as an "open attestation or acknowledgment; confession, profession." Implicit in this definition is the submission to an external authority and, possibly, an admission of culpability. Johnson's confession to her involvement in the murder adheres to this understanding of testimony. Immediately following this definition, however, is, another with a slight but important variation: "An expression or declaration of disapproval or condemnation of error; a protestation."[2] Testimony here signifies a petitioning against a situation or statement. Accordingly, *Stolen Life* provides a separate hearing for Johnson, enabling her to respond to the representation of her in the court, and for Wiebe to denounce the legal manoeuvrings that made her primarily culpable for the crime. It is between these two functions of testimony—as an act of confession, and as an act of protestation—that Johnson's testimony operates.

Away from its broader dictionary definition, testimony has acquired specific meaning within a number of critical contexts. Its currency in Holocaust accounts, Latin American documentary literature, illness narratives, and truth and reconciliation commissions indicates the transvaluation of this term away from its strictly legalistic sense. In their work on trauma and witnessing, Shoshana Felman and Dori Laub identify the psychoanalytic, literary, and historical dimensions of testimony that make it a germane mode for bearing witness to trauma.[3] Like the process of witnessing that Felman and Laub theorize, Johnson re-constructs traumatic episodes of her past and transmits them to Wiebe, who serves as a witness to her trauma. The merging of therapeutic and historical discourses that Felman and Laub identify as a key function of testimony corresponds to the different registers on which Johnson's traumatic past is recorded in *Stolen Life*. Johnson's individual experiences of trauma hold historical import by evoking a larger, collective experience of colonization. Testimony, as it is re-valued in *Stolen Life*, transcends its legalistic definition to bear witness to the injustices Johnson has suffered.

The collective significance of Johnson's life narrative calls to mind another instance of testimony that has emerged from political resistance movements of colonized peoples. Testimony, or *testimonio*, refers to a nascent literary form from Latin America, in which first-person accounts address a racial, cultural, or class struggle situation in which the narrator is actively and presently a part. Formed as a collaboration between a witness who gives an oral statement and a compiler who solicits, edits, and gives shape to the account, the *testimonio* involves a similar mode of production as the type of testimony Felman and Laub discuss. A crucial difference between the two, however, is that while the former bears witness to an event of the historic past, the *testimonio* engages a present, insurgent situation. *Stolen Life* is an interesting convergence of these two conceptions of testimony. Read beside Johnson's later testimony to her involvement in the crime, they provide information about her personal and cultural history that is not permitted in a legal context.

Collaboration

In the two instances of testimony described above, an interlocutive process between narrator and interviewer brings forth the resultant text. Johnson and Wiebe's text follows a similar model of exchange in its production, and so prompts a set of considerations pertinent to collaborative life writing. Collaborative life narratives cross a range of disciplines in the subjects they involve and the histories they document. Whether as "autobiography by those who do not write," as Philippe Lejeune calls it (1989), or "salvage ethnography," in James Clifford's terms (1986), collaborative life writing brings with it a rather troubled history because of the unequal power relationship traditionally at play in the production of the text. These collaborations typically involve a transaction between a narrating subject who does not have access to literary or publishing institutions and an editor who is representative of a more powerful social class. Recent collaborative life writing shows an acuity toward this inequity, and has developed an increasingly self-critical element. In *Stolen Life*, Wiebe demonstrates a similar sensitivity toward the different positions he and Johnson occupy in relation to one another. In a conversation with Johnson's counsellor, Wiebe expresses his reluctance toward this undertaking: "I'm an aging, professional man, exactly the kind of 'powerful White' who's so often created problems for her. Isn't there someone else who should work with her, a woman, a Native writer?" (1999, 41). Wiebe's uncertainty here reflects an awareness of the different, charged histories they bring to this text—histories that will have an inevitable impact on the production and reception of this work.

Wiebe's self-consciousness further needs to be contexualized within the voice appropriation debate in Canada. Emerging in the late 1980s and early 1990s, this debate has had a lasting impact on the activity and reception of non-Native authors writing about Aboriginal cultures. Encapsulated in the title of her 1988 article, Lenore Keeshig-Tobias's directive to "Stop Stealing Native Stories" (1990), this sensibility identified an urgent need for Native authors, artists, and critics to be the crafters of their own representations. A number of Native-led organizations emerged in response— among these, the Committee to Re-establish the Trickster,[4] The En'owkin International School of Writing,[5] and the founding of such presses such as Theytus Books. Although many eminent Native critics, including Keeshig-Tobias and Maria Campbell, have noted his sensitive handling of Native subjects and history, Keeshig-Tobias deems Wiebe incapable of "assuming a Native voice" (Lutz 1991, 80). She gravely adds that "the people who have control of your stories, control of your voice, also have control of your destiny, your culture" (Lutz 1991, 81). It is Wiebe's handling of Johnson's voice that Susanna Egan questions in "Telling Trauma: Generic Dissonance in the Production of *Stolen Life*," and her wariness of Wiebe's mediation is related to her criticism of this text's deployment of overlapping, conflicting genres.

Egan sees the different textual registers in *Stolen Life*—testimony, novel, and scriptotherapy[6]—as rubbing against each other, creating "dissonance" and leaving many issues, including Johnson's authorial agency and the work's generic integrity, unsettled. Her attention to the way a particular narrative mode controls the meaning of the text coincides with an argument put forth by Mark Sanders in his discussion of collaborative life writing. Sanders urges us to consider how narrative form "necessarily encodes, perhaps embodies, and ultimately transmits cultural presuppositions and ideological biases capable of creating or redirecting meaning for the text as a whole" (1994, 446). Though Sanders is speaking about dictated autobiography specifically, his emphasis on narrative form "as an independent signifier" (446) prompts a consideration of how Wiebe recasts Johnson's image and life within the narrative he shapes.

Stolen Life is a mediated text, which is not to say that it is unethical or politically condemnable, but that the reader needs to keep the knowledge of this sense of mediation at the front of their awareness. Wiebe is the relay—literally and literarily—between Johnson and the reader. We can never forget this, and the effects it has on the narrative. In his discussion of the ethics of collaborative life writing, G. Thomas Couser points out, "the inherent imbalance between the partners' contributions may be complicated by a political imbalance between them; often, collaborations involve partners whose relation is hierarchized by some difference—in race, culture, gender, class, age, or (in the case of narrators of illness or disability) somatic condition" (1998, 336). To Couser's listing I would add the physical and ideological limitations the prison places upon the incarcerated writer. Wiebe is Johnson's link—at times her only link—to the outside. What is more, he represents a link to Johnson's ancestral history, an ancestry that, she claims, includes legendary Plains Cree leader Mistahi Muskwa (Big Bear). In Johnson's initial letter to Wiebe, she describes her esteem for his writing of *The Temptations of Big Bear*: "*I was slapped in the face by how much you really knew or could understand*" [italics Johnson's] (Wiebe and Johnson 1999, 8). She entreats him, "*Please help me share what it is you know, and how you got it*" (9). "*In my own research I find everyone shutting up on me … run into special difficulties because of where I am*" [italics Johnson's] (8). Wiebe's value to Johnson is not initially as someone who can help write her life story, but as someone who can supply her with an extensive and impressive body of research about her larger collective of kin "*that has been sent all over the four winds* [italics Johnson's]" (9). Part of the challenge of writing Johnson's life story stems from the problems inherent to collaborative auto/biography: especially a collaboration that must contend with the occluding effects of the prison. Johnson's counselor points out to Wiebe, "'She's not capable of writing a publishable book, and never in P4W'" (1999, 40). It is not only psychic stress that Johnson has to work through but also material and physical constraints that preclude her ability to write. On his first visit to Johnson at Kingston's Prison for Women, Wiebe remarks how this obtrusive structure blots out the lives of those who enter it, "this stone place designed for lifetimes of confinement, where blurred shouts boom and echo along grey corridors and barred steel seems to be slamming continuously" (22). "The entire building seems to heave... breathing hard and blowing away the spirits of all the women it has sucked up," Wiebe says when he paraphrases Johnson on this topic (22). He recalls their first meeting in this place: "When the barred door slid aside on the dark, sounding corridors and stairs of P4W and I saw her for the first time, it seemed that, despite our long telephone conversations, she was materializing out of prison blankness, that she was coming towards me contained in a kind of silence that would surely be indecipherable to me" (21). What Johnson, in part, writes against is the silence that this place attempts to impose upon her. The challenge for both authors will be to translate what is "indecipherable." "Neither of us yet has a true conception of how difficult it will be to tell her story," Wiebe later reflects. "After forty years of working at writing, I think I know a bit about making stories, but I don't grasp the impossibilities of this one; not yet" (24).

Limit Cases, Trauma, and Witnessing

Stolen Life is an instance of what Leigh Gilmore calls a "limit-case"—writing that "breaks the frame" to "establish a lyrical position for the subject of trauma as one that entangles violence, memory, kinship, and law" (2001, 8). Limit-cases, Gilmore points out, often have no precedent. "In certain ways she doesn't grasp the magnitude of her own story," Johnson's counsellor (unnamed) tells Wiebe: "There's never been such a story out of P4W; dozens of women have died going in there, and it's closing soon. A kind of memorial, it needs a book" (1999, 41). Johnson's counsellor imagines Johnson's text as a less-told history of this prison, the reputation of which has been odious from the time of its early operation all the way to its closure. She sees this work as a tribute to the women whose lives were spent in that building, and her comments reveal the different exigencies bearing down upon Johnson's story even before it is written. Wiebe expresses his initial wonder at the type of writing that this book will be, given these multiple lines of relevance. "I know about writing certain kinds of books," he thinks to himself, "but I know I know nothing about the one this will have to be" (41). His response speaks to the difficulty not only of writing a text with a subject who is in prison, but also of finding a suitable narrative form for a story that has so many different values relevant to it. It is Johnson's traumatic past, however, that will pose the most significant challenge for this collaboration. What mode of writing can represent the memories that Johnson is about to disinter? As Johnson begins producing pages upon pages of "separate, lone memories, individual acts, but seemingly connected," she asks herself, "Do I really want to know and what am I to do with them?" (41).

The different genres and narrative modes that are used in *Stolen Life* reflect the difficulty of writing a life that has so many levels of signification, for it is a life that bears the weight of the post-contact history of Native peoples, of personal trauma inflicted by her own family members, and of a life sentence behind bars for murder. Thematically, historical causality can make these different levels fit together. "Why has she lived such a dreadful life, and why has she been so destructive to herself and those she loves? Why have they been so devastatingly destructive to her? How is it she became entangled in murder?" Wiebe asks (16), and then answers his own questions: "What I already know of her life makes it almost too horrifically representative of what has happened to the Native people of North America; of what her ancestor Big Bear most feared about the ruinous White invasion that in his time overwhelmed him, that jailed him in Stony Mountain Prison in 1885 for treason-felony, that is, for "intending to levy war against the Queen, Her crown and dignity" (16). Johnson's life story takes its place within a succession of cultural disinheritances and an ancestral legacy of criminalization. Four generations later, Big Bear's grim prophecy of the fate of his inheritors has come true. Cast within this continuum, Johnson's situation is easy enough to understand. The victim of extreme and, for many readers, unimaginable abuse, poverty, and racially motivated violence, Johnson struggled even for her daily survival. She later writes, "I see now that most children, growing up, are taught options, choices, personal strategies. I never was, and even though I understood that choices must exist, they couldn't mean anything to a dirty 'breed' like me. There were just two possibilities: get by, or commit suicide" (141).

"Get by" and "hang on" are the lessons that Johnson learned growing up. The first half of *Stolen Life* traces, in often horrific detail, Johnson's early, brutalized life. In addition to the difficulties inherent in growing up a "half-breed" in Butte, Montana—described as a mining city that lives by "eating its own guts" (1999, 80)—she was born with a double-cleft palate that limited her speech and required years of painful operations. She suffered sexual and physical abuse within the home and lost her eldest brother, whose death is suspected to have come at the hands of the police. The first half of the text consists of Wiebe's reproduced dialogues between himself and Johnson; Johnson's journal entries, which document her process of remembering traumatic fragments of her past; and Wiebe's narrativized re-creation of episodes of Johnson's life. This structuring is significant because, as Sanders reminds us, it steers our perception of Johnson's life and her later participation in the murder. The relationship between Wiebe and Johnson and the process of witnessing that they undertake together frame the narrative for the first half of *Stolen Life*. Dori Laub describes this process and the role of the listener/witness within it:

> To a certain extent, the interviewer-listener takes on the responsibility for bearing witness that previously the narrator felt [s]he bore alone, and therefore could not carry out. It is the encounter and the coming together between the survivor and the listener, which makes possible something like a repossession of the act of witnessing. This joint responsibility is the source of the reemerging truth. (1992b, 85)

Laub emphasizes the trust and reciprocity integral to the act of witnessing. For much of the text, the reader serves as "proxy witness" to Johnson's trauma, by which I mean the reader's mediation in the process of witnessing—a role also addressed by Felman who points out that the act of reading can be an act of bearing witness. In *Stolen Life*, the reader's role is similar to Wiebe's, except, of course, with one crucial difference: Johnson's account has already been filtered by Wiebe. In this regard, her story loses the immediacy of survivor testimony as it is re-worked into a coherent, chronological, and stylized narrative.

    Stolen Life is structured in such a way that the reader hears of Johnson's personal history and repeated victimization before s/he comes to know about her involvement in the murder. Johnson's indictment for first-degree murder remains in the background until the middle of the text, with the chapter "Three Days in September." Wiebe assumes the central narrative voice in this and the following two chapters discussing Johnson's case, and moves from being a witness to her trauma to being an advocate in a legal sense. As Johnson's advocate, his job is to piece together a coherent picture of the events from a mass of information. "From police and witness statements, trial records, and Yvonne's recollections," he self-reflexively explains, "I have tried to clarify a logical strand of facts" (252). Wiebe creates a narrative context modelled after judicial process—a process that allows "for the dialogue of oppositions to expose the factual truth" (314). This "factual truth," we can assume by Wiebe's re-opening of Johnson's case, was not produced in her trial. He collates the prosecution's presentation of information with Johnson's testimony to resolve some of the gaps and inconsistencies that emerge in his re-piecing of events. Shoshana Felman's description of the function of testimony within a judicial context is similar to Wiebe's use of it here: "Testimony is provided, and is called for, when the facts upon which justice must pronounce its verdict are not clear, when historical accuracy is in doubt and when the truth and its supporting elements of evidence are called into question. The legal model of the trial dramatizes, in this way, a contained, and culturally channeled, institutionalized, *crisis of truth*" [italics Felman's] (1992, 6). The very basis of this process, Felman points out, is a "crisis of truth." In *Stolen Life*'s treatment of the trial, Johnson's missing testimony produces this crisis; its absence casts doubt on the entirety and conclusiveness of the court's assemblage of information. But "what the testimony does not offer," Felman continues, is "a completed statement, a totalizable account of those events. In the testimony, language is in process and in trial, it does not possess itself as a conclusion, as the constatation of a verdict or the self-transparency of knowledge" (5). Testimony, as Felman describes it, is only ever partial. In a way that demonstrates this fissuring of truth, Wiebe brings in legal statements and transcriptions of court proceedings, which he counterpoints with Johnson's personal account. But, by this point in the text, Johnson has won the reader's confidence in her narration. While the reader's role is to adjudicate among the competing versions of truth brought out before him or her, the reading jury has already been tipped in Johnson's favour. The crisscrossing of perspectives, then, serves to undo the authority of the court proceedings that led to Johnson's conviction.

Wiebe's roles as narrator and advocate become conflated in the chapters that sort through the details of the murder. He reproduces witness statements and legal testimonies, but mediates between these various accounts to reserve for himself the ultimate authority in his reconstruction of the events: "I have studied [Johnson's version of events], at length, and researched more—including, of course, the trial records—and to create a reasonable account of this day I can only draw out the absolutely necessary strands of details, sketch what seem to be the most crucial and inevitable scenes. What is clear to us both is that, until the very last minutes before midnight, nothing criminal at all need ever have happened" (1999, 239–40). Wiebe's reconstruction of the events is not only "logical," it is "reasonable," "necessary," "crucial," and "inevitable." As narrator, he attributes motivations and emotions to the characters he represents. In his re-creation of a "cell shot," [official audio/visual recording of a detained subject's activities and conversations] in which undercover RCMP Constable Bradley sits with the co-accused Dwayne Wenger and Ernie Jensen, Wiebe interpolates, "in a minute Constable Jones will give Bradley the prearranged signal that will get him out of here, but even as he thinks this, he studies the two doomed men once more, carefully, with a trained eye and memory of a professional witness who knows he will be cross-examined by lawyers in a court of law. Poor buggers" (297). Wiebe fleshes out the skeleton of facts, and colours the events with emotional responses. He even re-creates a voice for some of the characters involved. His reconstruction of the events successfully conveys an impression of Johnson as someone who found herself involved in a crime not premeditatedly, but through the proliferation of suspicion that the murder victim had been molesting Johnson's daughter. In the end, Johnson emerges as someone caught up in a crime and set up for disaster by an untrustworthy relative, and by the vicissitudes of a night of heavy drinking gone awry. Wiebe relates the drastic turn Johnson's life takes after the hellish events that occurred under the influence of alcohol. In the aftermath of the murder, Johnson awakens to realize that "when the law-enforcement system seizes you as a criminal, the world changes. You may never recognize yourself again" (281). During sentencing, the adversary becomes the law, and Johnson stops being a perpetrator and starts being a victim. And it is her victimization—first at the hands of others and then by the legal system—that helps to soften her image as a cold-hearted murderer.

Near the end of the text, Johnson gives a detailed account of the night of the murder, and her confession marks a pivotal moment for the narrative since it is not collaborative. In terms of narrative effect, Johnson's protracted confession serves a few functions: first, it clears a space for Johnson's emergence as a protagonist of the narrative in the first two-thirds of the text. Next, the delay re-enacts the process that Wiebe must respect as Johnson's witness. He tells us "To write the whole story, I need to hear her memory of the basement, but I cannot push her. So, I wait" (1999, 309). The restraint exercised by Wiebe coincides with LaCapra and Laub's dictum that the secondary witness must abstain from inducing a reliving of the trauma. It is five years into their collaboration before Johnson divulges the details of the murder. In *Stolen Life*, her confession appears verbatim, with some elliptical omissions, from the five recorded audiotapes she gives to Wiebe. Before

offering her version of the events, Johnson emphasizes the spiritual importance of the telling: "I have taken Pauline Shirt as my Elder, and she is present with me at the Okimaw Ohci Healing Lodge while I tell this, for spiritual
support, guidance, counseling, and for friendship…. I do this in a ceremo-
nial way, and it is covered under the medicine, and I believe the spirits are
here to help me. My sole purpose in doing this is to give to the Creator"
(396). Confession, as a convention of the prison autobiography, typically
signifies "an attempt to rethink the author's 'crimes' in relation to [her]
own cosmology" (Davies 1990, 106). Johnson situates this tradition within
a specific spiritual context: her Cree cosmology. But when she asks the
reader, "Please try to hear me with your spirit" (396), she makes an appeal
to moral justice, and a gesture of confidence in justice as an indwelling,
universal value.

Legal Discourse and Testimony

The spiritual significance that Johnson attaches to her confession prompts
consideration of the public and private function of testimony. When Johnson refers to her "conviction of guilt, both legal and personal" (1999, 330),
she distinguishes between the separate jurisdictions of personal (spiritual)
and legal judgment. But, as Leigh Gilmore points out, the act of confession
sets out a double demand for the testifying subject. "Any self-representational
act," Gilmore observes, "is fully burdened by its public charge to disclose a
private truth" (2001, 14). Confession, while an intimate, introspective act,
inevitably directs itself outward. Gilmore explains, "The confession welds
together an official and a spiritual discourse in a way that conflates a functional boundary between the public and the private. This boundary dis-
solves under scrutiny in the confession, for just as one is compelled to
express one's private self, the official rules for doing so are always foregrounded" (2001, 14). Johnson calls attention to the demand that Gilmore
underscores in a witness statement describing her brother's rape of her,
when she says, "I have a hard time writing officially, as you would wish"
(1999, 336). With this statement, she appears to turn away from "official"
testimony and to take up the more intimate act of witnessing. As Laub
describes this process, "For the testimonial process to take place, there
needs to be … the intimate and total presence of an other…. The witnesses
are talking to somebody: to somebody they have been waiting for for a long
time" [italics Laub's] (1992a, 70–71). Johnson begins to witness when she
says, "For the first time, I get a sense someone hears me, or wants to" (1999,
336). Witnessing, as a private discourse addressed to another, offers John-

son a sense of legitimacy that is denied her within an official, legal context. When Johnson testifies formally before a court against her brother, her testimony is dismissed and the charges against him are dropped. The inclusion in *Stolen Life* of the court case in which Johnson testified to her rape provides a way of reading the central court case of this text—the murder of which Johnson is found guilty. Its role is to show that when Johnson does speak within a court of law, her credibility is dismissed. What is more, it demonstrates that the law does not protect Johnson as a victim.

While Johnson expresses difficulty with the official medium of legal testimony, she nevertheless comes forth with a very public text. When the court refuses to acknowledge the truths she forces into the open, she turns to writing to find this sense of acknowledgment. "This should not have to be spoken in public, or in a court of law," Johnson says of her charges against her brother. "At best it should have been talked through in my family only. If only that were possible" (1999, 333). Her writing intervenes in the silence both she and her family have maintained, a silence that has been crippling to Johnson's sense of herself as a subject. The importance of confronting what one has been reluctant to acknowledge is reinforced in the very first sentence of *Stolen Life* where Wiebe writes "to begin a story, someone in some way must break a particular silence" (3). In Dori Laub's words, "the 'not telling' of the story serves as a perpetuation of its tyranny" (1992b, 79). In such instances, "the events become more and more distorted in their silent retention and pervasively invade and contaminate the survivor's daily life. The longer the story remains untold, the more distorted it becomes in the survivor's conception of it, so much so that the survivor doubts the reality of the actual events" (79). With her investment in writing as a form of testimony, Johnson is able to affirm the reality of her flashbacks when she begins to doubt their veracity. Dominick LaCapra summarizes the special function of testimony in acknowledging what one has struggled to integrate cognitively. LaCapra's concern is not with life-narratives generally, but with testimonies to events that have collective, historical consequence. "Testimonies," he formulates, "are significant in the attempt to understand experience and its aftermath, including the role of memory and its lapses, in coming to terms with—or denying and repressing—the past" (2001, 86–87). Along with their function as historical documents, testimonies serve an individual purpose. In instances of trauma, especially, memory is a crucial nexus of self and subjectivity formation.

At what point does witnessing turn from an intimate, private discourse to a public act? One of the epigraphs to *Stolen Life* is a line from Albert Camus's *Myth of Sisyphus*: "But crushing truths perish from being acknowledged" (dedication). The invocation of Camus, the Algerian-born French writer who used his writing to bear witness to the traumas of the Second World War, invites consideration of Johnson's work as a similar testimonial act, one that testifies to a trauma that remains unacknowledged—publicly and individually. Both a "medium of healing" and a "medium of historical transmission," testimony bears witness to a personal and collective trauma (Felman 1992, 9). "Trauma is never exclusively personal," notes Leigh Gilmore. "Remembering trauma entails contexualizing it within history" (2001, 31). This thinking is echoed by Cathy Caruth, who puts it: "History, like trauma, is never simply one's own ... history is precisely the way we are implicated in each other's traumas" (1996, 24).

Johnson's trauma is also the trauma of her cultural community. The question that follows, then, is this: is this strictly Johnson's story to tell? In response to her insistence that she must tell her story to break the silence surrounding her abuse, Wiebe says, "'Yes—but it'll be hard. There are so many people in your life, no story is ever only yours alone'" (1999, 24). After some thought, Johnson counters, "'Maybe not only my story—but it is mine. Others maybe won't agree, but I want to tell my life the way I see it'" (24). Both Wiebe and Johnson anticipate opposition to her story during the collaboration, specifically from members of Johnson's family who resent the unflinching exposure of their private lives. Johnson understands that by speaking she will be rejected, even condemned, by those close to her. But while her disclosure of painful memories is an act of individual healing, it is not for her sake alone. She tells Wiebe, "I try to tell my sisters I've made a way for them to follow, I can take it, I've laid myself down like a bridge, all they have to do is walk over me" (24). Many of her family members, however, refuse the story she tells. In this way, Johnson's desire for collective belonging is upset by her most immediate collective: her family.

Johnson's rejection by her family undermines her characterization in this text as "representative," as standing in for a plural, collective "we." While her experiences speak to a larger, cultural struggle, a deeply personal, individual "I" emerges in many of the memories she recounts. Hers is a pathos of acute isolation that stems from early childhood due to her difference from others, marked by the physical deformity of a cleft palate. She explains:

My basic problem was the way I was born; in the centre of my face, where my nose, top lip, gums, and roof of my mouth should have been, there was only folded tissue that left a gap in my upper mouth. Even my teeth and inner-mouth bones were affected by this severe deformity. I've now had endless reconstructive surgery, but I still wonder what I would look like if

I'd been born like my sisters, all so neatly beautiful, and my brothers, so handsome as well. (1999, 29)

Johnson explains that this defect led to difficulty speaking and made communicating a frustrating ordeal. Johnson's image of herself as a mute child connects with the unspeakableness of many of her experiences:

> It was like being deaf but still hearing, speaking but speechless—it was there, heaping up inside me. I could not ask questions, just puzzle everything around inside my head, dreaming it, bouncing it back and forth, without any guidance to help me understand. So I learned by instinct.... To depend only on myself. There was no one else.
>
> My mind was my best, really my only, companion. But I think that then, on a deeper level, my spirit already knew and understood how much I was being hurt. The impact I wore in silence, and shed in tears. (30)

This is an early portrait of Johnson, whose alienation begins with an inability to express herself in the most fundamental of ways. Johnson internalizes her difference by removing herself from others. Her response, she points out, is to depend solely on herself. This self-dependency grows into apprehension, mistrust, and even hostility, toward others. Coupled with the abuse she suffers, Johnson's physical self-consciousness leads to social isolation. She tells Wiebe, "There are lots of reasons I don't want people close to me. My lip is only one" (31).

Alongside Wiebe's treatment of Johnson's life story as representative of an entire people and history, then, is a quietly divergent perspective told by Johnson, whose cleft palate—while perhaps a "manifest gift" of a potent ancestral legacy—results in her isolation from others, and whose individual experiences of abuse—though read collectively—is the source of a fierce mistrust. Johnson's conception of identity pulls her between two competing configurations: between a sense of place within her rather formidable ancestral history, and a painful awareness of her individual alienation. When Wiebe likens Johnson's silence in the courtroom to that of her ancestor— "Like her ancestor Big Bear at his trial for treason-felony in 1885, she did not speak a word in her own defence" (1999, 318)—he is looking past the individuality of the experiences that forced her into this state of silence. This silence is a behaviour that she learned early in response to the intimation of guilt. She summarizes her childhood by saying that "living was a long, silent secret where the very act of breathing already made me guilty of something" (78). Much of this guilt has to do with her gender, as the following sexual prohibitions reveal: "Never sit with your legs apart, never forget to wear long pants under your dress or they'll see your panties if you forget yourself and play as a child will play, never talk back, never, ever look them in the eye but listen to every sound, watch, be always alert and ready to outmaneoeu-vre danger before it's close enough to catch you" (78). Johnson learned at an early age how to recognize the approach of danger, and when she is arrested by police, her exercise of self-preservation is this learned silence. "They are in control," Wiebe narrates. "Except for one thing: her silence. Question, questions, let them pull out strands of hair, even offer them more—here, take it.... Long ago she knew this, as a tiny child she was taught this over and over: cry if you must, but don't speak a word. Not to anyone" (284). Wiebe's treatment of Johnson's silence as a means of maintaining a degree of control over her situation conflicts with my own interpretation, which sees Johnson's retreat into silence as continuous with her years of difficulty speaking and her helplessness to intervene in her victimization. Rather than being an expression of sovereignty, her silence forces her in a state of isolation where she is powerless to defend herself or to claim her innocence. While silence, as the legal code reminds us, is a right, it can also be an act of defencelessness. Moreover, it can be perceived as an admission of guilt, as the jury in Johnson's trial most likely read her silence to be in the courtroom.

The point to which I wish to return here is that the specificity of John-son's trauma complicates the organizing principle of this text, in which Johnson's experiences, including her present imprisonment, come to be read as representative of an entire people. Susanna Egan similarly ques-tions the "one single and forceful meaning" that this text emphasizes— "that Yvonne's long history of abuse, with its apparently natural result of crime and imprisonment, mirrors the history and present situation of her people" (2000, 22–23). Egan finds the thematic coherence into which John-son's life story is yoked "too tidy for the mess of trauma" (23), and her atten-tion to the limitations that trauma places on narrative reconciliation is consonant with what we know about trauma and its resistance to progres-sive structure and resolution. As LaCapra explains, "Working through trauma involves the effort to articulate or rearticulate affect and representation in a manner that may never transcend, but may to some viable extent counter-act, a reenactment, or acting out, of that disabling dissociation" (2001, 42). The resolution achieved by the end of Stolen Life runs counter to the contin-ual intrusion of traumatic memory in the life of the victim, however, and this narrative closure also fails to hold up in light of recent developments in Johnson's case. While evidently unable to "free" Johnson physically, the narrative repeatedly returns to her residency at the Okimaw Healing Lodge as a thematic end to her journey. The impression that Johnson has arrived to a place of origins and healing at the Okimaw Ohci Healing Lodge is undercut, however, by the fact that a few years after this text's publication, Johnson was transferred involuntarily to the Edmonton Institute for Women.[6] Clearly, one of the principle players that this text underestimated is Correctional Services Canada, whose power extends beyond the jurisdictions of this narrative to suspend the inmate's agency and self-determination at any time. Johnson's present state of imprisonment, like her traumatic past, is a condition that is impossible to transcend.

Egan remains similarly unconvinced by this narrative resolution, and by the historical continuum that attempts to hold together the different generic registers in *Stolen Life*. In the process of pointing out the generic incommensurabilities of this text, however, Egan dismisses the real, felt presence of this continuum in the lives of Aboriginal peoples a bit too hastily. I do find convincing the carceral succession underlying this text's thematic meaning, that is, Johnson's long history of abuse does have the logical outcome of crime and imprisonment, and this fate does mirror the history and present situation of many of her people. The insidious role the prison has played in the post-contact history of First Nations groups is no more apparent than in the disquieting numbers of Aboriginal inmates serving provincial and federal sentences.[8] Mohawk attorney and law professor Patricia Monture-Angus summarizes this historical condition when she declares "I have often been amazed that I landed at law school in Kingston, Ontario, only eight blocks (or so) from the federal Prison for Women. I have always felt that I should have properly landed on the other side of that high limestone wall" (1995, 47–48). As Monture-Angus attests, this continuum is an acting force on Aboriginal peoples. It reflects an historical patterning that has a reasonable and ineluctable place in the telling of Johnson's life story.

My reading of *Stolen Life* departs further from Egan's in the way I regard this text's deployment of multiple, overlapping narrative modes. While I agree with Egan's criticism of Wiebe's omniscience as narrator and the occasions where his voice too naturally fills in between one generic register and the next, I see in this text an awareness of its own weight. The different genres that Wiebe employs are evidence of the very difficulty of telling a story like this. Repeatedly throughout the work, Wiebe refers to the challenging process of amassing this text—a self-reflexivity that in fact undercuts Egan's appraisal of Wiebe as detached from the narrative, and as erasing his act of filtering from the narrative. In contrast to Egan's view that Wiebe "claims no personal need to tell this story... nor any personal involvement in it" (1999, 14), my own reading sees Wiebe's personal and professional stake as ever-present in this text—to the extent that his own motivations and desires imprint themselves on Johnson's life story.

Certainly, it is far easier to criticize a text like Stolen Life than it is to prescribe alternatives ways of presenting Johnson's life narrative. Johnson, we must also keep in mind, presided over the making of this text. To dismiss or overlook this point is also to dismiss her authority. As Couser points out, "The justice of the portrayal has to do with whether the text represents its subject the way the subject would like to be represented, with whether that portrayal is in the subject's best interests, with the extent to which the subject has determined it" (1998, 338). Interestingly, though, these methods of calibrating the ethical performance of a collaborative text belie the equity that Couser defends. Such criteria fail to take into account ethical considerations not reducible to the individual or individual life story. In cultural contexts where authorship and appropriation remain sites of ongoing struggle, consideration must reach beyond universal, humanist judgments—with their assumption of individual agency—to acknowledge the different values that authority, self-representation, and agency may hold. It is these very issues that have been at the centre of debate of Native literary self-representation.

Conclusion

Rather than seeing the different genres and narrative modes in Stolen Life as masking problems with authorship and story-making, one could view them as actively drawing attention to the problems with voice, authority, credibility, and truth. Stolen Life is an instance of the innovation and intervention currently overhauling traditional applications of auto/biography. Such a work, as Gilmore notes of limit-case narratives, points to the "new ways of representing the individual in relation to personal and collective histories of abuse that are becoming possible,... the new sorts of subjectivities, collective and personal identities, and the politics of aesthetics that emerge around self-representation and trauma" (2001, 48). Stolen Life lives up to Gilmore's assessment, generating dialogue about the "politics of aesthetics" surrounding this text's representation of trauma and the self constituted by that trauma. To what extent does Stolen Life live up to Gilmore's appraisal of limit-cases as authoring "representations of the self and trauma that refuse the deformations of legalistic demands" (44)? Although Johnson turns away from a legal medium, her account inevitably addresses a system that, she and Wiebe maintain, denied her justice. Johnson, however, never directly appeals to this system in her testimony; rather, it is Wiebe who represents her in the three chapters that sort through the legal proceedings of her case. Johnson appeals instead to the reader in a telling that emphasizes her healing, and in a context removed from her legal incrimination. When she does come forth with her confession, she situates it within a strictly spiritual context. Johnson and Wiebe manage the narrative in a way that allows her to circumvent the constraints that the law places upon self-representation. In doing so, they successfully structure an "alternative hearing," in Gilmore's terms: one that resists legal scrutiny and the singular judgment it imparts.

Notes

1 When asked about his reasons for advising Johnson not to testify, Crown Attorney Brian Beresh explains it is customary to keep the accused from testifying in cases where two stand charged with the crime so that their testimonies cannot be used against each other. Following this explanation, however, Beresh provides further reasoning supporting his decision. He tells Wiebe, "'Yvonne does not present well, [she] does not look too good'" (Wiebe and Johnson 1999, 318).

2 *Oxford English Dictionary*, 2nd ed., s.v. "testimony."

3 "Witnessing" and "testimony" are words that have also been applied to contemporary accounts by Native American writers. These accounts testify to a trauma that, in Dominick LaCapra's summary, "are just coming to a fully articulate voice in the present" (2001, 171). LaCapra suggests that the relatively recent emergence of these accounts is not only a result of the delayed effects of trauma but also the result of a reluctance on the part of North American dominant culture to look at a contemporary trauma in which it is implicated. Other critics have made the comparison between Holocaust testimonies and an insurgent body of Native American writing. See, for instance, Lilian Friedberg's "Dare to Compare: Americanizing the Holocaust" (2000).

4 Formed by 1986 in Toronto by Lenore Keeshig-Tobias, Tomson Highway, and Daniel David Moses, the CRET's aim was, in Keeshig-Tobia's summary, "to consolidate and gain recognition for Native contributions to Canadian writing—to reclaim the Native voice in literature" (1998, 3). This political and cultural mandate was carried out through the publication of *The Magazine to Re-establish the Trickster*, as well as through seminars, performances, and workshops.

5 Located in Pentincton, British Columbia, and directed by Jeannette Armstrong, the En'owkin School of Writing offers a creative writing program for Native writers.

6 Egan borrows this term from Suzette Henke, who describes scriptotherapy as "the process of writing out and writing through traumatic experience in the mode of therapeutic reenactment" (Henke 1998, xii). "Through the artistic replication of a coherent subject-position," Henke formulates, "the life-writing project generates a healing narrative that temporarily restores the fragmented self to an empowered position of psychological agency" (xvi).

7 Johnson's involuntary transfer was posted on the website of Joint Effort, a British Columbia-based activist group concerned with the treatment of female prisoners. See "Current Issues for Women in Prison."

8 While Aboriginal peoples make up 2.8 percent of the general population, they account for approximately 18 percent of the federal prison population (Correctional Services Canada Aboriginal Offender Statistics, 2002) and 32 percent of the total inmate popula-

tion in provincial, territorial, and federal prisons (Canadian Centre for Justice Statistics, 1999). The problem of overrepresentation is far greater in the Prairie provinces. In Saskatchewan, the Native incarceration rate is over nine times the proportion of the general population they represent, and in Manitoba, over six times their proportion in the general population (Canadian Centre for Justice Statistics, 1999).

References

Camus, Albert. 1955. *Myth of Sisyphus, and other essays.* Trans. Justin O'Brien. New York: Knopf.

Canadian Centre for Justice Statistics. 1999. *Adult correctional services in Canada 1997–98.* Ottawa: Minister of Industry.

Caruth, Cathy. 1996. *Unclaimed experience: Trauma, narrative, and history.* Baltimore: Johns Hopkins Univ. Press.

Clifford, James. 1986. On ethnographic allegory. In *Writing culture: The poetics and politics of ethnography,* ed. James Clifford and George Marcus, 98–121. Berkeley and Los Angeles: Univ. of California Press.

Correctional Services Canada. 2002. Aboriginal Offender Statistics < http://www .csc-scc.gc.ca/text/prgrm/correctional/abissues/know/4_e.shtml >.

Couser, G. Thomas. 1998. Making, taking, and faking lives: The ethics of collaborative life writing. *Style* 32(2): 334–50.

"Current Issues for Women in Prison." 25 February 2003. Joint Effort. 6 July 2003. < http://www.vcn.bc.ca/augusto/current.htm >.

Davies, Ioan. 1990. *Writers in prison.* Toronto: Between the Lines.

Egan, Susanna. 2000. Telling trauma: Generic dissonance in the production of *Stolen Life. Canadian Literature* 167: 10–29.

Felman, Shoshana. 1992. Education and crisis, or the vicissitudes of teaching. In *Testimony: Crises of witnessing in literature, psychoanalysis and history,* ed. Shoshana Felman and Dori Laub, 1–56. London and New York: Routledge.

Friedberg, Lilian. 2000. Dare to compare: Americanizing the Holocaust. *American Indian Quarterly* 24(3): 353–80.

Gilmore, Leigh. 2001. *The limits of autobiography: Trauma and testimony.* Ithaca, NY: Cornell Univ. Press.

Henke, Suzette. 1998. *Shattered subjects: Trauma and testimony in women's life-writing.* New York: St Martin's.

Keeshig-Tobias, Lenore. 1988. Let's be our own Tricksters, eh. *The Magazine to Re-establish the Trickster: New Native Writing* 1(1): 2–3.

———. 1990. Stop stealing Native stories. *Globe and Mail,* 26 January, A7.

LaCapra, Dominick. 2001. *Writing history, writing trauma.* Baltimore: Johns Hopkins Univ. Press.

Laub, Dori. 1992a. Bearing witness or the vicissitudes of listening. In *Testimony: Crises of witnessing in literature, psychoanalaysis, and history,* ed. Shoshana Felman and Dori Laub, 57–74. London and New York: Routledge.

———. 1992b. An event without a witness: Truth, testimony and survival. In *Testimony: Crises of witnessing in literature, psychoanalaysis, and history,* ed. Shoshana Felman and Dori Laub. London and New York: Routledge.

Lejeune, Philippe. 1989. *On autobiography*, ed. Paul John Eakin. Trans. Katherine Leary. Minneapolis: Univ. of Minnesota Press.

Lutz, Hartmut. 1991. Interview with Lenore Keeshig-Tobias. In *Contemporary challenges: Conversations with Canadian Native authors*. Saskatoon, SK: Fifth House.

Monture-Angus, Patricia. 1995. *Thunder in my soul: A Mohawk woman speaks*. Halifax, NS: Fernwood.

Sanders, Mark. 1994. Theorizing the collaborative self: The dynamics of contour and content in the dictated autobiography. *New Literary History* 25: 445–58.

Wiebe, Rudy. 1973. *The temptations of Big Bear*. Toronto: McClelland and Stewart.

Wiebe, Rudy, and Yvonne Johnson. 1999. *Stolen life: The journey of a Cree woman*. Toronto: Vintage Books. (Orig. pub. 1998.)

ANN FUDGE SCHORMANS 🐿

Biographical versus Biological Lives: Auto/biography and Non-Speaking Persons Labelled Intellectually Disabled

> While his spirit remains strong, his features are soulful.
> What has this boy seen in his short life? How would he
> recount his story? I only know that his words would rivet
> me and that I would listen gratefully, in rapture, for hours
> on end.   —*Edelson* 2000, 189

I SHARE EDELSON'S SENTIMENT, yet strong-
ly disavow that she and I are unique in this regard. This wish is one voiced
by innumerable parents, carers, and others who share relationships with persons having intellectual dis/Abilities[1] and concomitant communication
impairments. If suddenly possessed of the gift of speech, what would these
people tell us, or is this even a fair question? Is speech a prerequisite to our
receiving their stories? To our education as to who they are? To their gift to
us of the chance to know them and to learn from them? Or can their stories
be told in alternative ways, ways that can be equally valid and valued to the
spoken account? This essay, then, will begin a nascent examination of some
of the issues involved in the writing of the life stories, or auto/biographies,
of non-speaking persons labelled intellectually dis/Abled.

In asking these questions, I am foregrounding ontological and epistemological concerns, as the constructs of existence and essence, being and
knowing, and the conceptualization of non-speaking persons labelled intellectually dis/Abled as "knowers" and as "knowable" must be addressed.
There is a lack of historical information regarding the status of this group
as both subjects and objects of knowledge. What information does exist
exposes the record of devaluation that is their history as both "knowers" and
"knowable."

Knowing and Being Known

Persons labelled dis/Abled have long been the objects of knowledge. Hippocrates, Plato, Aristotle, and early Christians shared an understanding of dis/Ability as arising from divine or demonic origin (supernatural, not human, flesh without soul), and held perceptions of the dis/Abled as being without wisdom or reason and, therefore, without humanness (Wizner, 1997; Young and Quibell, 2000). Later, the Renaissance belief in the educability of persons labelled intellectually dis/Abled, along with recognition of their humanness and their inclusion in the "rank" of knowing subjects, was short-lived when this group failed to respond as hoped to the instructional measures that were implemented for them. Institutions created during the Renaissance to educate and protect people with intellectual dis/Abilities from an "uncaring society" were converted during the time of Enlightenment to warehouses of custodial control. These places were intended to protect a "normal" society from the depravity of a deviant underclass, as the Enlightenment emphasis on individualism and reason coalesced with the elevated status accorded to intelligence, beauty, and perfection. It further combined, in the nineteenth century, with a Victorian moral structure to disqualify inclusion of persons labelled intellectually dis/Abled, and to foster the doctrine of human degeneration which underpinned eugenics. This connection was bolstered by Langdon Down's connection of human evolution, race, and intelligence in his study of persons labelled intellectually dis/Abled, an association now rooted in the genealogy of intellectual dis/Ability (Radford 1994).

Subjugation of persons labelled intellectually dis/Abled as knowers persisted throughout the modern era as a positivistic valuation of objective scientific knowledges, conjoined with tenacious belief structures as to the value of reason and intelligence. The effects of industrialization and market forces perpetuated individual pathology, custodial models, and discourses of intellectual dis/Ability (Enns 1999; Radford 1994; Young and Quibell 2000). Insistence upon the authority of diagnostic labels, the ascendancy of "expert" knowledges, and of standardized measures of intelligence that categorized persons labelled intellectually dis/Abled as "lesser"— devoid of the capacity and means of knowing—solidified their exclusion as knowers and their identification as "other" (Atkinson and Walmsley 1999; Radford 1994). Citing Gaventa (1993), we have since entered a post-industrial epoch with ideological underpinnings that continue to reify dominant, scientific, expert knowledge. Knowledge is created both for innovation and social control. Control and subjugation of other knowledges are managed by the "knowledge elite" through mechanisms of "expert power," serving to separate powerful expert "knowers" from the rest. The inevitable outcome is the embedded objectification of persons labelled intellectually dis/Abled and their devaluation as knowers.

However, as we know from feminist and critical race theorists, oppressed groups do possess knowledge: knowledge that has been subjugated, repressed, and summarily dismissed. Eagle (2001) posits the same for this particular group. Critical explication of the veracity of standardized assessment measures challenges their worth as an accurate evaluation of the intelligence of non-speaking persons labelled intellectually dis/Abled, leading us to conclude that we cannot assume people "do not know" simply on the basis of an IQ score. Yet these normalizing judgments, based as they are upon a normal/abnormal dichotomy, continue to regulate what passes for knowledge, both from and about persons so labelled. These discursive truths of intellectual dis/Ability have discounted disparate truths, alternate understandings, and indicators of intelligence that fall outside this regulative frame, and are not consistent with standardized test scores and the "mentally retarded" label (Clear 1999; Peter 2000).

Further, intelligence is considered to be co-extensive with speech. Verbal and written communications are esteemed, prioritized, and valued as "truth" and the "official version" (Bogdan and Taylor 1989; Stern 2000). General adherence to "normal" child development models presumes that all children develop "normal" language competencies, and suggests that those who fail to become language competent fail similarly to share this essential feature of being human (Shapiro 1984). The verisimilitude of such ideas is, however, confounded by Polanyi's construct of tacit knowledge (1959); by aspects of Piaget's genetic epistemology (Piaget and Inhelder 1969); Stern's work on the interpersonal world of the infant (2000); and Bogdan and Taylor's social construction of humanness in severely dis/Abled persons (1989). These works suggest that intelligence exists independently of verbal articulation, and distinguish between "thinking" and "communicating thought." Non-speaking persons—even those with severe intellectual impairments— are believed to convey knowledge, understanding, and their subjective experiences in alternative ways. Re-conceptualized as both "shaped by" and "shapers of" their worlds, they are granted agency in their own experiences, interactions and understandings of the world. Baum (1999) extends this belief, positing that this group, through the use of pre-verbal and non-verbal modalities and artistic languages, are capable of understanding and exploring the question of "who am I?" thereby becoming "subject," "object," and the "means of knowing" of their own knowledge. Although less precise than verbal or mathematical languages, artistic language can be communicated at levels for which no other language is adequate or available (Imre 1984).

What then of our capacity, as non-dis/Abled persons, to access, understand, and facilitate the articulation and dissemination of the knowledge held by non-speaking persons labelled intellectually dis/Abled? The means of "knowing" thus shifts from dependence upon traditional verbal and written expressions of knowledge to an understanding of the alternative ways members of this group articulate, acknowledging the tremendous diversity inherent within this population in terms of both level of ability and the forms of communication utilized. Non-speaking persons labelled intellectually dis/Abled employ a mélange of communication tools including photographs, concrete objects, picture symbols, gestures, consistent sounds, sign language, augmentative communication systems and/or symbolic messages made possible through art, dance, and play. Persons with more severe impairments may be restricted to more behavioural communication strategies (e.g., facial expressions, body postures, and voluntary movements). Nonetheless, there are ways to hear the idiosyncratic voice of the non-verbal person, even when there is no written or spoken text for that voice (Woodill 1994), without the threat of losing the power of the message (Garbarino and Stolt 1989). The onus is on the receiver to listen, learn, and grasp what is being conveyed, a shift that entails extended observation, relationship, and concurrent recognition of members of this group as "competent communicators" (Mar and Sall 1999).

> When she was ill, I saw the great deal of pain she went through and I was often the only person she could show it to. She let me know very clearly that she was hurting and I often mistook this as personal dislike for me. I realize now that she was communicating with me the only way she knew how and that I wasn't picking up very well on what she had to say. (Schafer 1999, 299)

The Potential Uses of Auto/biography

A growing interest has developed in auto/biography as a research perspective, methodological strategy, and/or form of data. Addressing the epistemological concerns of what and how we come to know about non-speaking persons labelled intellectually dis/Abled, auto/biography would appear to have potential as a means of redress for the historical exclusion of this group of persons. According to Couser, the questions of "who gets a life and who doesn't: whose stories get told, why, by whom, and how" are currently occupying centre stage in recent discussion of auto/biography and other forms of life writing (1997, 4). The postmodern disenchantment with meta-theory, with the "disappearing" individual, and an over-determined view of reality created by attempts to impose order upon a messy world (Booth and Booth 1996; Evans 1993; Harrison 1993), have led postmodern theorists to accede primacy to the particular. As suggested by Evans (1993), this new primacy is relevant to a discussion of auto/biography in that postmodernism has granted a new respectability to individual lives, and to documenting the individual lives, and histories of those marginalized persons who, because they were not "great men," were previously silenced. Evans further asserts that, in the social sciences literature, the "person has, in a sense, become the new heritage industry" (6), with auto/biographies serving to illuminate the individual and, in so doing, facilitate an understanding of the general. In the "telling" of postmodern life stories, people are able to place themselves outside of "the unifying general view," and/or the reductionist professional purview that serves to categorize people (Frank 1995, 13). The resultant emergence of a potentially liberating pluralism "extend(s) the boundaries of what is acceptable, even if normality remains as rigidly fixed as ever" (Evans 1993, 6).

In contrast to feminist and sociological traditions of utilizing life histories and personal accounts to expose hidden spheres of culture, social interactions, and individual perceptions (Harrison 1993), the potential auto/biography holds for people who have been labelled intellectually dis/Abled has only been recognized very recently (Atkinson et al. 1999). The referent, "intellectual dis/Ability," remains a demeaning concept engendering personal, social, political, and economic consequences for those so labelled. Yet there has been little examination of this group of persons' lived experiences, their informal discourses, or "disability" life stories (Allan 1996). Historical analyses reveal limited interest and a strong bias towards the written accounts and voices of others (parents, carers, professionals, administrators, and bureaucrats). Largely absent are the voices of the labelled persons, the "insider stories" (Goodley 1996; Woodill 1994), especially those persons with intellectual dis/Ability who experience additional communication impairments. This group is effectively invisible to the larger society because they often do not get the chance to represent themselves.

Arguably, the most commonly understood reason for the exclusion of the "voices" of non-speaking persons labelled intellectually dis/Abled is the aforementioned devaluation of their capacity as knowers and communicators. Theirs "are the ultimate 'lost voices' in terms of auto/biographical records" (Atkinson et al. 1999, 203). The label, "intellectual dis/Ability," is perceived to negate one's potential to analyze one's own life situation; to possess insight or to understand who one is and what one may wish to become; and to coherently express or articulate these self-perceptions and wishes to the world. Determined to be incapable of insight and the physical and creative potential necessary to facilitate expression, non-speaking labelled persons are summarily denied the opportunity to do so (Atkinson et al. 1999; Lea 1988; Minkes, Robinson and Weston 1994). Because they frequently cannot read or write, they are particularly subject to representation by others (Atkinson et al. 1999). Systemic devaluation and exclusion of languages other than verbal or written languages regulates and makes irrelevant the knowledge they have about themselves. This group is more readily perceived as a source of data for a (non-labelled) researcher's narratives, as opposed to persons with their own stories to tell (Booth et al. 1996).

The specifics of the experience of socially constructed identities can be learned from the stories of *speaking* persons labelled intellectually dis/Abled. This group of persons has their own understandings of their selves, their situations, and their experiences: an understanding that frequently diverges from that of their families and/or the professionals involved with them (Aull Davies and Jenkins 1997), and which may, in fact, be more reliable and superior (Lea 1988). Thus the words, and the informal, anecdotal, and more personal elements of the labelled individual's life story, can be viewed as a source of understanding for non-labelled persons by which we can overcome our ignorance of the lived experiences of this marginalized group, and come to know them more intimately. Such intimacy is proffered to assist our learning, thus rendering ableist categories irrelevant and forcing us to acknowledge the humanity of labelled persons and the potential of lives that, as a society, we continue to stifle (Bogdan et al. 1976; Goodley 1996).

Auto/biographical methodology, the telling of one's own life story, can be used with non-speaking persons labelled intellectually dis/Abled if consideration and attention is accorded to the variable ways in which this group communicates. The myriad means of expression result in any number of alternative auto/biographical "texts." These texts, however, can assist labelled persons to deconstruct the dominant stories that they have lived by, to reverse the colonization of their life stories through revisions of "official" institutional versions or the production of their own alternative experiential versions. These versions would have the power to begin to transform conceptions of individual and group history and be a record of marginalized or neglected stories which speak to the reader of inclusion and achievement, as well as of segregation and institutionalization (Bredberg 1999; Gilman et al. 1997; Goodley 1996). Stalker asserts these versions are a more authoritative account of the lived experiences of people traditionally represented in very stereotypical ways (1998). Those telling the stories can claim an authentic identity and begin to shed the labelled identity constructed for them by more powerful others (Atkinson et al. 1999). Reflecting feminist ideology and practice, this would demonstrate this particular marginalized group to also have a history, to be makers of history and not be just victims of it (Evans 1993). Life histories told from the lived experience of the narrator are invaluable as they do not fracture life experiences but, instead, provide a way of evaluating the present, re-evaluating the past, and anticipating the future (Cotterill and Letherby 1993). If these stories are acknowledged and accepted by a wider audience, the previously marginalized ideographic knowledge stemming from the labelled individual's personal experience can supplant the historically privileged nomothetic knowledge of the professional "experts." Thus, auto/biographical techniques possess the power to render visible a group of persons previously invisible in their own communities (Atkinson et al. 1999), and to turn the cultural practice of objectification upon itself through individual agency and the re-authoring of life stories (Gilman, Swain, and Heyman 1997).

In ways which recall earlier feminist and civil rights activism, reclaiming one's history and self-representation are integral parts of the resistance of dis/Abled people to oppressive attitudes and practice. There is a growing recognition of the need to involve persons with dis/Abilities in decision-making with respect to the services they require, and a concomitant realization that this will require a more concerted and flexible effort to ascertain the perceptions and wishes of those persons with communication impairments (Minkes et al. 1994). At a more basic level, it is imperative we allow those people, about whom so much has been written, the opportunity to represent themselves to ensure their well-being. This idea is expressed clearly by a parent in the following: "I wonder if Jake can feel the seizures. They look so violent. Does it hurt? Is he suffering? The staff suggest that seizures are like an electrical storm in the brain and that he can't feel them. But how do they know, I wonder?" (Edelson 2000, 39).

A lack of voice and the ability to self-represent is also premised to be a threat to the very safety, and, indeed, even the survival of some non-speaking persons labelled intellectually dis/Abled. In Canada, this threat is exemplified in the death of Tracy Latimer at the hands of her father, Robert: "Because she [Tracy Latimer] couldn't speak, the assumption was that she couldn't comprehend and, if she couldn't comprehend, her death really wasn't as monstrous as the killing of someone who could" (Enns 1999, 47).

The Historical and Contemporary Misuse of Auto/biography

Despite the obvious benefits, and indeed necessity, of auto/biographical accounts of the lived experience of dis/Ability, what we have instead is a preponderance of institutional accounts. Much of the history of dis/Ability has been culled, not from the experiences of persons so labelled, but from within institutional practices. In a misguided attempt to address the perceived problems "posed" by dis/Ability to the greater society, these "biographical" accounts are written almost exclusively from the perspective of the non-dis/Abled "expert." Indicative of their positivistic epistemological foundations, these writings typify those of the history of science. They are written by scientists and not by historians or the "makers" of the history themselves (Bredberg 1999). Such accounts are proffered to possess some value in the sense that they afford the reader an initial overview of the historical clinical treatment of persons labelled dis/Abled. Further, a more critical reading explicates the attitudes of the authors (attitudes perhaps extendable to the larger cultural context in which they are situated) about dis/Ability and similarly labelled persons (Bredberg 1999), and the frequently appalling service features, and adverse and disabling life conditions, this group has been subjected to (DiTerlizzi 1994).

Unfortunately, the negative implications of these narratives far outweigh their apparent benefits. Bredberg (1999) notes the one-sided nature of such accounts of the experience of dis/Ability. Labelled persons are presented as depersonalized objects of institutional care and action, thus sustaining individual pathology and deficit models of dis/Ability while suppressing the structural features inherent in the construct of dis/Ability. Case file accounts are granted legitimacy, demarcated as the "official" version, and invested with the status of truth (Gilman et al. 1997). They silence, objectify, pathologize, label, and marginalize the voices of labelled individuals, while simultaneously exalting and privileging "expert" voices and knowledges which uphold dominant discourses (Bredberg 1997; DiTerlizzi 1994). Life stories are thus constructed within cultural, structural, and institutional contexts that figure in the privileging of dominant discourses and the non-selection of contradictory events, ideas, and feelings (Gilman et al. 1997).

In the field of dis/Ability studies, Atkinson and Walmsley (1999) posit a distinction that I find relevant here. They argue that it is possible to differentiate between true auto/biography and auto/biographical accounts (or auto/biographical "fragments"). These two narrative forms are distinguishable in terms of authorship, style, and content. Described as a full and flowing life story, true auto/biography is initiated, shaped by, attributed to, and owned by the author. Characterized as "survivor stories," true auto/biographies dwell upon the ordinariness of labelled people's lives, even when those lives have been lived in extraordinary circumstances (i.e., institution-alization), affording the reader a rounded picture of the author as a person with a history, culture, class, and gender, as well as an impairment.

Clearly more biographical in nature, auto/biographical fragments are initiated, written, and owned by someone else (i.e., a researcher, profes-sional, or parent). A potent example of the fragmented auto/biography is the institutional account: the case file. The emphasis within these accounts on the impairment as a defining feature marking the labelled person "different" spurs an interpretation of these accounts as "victim stories" (Atkinson et al. 1999). This fragmentation occurs for a purpose, a purpose established by someone other than the labelled subject. This type of document describes persons labelled intellectually dis/Abled in very specific ways, for very spe-cific purposes, to fulfill governmental regulations, or to support legisla-tion, justify institutional care and segregation. It is the performative function, the implicit, if not explicit, purpose, of these auto/biographical fragments to highlight only those aspects of a life that meet these ends and to dictate what gets written and how. In assessing their value we need then to ask of these documents a series of questions. Who is the author? What is her/his relationship to the labelled individual? Are there issues of power and author-ity at play? What was the purpose of the account? Why was it written at this point in time? Who is reading it and why? What types of 'evidence' or data sources were used and why were they chosen? What (and whose) interpre-tation of the labelled person and/or the written account is being made? And what impact might that have on the labelled individual (Atkinson et al. 1999)?

Employing Foucault's concepts of the professional/institutional "gaze" and the case file as a "dossier," these biographical accounts can be under-stood as technologies of power which serve to socially construct labelled per-sons as subjects and objects of knowledge and power through professional and institutional disciplines and discourses (Allan 1996; Bredberg 1999). Through institutionalized hierarchical observation, normalizing judgments and professional assessments, these biographies reduce the individual to a "case." As such, s/he can then be described, judged, measured, compared with others, trained, corrected, classified, normalized, or excluded (Allan 1996).

Gilman, Swain, and Heyman (1997) and DiTerlizzi (1994) lament the lack, loss, or unavailability of personal details, life experiences, and life his-tory materials contained within these professional biographical accounts. Focused on the institutional perspective, little or no space is accorded the experiential perspective of the labelled individual, or to vernacular accounts demonstrating non-institutional responses to the labelled person within the larger society (Bredberg 1999). Alarmingly, for many labelled persons (i.e., those having resided in state hospitals, group care, or the child welfare system) these case files are often the only records of their lived experiences. Further, they frequently contain little information of much use to the individual and/or their carer. Conversely, case files appear to have greater significance and value for the professions and institutions that produce them. Appealing and (because of client confidentiality) available only to a narrow readership, they are little more than a vehicle for the presentation of the "expertise" of the professional author (DiTerlizzi 1994; Gilman et al. 1997), begging the question "whose auto/biography is it?" The little history this group does have is not so much their own as it is the history of others acting either on their behalf or against them (Atkinson et al. 1999).

Others suggest that it is in the labelled individual's "best interests" not to have background information "on record" as it may perpetuate negative stereotypes and prejudice staff to see the individual in a certain light (DiTerlizzi 1994), a view which ignores the problematic nature of what information does and does not get recorded. In the absence of sufficient biographical information, staff persons often rely upon their own intuition and/or informal networks of information sharing among staff. However, such informal information may prove little more than innuendo, gossip, or horror stories (Gilman et al. 1997). A lack of biographical and life history material has additional consequences as well. Interventions (even those that are ineffective or harmful) may be repeated if there is no record of their previous use. Similarly, time may be wasted completing assessments that have already been done (DiTerlizzi 1994). Unsupported judgments made as to the potential of non-speaking labelled persons may serve to underestimate or overestimate their capacities. With no information, there can be no recognition of past accomplishments. Nor can there be an understanding of just who this person is; a fuller understanding of the person's identity is lost, along with his or her history (Atkinson et al. 1999).

The absence of personal background information in the files may be interpreted as professional dismissal of the relevance of this information to "expert" interventions. A second interpretation is that they are records of "often harrowing accounts of oppressive and dehumanizing practices at the hands of professionals and others, and may well be regarded, by some, as best forgotten" (Gilman et al. 1997, 680). Ignorance of the individual histories of labelled persons is dehumanizing. Eradicating a person's humanity allows for professional distancing, and for dividing and objectifying practices to take root. Gilman, Swain and Heyman (1997) suggest that while physically dis/Abled persons wish to reclaim the right to define themselves as "dis/Abled" on their own terms, the struggle of persons labelled with intellectual dis/Abilities against the colonizers of that label is a different one. Their fight is against this denial of their humanity that threatens their very existence and, as a consequence, they want recognition of themselves as people first: a recognition abetted through the recording of their own personal histories.

Nonetheless, accounts written from this institutional perspective prevail as a consequence of the historical (and contemporary) role of professional agencies and institutions in the lives of this group. As these institutions were most involved with the "problem" of dis/Ability, they have been in a position to record, preserve, and pass on this form of biographical account of persons labelled intellectually dis/Abled: the undesired outcome being the over-abundance of this (largely non-accessible) type of material, leading to a loss of personal histories, and the misrepresentation of intellectual dis/Ability and of persons so labelled (Bredberg 1999). This outcome is more troubling when one considers the questions regarding the validity and relevance of the information contained within these institutional accounts (Gilman et al. 1997).

Potential Barriers and Strategies in the Use of Auto/biography

A social model of dis/Ability "creates a vision whereby it is possible to imagine a group of people with learning difficulties getting together themselves, identifying the need for a research project, designing it, employing interviewers and overseeing its execution, or even doing it themselves" (Stalker 1998, 15). The inference is that what is required to realize this vision is for labelled persons to overcome the social, political, economic, cultural, and material disabling barriers that are preventing them from doing so. Of relevance to the task of collecting auto/biographical and life history information from the population group of interest here, is the criticism levied at the model's failure to address the very real problems experienced by people with certain impairments: problems not readily amenable to social manipulation (1998). Booth and Booth (1996) conclude that the challenges posed by impairment are not insuperable barriers to non-speaking labelled persons telling their stories. It is possible to give voice to people without words, and to gain access to the lives of even the most inarticulate subjects. However, both the socially constructed barriers and the challenges stemming from the impairment must be acknowledged and addressed.

Booth and Booth (1996) present the reader with a paradox: those individuals most in need of having their stories told may be the least able to tell them. It is generally accepted that people require good verbal articulation skills for narrative or storytelling (perhaps reflecting an inherent ableist bias in the methodology). The restricted language skills and inarticulateness common to this group serves then to discount non-speaking persons labelled intellectually dis/Abled from this task. Unresponsiveness, defined as a limited ability to answer some types of questions, similarly impedes accessing their stories. Are verbal articulation and response skills a function of the impairment alone, or are they also impacted by social isolation, learned habits of compliance and helplessness, loneliness, low self-esteem, and the experience of oppression? Would attention to these socially constructed barriers improve communication performance?

A strong orientation to the present and difficulty understanding the concept of time pose additional problems as some members of this group struggle with dates, numbers, and the passage of time. Again, Booth and Booth (1996) query the impact of factors external to the impairment on the creation of this "problem." Especially for those non-speaking labelled persons experiencing long-term institutionalization, their lives may have lacked recognition of many of the milestones (i.e., birthdays, school graduation) people use to order their past and the many props they use (i.e., photos, possessions) to mark the passage of time, necessitating, in auto/biography, a shift to different markers. A related challenge stems from this group's operation from a concrete frame of reference (Booth et al. 1996). Many find it hard to generalize from one experience or situation to the next, or to think in abstract terms. Juxtaposed with the trial of understanding time, this concrete frame of reference impacts upon the referential and evaluative functions of narrative auto/biographical methods. It may prove arduous to reconstruct past events in a chronological order, entailing a shift instead to a non-chronological narrative form.

It is proffered to be difficult for many in this group to look back on the past with the degree of reflexivity required to reconstruct the meaning of the past in order to give meaning to the present (Booth et al. 1996). I can, however, provide a contrary, and personal, example involving my (foster) daughter, a child with Down syndrome who was non-speaking as a consequence of a stroke at infancy. She had been institutionalized at the age of five years, placed in a group home at age seven, and moved into my home (where she was the only child) shortly after her eleventh birthday. The following Christmas, I attempted to take her to visit the group home for a Christmas party. She refused to go. She was adamant. Using several of the behavioural indicators in her repertoire, she quite clearly communicated that she had absolutely no intention of going to the home, even to visit. Interpreting her behaviour as indicative of her preference for her present life situation to that of her past one, I acknowledged what she was telling me and accommodated her wishes.

Memory impairments may be a factor in recounting life history, as many persons with intellectual impairments are believed to have deficits in various types of memory. One controversy concerns whether the memories of labelled persons are qualitatively or quantitatively different from memories of non-labelled persons. Vakil et al. (1997) suggest that the problem may be quantitative, lying in the rate of memory acquisition as opposed to the quality of acquisition. Fletcher and Bray (1995) posit that researchers may have underestimated and misrepresented the memory capabilities of many persons labelled intellectually impaired. The heterogeneity of this "group," and the various syndromes and etiologies involved in intellectual impairment, combined with our astounding lack of knowledge into how the brains of this group of persons work, would dictate that any generalizations are dangerous, and that memory (and many other qualities) would need to be assessed on an individual basis. Adaptive skill deficits in the area of communication are one of the defining characteristics of this group, yet much variation exists here as well and acknowledgment is granted that we know very little about the actual communication skills and needs of this population (McLean, Brady and McLean 1996; Rodgers 1999). Research completed to date has examined only specific subgroups. The consequence of this is that while we have detailed description of the non-verbal communication patterns of some individuals, we really do not know how typical these patterns are across the larger group. Nor do we yet understand if, and how, secondary impairments (i.e., hearing, vision, motor, orthopedic, and/or behavioural), as well as gender, class, race, and age may complicate accessing these life stories (McLean et al. 1996).

As noted earlier, non-speaking persons labelled intellectually dis/Abled frequently make use of a variety of symbolic and intentional communication methods and modalities. Each presents its own challenges. The slower pace with which many of these alternative systems can be used reduces the volume of information communicated. Augmentative communication systems are considered instrumental in enhancing a user's abilities to engage in conversation, yet there is a tendency for the user to remain in the position of "respondent," as opposed to "initiator," of conversations. In addition, the quantity and quality of the vocabulary available to users of alternative or augmentative systems may not be sufficient for them to tell their own stories (Romski, Sevcik and Adamson 1999).

Acquiescence and the desire to please are possible (if not probable) outcomes for people whose lives are controlled by others (Stalker 1998), and may also factor in the challenges posed by the notion of informed consent. Seen as critical to participatory and emancipatory approaches with labelled persons, Stalker (1998) and Rodgers (1999) query the demands of ethical review boards and others that "consent" be obtained from someone other than the labelled person her/himself, a requirement that reinforces the "eternal child" stereotype of persons labelled intellectually dis/Abled. Consent is further viewed as subject to the influence of market considerations and the purposes of academia and/or service providers, rather than to the ethical imperative of emancipatory approaches (Rodgers 1999). Nonetheless, the debate continues as to whether all non-speaking persons labelled intellectually dis/Abled are capable of understanding the concept of "consent." Rodgers (1999) asserts that, with careful explanation, many can make informed decisions. For those with more profound impairments this may not be possible, thus necessitating reliance upon others to act on their behalf. We must then ask who is best suited to decide for the individual, and who makes this determination? Is it even acceptable to have a substitute decision maker? Does the need to access the individual's story outweigh their right to self-determination? Are we making an ethical, moral, or pragmatic choice? Again, who decides?

Goodley admits there exists a wide chasm between the abstract theory of empowering the self-representation of a non-speaking person labelled intellectually dis/Abled and actually doing so (1996). A purview of a sample of the literature pertinent to research with persons labelled intellectually dis/Abled (speaking and non-speaking) illuminates a number of demonstrably effective strategies. The constraints imposed within this chapter permit little more than a naming of some of these.

Very few people actually write their own auto/biographies unaided. Non-speaking persons labelled intellectually dis/Abled, as a result of their limited access to speech and the written word, however, require more than a "ghost writer." They may need an initiator, facilitator, interpreter, and scribe (Atkinson et al. 1999). A greater responsibility lies with the one hoping to access (or facilitate a labelled person's wish to articulate) this material. The investigator must try harder; probe more fully; pay closer attention to the form of the questions, to the language being used, to what is being communicated; 'test' the individual's abilities to understand and express themselves prior to beginning; and explore the efficacy of a myriad of questioning techniques (Booth et al. 1996). Rapport, familiarity, and relationship, established over repeated contacts, are key constructs implicated in the efficacy with which the investigator will be able to understand and correctly interpret such non-verbal communications as smiles, eye contact, facial expressions, body language, and looking away (Booth et al. 1996; Minkes et al. 1994). Attention to silences, both expressive (waiting to be broken) and closed (waiting to be passed over), may be warranted (Booth et al. 1996).

A more creative, flexible, and less rigid approach is essential (Minkes et al. 1994): one utilizing not only the skills and tools of social science research, but those of the novelist, artist, and poet as well (Goodley 1996). Discretion must be granted to the investigator to approach each individual in a unique manner. In addition to recognizing labelled persons as competent communicators, able to participate in activities whereby their opinions, stories, choices, and preferences are sought, acceptance and facilitation of their idiosyncratic communication methods are a prerequisite to success. Visual cues, prompts or aides, in the form of photos (of people or places), pictures (of everyday objects), and/or concrete objects can increase response rate and the intelligibility of answers (Minkes et al. 1994; Stalker 1998). In opposition to accepted narrative methodological dictum, more direct and structured questioning may be demanded. Questions relating directly to the individual's own experience; a menu approach to questioning, allowing the investigator to gradually eliminate alternatives until the most likely interpretation is achieved; an interview schedule consisting entirely of "yes"/ "no" questions; concrete questions pertaining to likes, dislikes, and activities; or some combination of strategies are frequently the only means by which to elicit information (Booth et al. 1996; Minkes et al. 1994). Interviews eliciting a limited harvest of data, or awareness that some "answers" are not factually correct, does not invalidate the information provided (Rodgers 1999). Interviewing inarticulate subjects necessitates unorthodox methods (Booth et al. 1996).

Perhaps the most frequently used strategy is, in its own right, one of the greatest dilemmas facing those attempting to access the life stories of non-speaking persons labelled intellectually dis/Abled, and relates to the understanding of what is being communicated. Research attests to the importance of familiarity with the non-speaking person and with their style of communication, and the impact of both familiar and non-familiar communication partners and contexts (McLean et al. 1996; Minkes et al. 1994; Rodgers 1999; Stalker 1998). The person solicited to convert the life story to text (i.e., researcher, biographer) is not necessarily the best equipped to access the "words" of the labelled person. Establishing the degree of familiarity between researcher and subject demanded in this context is highly labour intensive. Utilization of the "informant" technique, employing the person most familiar with the labelled person in the role of interviewer, may yield more fruitful data. A person who regularly interacts with the subject arguably has a more representative and complete knowledge of both the subject and her/his typical communication performances (Minkes et al. 1994; Rodgers 1999), thus according ecological validity to the information provided (McLean et al. 1996). Familiarity may also facilitate the labelled person to communicate more freely and willingly than would be possible with a stranger. Selection of an interviewer in a position of authority over the labelled person (i.e., staff, parent, teacher) however, may impact upon the efficacy of the endeavor (Minkes et al. 1994). Furthermore, those closest to the labelled person may be prone to underestimate their abilities, and are often surprised at the amount and sophistication of information that labelled persons can provide about their own lives and experiences. They can prove a hindrance rather than a help should they attempt to take over the process, answer for the labelled person, challenge or correct the labelled person's answers, provide what they feel the right answer should be, or pursue their own agendas (Rodgers 1999), thereby assuming ownership and facilitating misrepresentation. Again, whose auto/biography is it?

In the event of monosyllabic responses, limited or no verbal content, or information provided in picture or symbolic form, it may be that the only way to collect and textualize the stories is to actually "loan" people the words. It may be necessary to insert words not actually spoken to convey or reflect the affective content or perceived intent of the non-spoken communication (Booth et al. 1996; Stalker 1998). Developing the narrative may be possible only through creative guesswork and through piecing the story together from a variety of data sources, i.e., the communication of the labelled person, family, carers, significant others, staff and professional reports, and case files (Dickinson 1993; DiTerlizzi 1994; Goodley 1996). The risks are many. As a process, this contravenes accepted standards for validity and rigor. It is dependant upon the subject, to the extent they are able, to reject a false narrative hypothesis, and to confirm or disaffirm whether the researcher/biographer "got it right" (Booth et al. 1996). The danger exists that the researcher/biographer (involuntarily or willingly) will impose her/his own assumptions, understandings, or ambitions upon the emerging stories (Goodley 1996). Examining auto/biography through a dis/Ability lens, however, unsettles the imperative for the individual to speak alone, and demands a shift towards explicitly co-constituted narrative accounts that highlight the interactive basis upon which the account is created.

Conclusion

While hopefully having established that non-speaking persons labelled intellectually dis/Abled do possess valuable knowledge, the dilemma of accessing these narratives is far from being resolved. What else can we do to facilitate articulation and understanding? How can we be sure that we "got it right"? Do we cling to our subjunctivizing terms, claiming no more than a perspective on another's subjective state of mind? Davies (1993) proffers a comparison with psychoanalytic psychiatry, suggesting we utilize the "signs" that satisfy psychiatrists that the interpretations they offer their clients of the unconscious content of their brains are correct: intellectual recognition, strong emotional reaction, and a flood of associations. Maybe it is little more than the "eureka" factor. Certainly for many of us sharing close relationships with non-speaking persons labelled intellectually dis/Abled, there is a sense that you "just know." But this does not bode well with demands for scientific rigor.

For auto/biography to become a viable option to capture the narratives and life stories of this group, more careful scrutiny is demanded: of the "how to" aspect of auto/biography with non-speaking persons; of questions pertaining to definitions of, and boundaries between, autobiography or biography; of issues of "truth" and validity of content; of the role of the researcher and answers to the question of "whose auto/biography is it"; of the line between fact and fiction, and the deliberate use of fictionalized auto/biographical representations of labelled persons; of the impact of auto/biographical processes and the textualization of life stories on the labelled person themselves; and the potential for auto/biography as a context for empowerment and combining social and individual worlds. And this is but a beginning, as Schaefer points out:

> With Cath my dependence on words has lessened. I needed to understand how unnecessary words are before I could let go of trying to build our friendship on what I said with them. I had to realize we weren't going to have a close relationship unless we were on equal ground, and we gradually achieved this through living together and sharing numerous life experiences. Many people see Cath as being limited in what she can say because she doesn't use words, but I feel quite the opposite. I can't use words to say half of what I'd like to because I'm using this medium to communicate about a friend whom I don't think of in these terms.... Between Cath and me, language has become an experience of touch, sight and sound ... I think ... about the things she says with her eyes that no one could ever say to me with words. (Schaefer 1999, 299).

Much can be surmised from the above quotation. The author demonstrates the necessity (and possibility) of a radical shift, both in our definition and understanding of what constitutes "communication," and in the way in which we "hear" that communication. The non-speaking person labelled intellectually dis/Abled is reconceptualized as a competent communicator, a transgressive rupture of the dominant discourse that continues to occupy a prominent place in her life. In such a context, auto/biography is possible and the "telling," as a product of communication, is a process with the potential to affect both the producer and the listener (Whyte and Ingstad 1995).

Notes

1 Consideration of semiotics prompts the use of the sign "dis/Ability." "Dis/Ability" vis-à-vis "disability" foregrounds "disability" as the focus while simultaneously allowing the reader to consider and appreciate the "ability" that was previously obscured (Rogers and Swadener 2001). Use of this particular formulation explicates the epistemological and ontological foundations embedded within this work.

References

Allan, Julie. 1996. Foucault and special educational needs: A "box of tools" for analysing children's experiences of mainstreaming. *Disability and Society* 11(2): 219–33.

Atkinson, Dorothy, and Jan Walmsley. 1999. Using autobiographical approaches with people with learning difficulties. *Disability and Society* 14(2): 203–16.

Aull Davies, Charlotte, and Richard Jenkins. 1997. "She has different fits to me": How people with learning difficulties see themselves. *Disability and Society* 12(1): 95–109.

Baum, Nehama. 1999. How to break the spell of ill-being and help kids achieve a better quality of life. *Exceptionality Education in Canada* 9(1 and 2): 129–45.

Bogdan, Robert, and Steven Taylor. 1976. The judged, not the judges: An insider's view of mental retardation. *American Psychologist* 31(1): 47–52.

———. 1989. Relationships with severely disabled people: The social construction of humanness. *Social Problems* 36(2): 135–149.

Booth, Tim, and Wendy Booth. 1996. The sounds of silence: Narrative research with inarticulate subjects. *Disability and Society* 11(1): 55–69.

Bredberg, Elizabeth. 1999. Writing disability history: Problems, perspectives and sources. *Disability and Society* 14(2): 189–201.

Clear, Mike. 1999. The "Normal" and the "Monstrous" in disability research. *Disability and Society* 14(4): 435–47.

Cotterill, Pamela, and Gayle Letherby. 1993. Weaving stories: Personal auto/biographies in feminist research. *Sociology* 27(1): 67–79.

Couser, G. Thomas. 1997. *Recovering bodies, illness, disability, and life writing.* Madison, WI: Univ. of Wisconsin Press.

Davies, Michele L. 1993. Healing Sylvia: Accounting for the textual "discovery" of unconscious knowledge. *Sociology* 27(1): 110–20.

Dickinson, Hilary. 1993. Accounting for Augustus Lamb: Theoretical and methodological issues in biography and historical sociology. *Sociology* 27(1): 121–32.

DiTerlizzi, Michele. 1994. Life history: the impact of a changing service provision on an individual with learning difficulties. *Disability and Society* 9(4): 501–17.

Eagle, Rita. 2001. *Assessing and accessing intelligence in individuals with lower functioning autism*. Paper presented at Eclipse Conference, Toronto, Ontario.

Edelson, Miriam. 2000. *My journey with Jake: A memoir of parenting and disability*. Toronto: Between the Lines.

Enns, Ruth. 1999. *A voice unheard: The Latimer case and people with disabilities*. Halifax, NS: Fernwood.

Evans, Mary. 1993. Reading lives: How the personal might be social. *Sociology* 27(1), 5–13.

Fletcher, Kathryn L., and Norman W. Bray. 1995. External and verbal strategies in children with and without mild mental retardation. *American Journal on Mental Retardation* 99(4): 363–75.

Frank, Arthur W. 1995. *The wounded storyteller: Body, illness, and ethics*. Chicago: Univ. of Chicago Press.

Garbarino, James, Frances Stolt, and the Faculty of the Erikson Institute. 1989. *What children can tell us*. San Francisco: Jossey-Bass.

Gaventa, John. 1993. The powerful, the powerless and the experts: Knowledge struggles in an information age. In *Voices of change*, ed. Peter Park, Mary Brydon-Miller, Budd Hall, and Ted Jackson. Toronto: OISE Press.

Gilman, Maureen, John Swain, and Bob Heyman. 1997. Life history or "case" history: The objectification of people with learning difficulties through the tyranny of professional discourses. *Disability and Society* 12(5): 675–93.

Goodley, Danny. 1996. Tales of hidden lives: A critical examination of life history research with people who have learning difficulties. *Disability and Society* 11(3): 333–48.

Harrison, Barbara, and E. Stina Lyon. 1993. A note on ethical issues in the use of autobiography in sociological research. *Sociology* 27(1): 101–109.

Imre, Roberta Wells. 1984. The nature of knowledge in social work. *Social Work* 29(1): 41–45.

Lea, Susan J. 1988. Mental retardation: Social construction or clinical reality? *Disability, Handicap and Society* 3(1): 63–69.

Mar, Harvey M., and Nancy Sall. 1999. Profiles of the expressive communication skills of children and adolescents with severe cognitive disabilities. *Education and Training in Mental Retardation and Developmental Disabilities* 34(1): 77–89.

McLean, Lee K., Nancy C. Brady, and James E. McLean. 1996. Reported communication abilities of individuals with severe mental retardation. *American Journal on Mental Retardation* 100(6): 580–91.

Minkes, John, Carol Robinson, and Clive Watson. 1994. Consulting the children: Interviews with children using residential respite care services. *Disability and Society* 9(1): 47–57.

Peter, Dimity. 2000. Dynamics of discourse: A case study illuminating power relations in mental retardation. *Mental Retardation* 38(4): 354–62.

Piaget, Jean, and Barbel Inhelder. 1969. *The psychology of the child.* New York: Basic Books.

Polanyi, Michael. 1959. *The study of man: The Lindsay memorial lectures.* London: Routledge and Kegan Paul.

Radford, John P. 1994. Intellectual disability and the heritage of modernity. In *Disability is not measles: New research paradigms in disability,* ed. Marcia H. Rioux and Michael Bach. North York, ON: L'Institut Roeher Institute.

Rodgers, Jackie. 1999. Trying to get it right: Undertaking research involving people with learning difficulties. *Disability and Society* 14(4): 421–33.

Rogers, Linda J., and Beth Blue Swadener, eds. 2001. *Semiotics and dis/ability, interrogating categories of difference.* Albany, NY: State Univ. of New York Press.

Romski, Mary Ann, Rose A. Sevcik, and Lauren B. Adamson. 1999. Communication patterns of youth with mental retardation with and without their speech-output communication devices. *American Journal on Mental Retardation* 104(3): 249–59.

Schaefer, Nicola. 1999. *Does she know she's there?* Markham, ON: Fitzhenry and Whiteside.

Shapiro, Theodore. 1984. An epistemological basis for clinical practice: Learning from deviance. In *An epistemology for the language sciences,* ed. A.A. Guiora, 141–58. Ann Arbor: Univ. of Michigan.

Stalker, Kirsten. 1998. Some ethical and methodological issues in research with people with learning difficulties. *Disability and Society* 13(1): 5–19.

Stern, Daniel N. 2000. *The interpersonal world of the infant.* New York: Basic Books.

Vakil, Eli, Edna Shelef-Reshef, and Rachel Levy-Shiff. 1997. Procedural and declarative memory processes: Individuals with and without mental retardation. *American Journal on Mental Retardation* 102(2): 147–60.

Whyte, Susan Reynolds, and Benedicte Ingstad. 1995. Disability and culture: An overview. In *Disability and culture,* ed. Benedicte Ingstad and Susan Reynolds Whyte, 3–34. Berkeley and Los Angeles, California: Univ. of California Press.

Winzer, Margaret A. 1997. Disability and society before the eighteenth century: Dread and despair. In *The disability studies reader,* ed. Lennard J. Davis, 75–109. London and New York: Routledge.

Woodill, Gary. 1994. The social semiotics of disability. In *Disability is not measles: New research paradigms in disability,* ed. Marcia H. Rioux and Michael Bach, 201–26. North York, ON: L'Institut Roeher Institute.

Young, Damon A., and Ruth Quibell. 2000. Why rights are never enough: Rights, intellectual disability and understanding. *Disability and Society* 15(5): 747–64.

LJILJANA VULETIC 🦋
and MICHEL FERRARI

A Transfer Boy:
About Himself

Men—each one of whom represents a unique and valuable experiment on the part of nature—are therefore shot
wholesale nowadays.... But every man is more than just
himself; he also represents the unique, the very special
and always significant and remarkable point at which the
world's phenomena intersect, only once in this way and
never again. That is why every man's story is important,
eternal, sacred; that is why every man, as long as he lives
and fulfills the will of nature, is wondrous, and worthy of
every consideration.   —*Hermann Hesse* (1965)

MANY PHILOSOPHERS AND PSYCHOLOGISTS
interested in studying people, rather than people's minds alone, believe
that *self-narrative* (or autobiography) is the best method for conducting such
inquiry.[1] Moreover, this method has been used successfully in studying both
"typical" and "atypical" persons—including small children (Nelson 1989),
adults (McAdams 1993), people with traumatic brain injury (Nochi 2000),
and people with breast cancer (Langellier 2001).

Psychological studies of people diagnosed with autism, however, are
still grounded in a positivistic paradigm of science. Except for a few clinical reports, these studies still are mostly about what these individuals "have"
(i.e., "autism," considered as some isolated difference in their "kind of
mind" that can be easily operationalized and studied under controlled experimental conditions), and not with their personal experiences or way of
being. Fortunately, over the past fifteen years or so, some people diagnosed

with autism have written about themselves, providing a different much richer, and more fascinating, picture of what their lives are like.

In this essay, we introduce an unusual child who has been diagnosed with autism: a thirteen-year-old boy named "T." Unlike the medical/scientific approach to understanding autism, we aim to understand people diagnosed with autism by presenting T's own perceptions of himself through his autobiographical writings, and to see how those differ from the writings of his best friend, who has no such diagnosis.

What Is Autism?

Scientific Perspective

The scientific diagnosis of autism refers to a set of mental disorders characterized by "impairments in social interaction, verbal and non-verbal communication," and "a pattern of repetitive behaviors" (American Psychiatric Association 1994). Autistic symptoms range from mild to severe. For example, impairments in social interaction range from almost complete social withdrawal and isolation to active but slightly odd social approaches. Similarly, communication impairments vary from no speech to no or only slight delay in language development and slight difficulty in initiating and/or maintaining a conversation. Behaviour too may range from solitary play (e.g., spinning objects and lining things up) to repetitive and stereotyped activities. Some sixty years ago, Kanner and Asperger[2] independently described the first cases of children with this pattern of impairments. Both Kanner and Asperger referred to their cases as autistic (from *autos* the Greek word for self).[3] In recent years, it has been recognized that Kanner and Asperger described two distinct disorders that fit the same general category. The latest revision of the *Diagnostic and Statistical Manual of Mental Disorders* (DSM-IV)[4] uses the terms Autistic Disorder and Asperger's Disorder for these two disorders, respectively. The term "Pervasive Developmental Disorders"[5] is proposed as a general category term under which these disorders are classified, and includes three other disorders: Rett's Disorder, Childhood Disintegrative Disorder, and Pervasive Developmental Disorder Not Otherwise Specified (PDDNOS).

Even though most people diagnosed with autism are mentally retarded, about 30 percent are in the intellectually superior range (American Psychiatric Association 1994). Furthermore, regardless of their general level of intelligence, the cognitive skills of individuals diagnosed with autism are usually uneven. Thus, it is often the case that individuals diagnosed with autism perform at the superior range on cognitive tasks such as block design and visual discrimination (Happe 1994; O'Riordan and Plaisted 2001), and have exceptional rote memory (e.g., for facts, numbers, dates, routes, bus and train timetables, etc.)[6] or visual thinking skills (Grandin 1995). In addition, many people diagnosed with autism posses extraordinary drawing, music, mental calculation, and calendrical skills in spite of mental retardation (i.e., idiot savants).[7]

It is currently believed that autism is a neurobiological disorder with multiple etiologies, both genetic and nongenetic. A number of structural, functional, and neurochemical abnormalities have been reported (with many inconsistent and contradictory findings) that may be connected (Tager-Flusberg, Joseph, and Folstein 2001).

In spite of significant progress in the study of autism over the past sixty years, science is far from having a complete understanding of the abnormal (diminished or enhanced) features that define autism, and there are many hypotheses about its nature and origin. We will limit this review to only one such feature—Theory of Mind—which we believe is challenged by autobiographical accounts of autistic individuals—including T's.

According to Theory of Mind (TOM) deficit hypothesis, the core deficit in autism is the inability to attribute mental states (such as intentions, desires, and beliefs) to self and others (Baron-Cohen, Leslie, and Frith 1985). Research has shown that most people diagnosed with autism do not pass TOM tasks, most of which require attributing false beliefs to others (Baron-Cohen 2000; Baron-Cohen, Leslie, and Frith 1985). This finding is in sharp contrast to the performance of typically developing children over four years of age, or of children diagnosed with mental retardation matched on mental age. On the basis of this research Baron-Cohen (1995, 1) has suggested that people diagnosed with autism are *mindblind*, ("blind to things like thought, beliefs, knowledge, desires, and intentions").

Subjective Perspective

In the last fifteen years or so, many people diagnosed with high-functioning autism (or Asperger syndrome)[8] have written books and scientific papers, and spoken publicly, about their life experiences and about what it means *to be* autistic.[9] In this section, we briefly review their own view of autism. People diagnosed with autism[10] feel that they are misunderstood by scientists. For example, Liane Holliday-Willeys, a doctor of education, writer, and researcher, wrote, "Autism touches many, and yet, it is one of the most *misunderstood* developmental disorders" (1999, 13: emphasis added).

Edgar Schneider, a retired mathematician and computer programmer, at the end of his autobiography wrote "I hope that I have been able to give some ideas of what autism is all about, because it has to be the most misunderstood disability there is" (1999, 116: emphasis added). Another person diagnosed with autism, Donna Williams, author of four autobiographical books, a manual on autism, and a book of poetry and prose, expresses her view on autism in the following way:

> Autism is a label which describes outer behaviours, not inner realities.... "Autism" is simply an *internal human "normality" with the volume turned up.* We all have experienced moments when we aren't quite aware or when we are too aware to handle the world. Or moments when we aren't quite aware of the company we are in or so overly aware of it that it gets hard to function.... For me, *the experience of "autism"* is not of any of these things in themselves, but rather the frequency and extremity with which they are experienced and the *degree* to which these experiences affect how one expresses oneself and *relates to one's inner world and the outer world.* It's a matter of whether you visit these states or whether you've lived there. (1998, 9–10: emphasis added)

Donna Williams also addresses other scientific misconceptions about autism. For example, she writes:

> Those seeking to test people with "autism" might begin by daring to imagine that these people may not be *lesser-developed versions of non-autistic people* but, rather, people who HAVE developed, sometimes substantially, along a very different track from non-autistic people. Looking at how "autistic" people measure up to non-autistic people according to a non-autistic developmental path tells the researcher nothing about how far the same person may have developed a whole range of adaptations, compensations and strategies along an "autistic" track. (1996, 235: emphasis added)

Jim Sinclair, disability educator and consultant, also protests, "Autism is not an appendage." He elaborates:

> Autism isn't something a person has, or a "shell" that a person is trapped inside. There's no normal child hidden behind the autism. *Autism is a way of being.* It is pervasive; it colors every experience, every sensation, perception, thought, emotion, and encounter, every aspect of existence. *It is not possible to separate the autism from the person*—and if it were possible, the person you'd have left would not be the same person you started with. (1993, n.p.: emphases added)

What all of these subjective perspectives on high-functioning autism show is that these people have a rich inner life—one that should be considered on its own terms. This is what we hope to do in discussing the case of T.

T's Auto-biographical Writings

We will focus on three pieces of T's autobiographical writings.[11] The first was written in school few years ago; the other two were written more recently at the request of the first author.[12] For the purpose of comparison, an autobiographical essay written by T's best friend is also discussed.[13]

"Transfer Boy" (1998) This essay was written when T was nine years old in response to his (then) new teacher's request that he write about himself, as a way to introduce himself to her through his hobby. In the upper left hand corner, T drew a subway transfer with a face, colored in green and labeled "transfer boy." In the body of the text T wrote:

> I am a green Transfer. I eat a lot of other transfers. I look as a real transfer, but I have eyes. I am afraid of fire and seessiors [sic scissors].[14]

"Why I Like Transfers" (1999) When the first author recently asked T to write about why he likes transfers, he wrote:

> I started collecting transfers in week 29, 1995. I thought They are nice for me to collect, so I made a rule. I don't show my transfer If an adult dos'nt [sic] tell me to show my transfer. I like to collect transfers because I can use them as busies [sic buses] or as very nice things.

"Who I Am" (2001) When the first author more recently asked T to describe himself as he would to somebody who does not know him, he wrote the following:

Who I Am

I am a person who knows and likes about different kinds of transportation. I collect lots, lots and lots of transfers from different buses, subways and streetcars, and trains. I also collect maps and schedules.

I love having car toys and I make cars as buses by writing different destinations that I know and putting them in the cars. I can also make cars as airplanes by putting wings on the cars and writing the company and the plane destination on a piece of paper and putting that piece of paper and putting that piece of paper on the car.

At school, during lunch recess, I help the caretakers in the school by washing desks in the classes. I love this job.

I like drawing airplanes and building models. I also collect plane tickets and schedules. When I make my own plane schedule, I take information from the internet and I make my own schedules. I collect books with airplane pictures and in those books, there are pictures of airports showing the gate numbers and terminals (like a plan). I like watching movies, especially Home Alone, with airplanes and bad guys. The bad thing about that is that I hear, for example, "I'm gonna kill that kid," and I say, "I'm gonna kill you!" (This is a joke, of course)! and I get punished.

I go on Sunday, with Lilliana to Ontario Science Centre. There, me and my friend play and learn!

Consider the difference between this autobiography and what T's best friend, K, wrote about himself on the same occasion, when given the same instructions as T—that is, to describe himself as he would to somebody who does not know him:

Who I Am

I am a kid. I am 12 year old. I am in grade 6. I like tools. I am very smart when it comes to fixing things. I like to learn. Math and science are the subject that I like the most. But I bet that I am the only kid in my school that knows a lots about tools. I know more then 200 kinds of tools. I have a best friend. [His] name is Mr. T. So now I am going to talk about my favorite tv show, Pokemon & Alglomon.

Many things could be said about T's autobiographical writings; however, we will limit our discussion to only a few issues. First, there is a single reoccurring theme in T's autobiographical writings: public transportation systems (PTS). In a three-year time span, T did not change his perception of himself as a "transfer boy." Indeed, T's "Transfer Boy" essay could be viewed as his imaginative self-definition, in which he identifies with an object he values the most—a PTS transfer. Further, in T's description of why he likes transfers, we find T has an extraordinary visual memory for numbers. We also learn that transit transfers are, most of all, "very nice things" for T. Indeed, in T's most recent essay, he wrote almost exclusively about *things he likes* (and *knows about*), with the exception of mentioning the punishment he gets for one of the things he likes to do. Note that the way in which T wrote his autobiographical essay is consistent with what he believes one should talk about when talking about oneself—he said one should talk about *what* one likes. Thus, he introduced himself as a person who "*knows and likes about different* kinds of transportation," and as a person who collects various items related to this topic. He also told us that he makes his own plane schedules, based on the information he finds on the Internet. He also wrote about playing with car toys by turning them into buses or airplanes, and about drawing airplanes and making plane models. In addition, T wrote about three topics besides PTS: (1) watching movies (especially "Home Alone, with airplanes and bad guys"); (2) his "job" (i.e., school caretaker's helper), which he loves; and (3) going to the Ontario Science Centre with his friend and the first author—where he can "play and learn." In regard to the movies, T mentioned his favorite movie, and explained why he likes it. He wrote that there are airplanes and bad guys in it, that he likes to repeat what the characters say in the movie, and that this way of having fun can get him into trouble.

A content analysis of T's most recent essay revealed that it is mostly about his interest in PTS (i.e., 65 percent of all the words, or 157 out of 242 words). T used 45 words (19 percent) to describe his second interest (i.e., watching the movies), 40 words (16 percent) to describe his "job" (22 words, or 9 percent) and 18 words (7 percent) to describe visits to Ontario Science Centre. Thus, he spent more time (and words) describing his main interest than all other areas of interest combined. T's descriptions of different interests also differ in the details he provided about them. T took time to explain what he collects, and how he plays PTS games, but did not do so for his visits to the Ontario Science Centre, about which he just said he liked to "play and learn"; for him, it was not important to explain how. And even though he said he "love[s]" his job, he did not go into any detail about what it is that he does, or loves about it. On the other hand, he did find it necessary to mention what it is about movies that he likes. And here, again, we find PTS (in this case, airplanes), and interesting things to repeat (connected to his interest in having fun with sounds). Therefore, one may take these differences as an indicator of the centrality of the interest in PTS in T's life. And even though T does not elaborate a lot on his having "fun with sounds," the fact that it seems to persist in spite of "punishment" seems to indicate its importance.

We also notice some absences from T's most recent essay. First, there are very few people in it. In fact, only two people were mentioned (his best friend and the first author), and this was done only in the last paragraph. One cannot but wonder whether the last paragraph was just added for the person for whom he was writing—the first author.[15] School too is only just mentioned, and then only as the place where his "job" takes place: not in relation to learning and/or friendships, as one might expect.

Finally, when we compare T's essay to that of his best friend, we find both similarities and differences. K also wrote about things he likes, and also included the most detail about his main interest—tools. Similarly, as T wrote about watching movies, K wrote about his favourite TV show. In addition, K also mentioned his best friend, and with no details. Unlike T, however, who starts with things that feel central to him—his interest in PTS—and his lived experiences, K introduces himself in a more general way—as a "kid." He then proceeds with two more generalizations about himself, neither of which were even mentioned by T: his age and school grade. In addition, contrary to T, when K wrote about school it was related to learning—what he likes to learn the most. It is interesting to note that K mentions even fewer people than T—in fact, only one (his best friend, T). Finally, even though we find a greater variety of self-related themes (that is, more breadth) in K's account, we find much richer descriptions of the "important" themes (more depth) in T's account.

What We Learned about T from Himself

To attempt a portrait of T as a person using the information he provided in his three autobiographical writings, we use two different (although related) criteria of defining a person: what one likes, and what one remembers.

One Is What One Likes

When the first author recently asked T about the best way to describe a person, he said that people are best described by what they like. From this perspective, then, T's is best described as *a person who likes* PTS. In his autobiographical writings, T portrayed himself as a person who *knows and likes* things about PTS, *collects* items related to PTS, and *plays* PTS games. Therefore, one might say that PTS is at the centre of T's personal gravity. Further support for this conclusion is found in the fact that T often refers to himself as a "transportation expert," "PTS expert," or "PTS person," and in his poetic label in his school essay from a few years ago—"transfer boy."

T's need to have fun with sounds is also at the centre of his personal gravity. Even though this need is not as apparent in his autobiographical writings as is his interest in PTS, the fact that he is ready to get into trouble over his attempts to satisfy this need suggests that it is important to him. Not only that, in a conversation with the first author, T mentioned that his friend V does not want to sit with him on the school bus after he embarrassed him by saying "You little...!" (which he said in a way he heard in his favourite movie, *Home Alone*).

In his most recent autobiographical essay, T talked about two additional areas of interest: his caretaker's job, and learning and having fun in the

Ontario Science Centre. Even though he did not say a lot about them, the fact that he loves his "job" tells us that what he is doing is important to him, and the fact that he mentioned the visits to Ontario Science Centre with his friend and the first author suggests that they are also of some importance to him. However, it seems unlikely that these two areas are among his main interests, and seem instead to belong to the fringe of T's personal gravity. This area on the fringe of his personal centre may be analogous to Vygotsky's notion of the *zone of proximal development* (1934). From this Vygotskian perspective the most interesting indicator of a child's level of development is not found in what s/he can do independently, but rather in what s/he can do with the help of others. Similarly, the most important area of T's personal, or life space—to use Kurt Lewin's phrase (1951)—may not be what T is most interested in on his own, but what he *can become interested in* with the help of others.

In sum, when we apply T's own criterion for defining a person, we find his personal gravity centres on his interests in PTS and funny sounds. On the fringe of T's personal centre, we find his interests in helping the caretakers in school, and learning and having fun in the Ontario Science Centre. Still, it is worth mentioning that some things never came up in T's accounts of himself. These include computer games, sports, literature, science (or any other school subject), clothes, and other interests that children of his age would usually mention. These areas of life seem to belong to T's most remote personal areas.

One Is What One Remembers[16]

The way we define ourselves to ourselves and to others through our autobiographical narratives (i.e., how we form our personal identity) depends crucially on our memory (Freeman and Brockmeier 2001; Locke 1690). Freeman and Brockmeier (as well as Taylor [1989]) argue that how we evaluate our past is inseparable from our conceptions of what a good life is, or should be. Clearly, T organizes his autobiographical narratives around PTS themes and funny things to remember. So applying the second criterion for defining a person provides the same basic portrait of T as a person who likes PTS and "funny things." However, Freeman and Brockmeier suggest that these interests of T not only have a psychological and aesthetic meaning, as organizing forces of his life and sources of information about what is beautiful in life, but also an ethical dimension, informing T about what a good life is.

T as a Person

Let us now briefly summarize what we have learned about T in this study, and suggest some ways to utilize this knowledge.

The Centre of T's Personal Gravity

From T's autobiographical writings, we have learned that two interests (or needs) are at the centre of his personal gravity: interest in public transportation systems (PTS) and a need to have fun with sounds.[17] T seeks every opportunity to engage in activities related to PTS or to have "fun with sounds."

That special interests form the centre of personal gravity of people diagnosed with autism is also clear from their autobiographical writings. For example, Temple Grandin (1992, 1997, 1986) has written and lectured extensively about this fact. From Grandin's perspective, the best way to help people diagnosed with autism is to use their interests to engage them. She writes, "Parents, teachers, and therapists should work *with* fixations and not against them" (1986). And in saying this, she spoke from her own life experience, in which she built a successful career on her "fixations." Holliday-Willeys also wrote about her love for imitating other's voices and using this love in a constructive way in drama classes (1999). We too believe that those working with children diagnosed with autism should take these examples as guides in their efforts to help them. In T's case, science projects seem related to PTS topics, drama classes, and "family theatre," and provide ways to expand his main interests.

The Fringe of T's Personal Gravity

On the fringe of T's personal gravity, we found interests in helping others (such as caretakers at school) and in learning and having fun at the interactive science museum. We believe these interests point to ways in which others may enrich T's life.

In his autobiographical essay, T said that he loves his caretaker's helper "job." From the first author's conversation with him, this job seems to meet two of his needs: to help others, and to receive recognition. It is important to T to feel helpful. But although real recognition for his help with cleaning school desks must have felt wonderful to him, T's other interests not only could be used in other school-based "jobs" to provide him with a feeling of pride for his competencies and recognition by others, these jobs could further expand his interests. For example, T loves labels—any kind of labels in his environment, such as prices and book labels. At home, T has his own library with books labeled the way library books are, with labels marked mystery, adventure, fiction, and so on. He also has a page with information about the author, title, and borrowers of the book (e.g., the date due, the borrower's name, and room number for the books from the school library). As we have seen from autobiographical accounts, interest in labels is very common among people diagnosed with autism. So, if T were assigned to help a school librarian, not only would he feel helpful and recognized, but he would also further develop his "librarian skills."

In his autobiographical essay, T mentioned going to the Ontario Science Centre, where he can both "have fun and learn." Although T did not elaborate much on this, we believe that T points out an important, and often overlooked, element of learning and teaching—fun. T, and all those diagnosed with autism who wrote autobiographies—greatly need to have fun whenever possible. Moreover, they quickly learn things that (for whatever reason) they find "funny." This suggests that those of us who want to help children diagnosed with autism broaden their perspectives, knowledge base, or social skills, should consider "fun" an important aspect of the teaching process.

Conclusion

According to the Theory of Mind deficit hypothesis of autism, people diagnosed with autism are severely deficient in their ability to self-reflect, produce self-report, and understand themselves in general (Baron-Cohen 1989, 1995, 2000; Baron-Cohen, Leslie, and Frith 1985). However, autobiographical accounts and case studies of people diagnosed with autism clearly show that these people are capable of sophisticated self-knowledge. They can report about their own mental states and experiences, including their expertise in the areas of specific interest, their needs, feelings, specific experiences, and many other aspects of self.

As T's and other autobiographical writings indicate, there is much more to people diagnosed with autism than the experimental psychology of autism suggests. By saying this, we do not mean to say that nothing we have learned from experimental studies is important, but only that, as Cytowic wrote, "A knowledge base is vital, but so is understanding real people, their needs, their feelings, and what their illnesses mean to them" (1993, 12). Autobiographical writings of people diagnosed with autism suggest that understanding such persons requires methods like those used for studying any other "kind" of person: narrative methods like autobiography.

Notes

1 See Gordon W. Allport (1937); Jerome Bruner (1990); Michel Ferrari and Ram Mahalingam (1998); Mark Freeman and Jens Brockmeier (2001); Alasdair C. MacIntyre (1981); Dan P. McAdams (1995); Keith Oatley (1992); Donald Polkinghorne (1988).

2 Hans Asperger (1991); Leo Kanner (1943).

3 Kanner's original term was "early infantile autism" and Asperger's—"autistic psychopathy."

4 The DSM-IV is the official diagnostic manual in North America for mental disorders.

5 This term is used by mental health professionals in North America, while the term *autistic spectrum disorder* is preferred in Europe.

6 See Tony Attwood (1998); Uta Frith (1989).

7 See Leon K. Miller (1999); Bernard Rimland and Deborah Fein (1988).

8 Note that what is said in this and subsequent sections refers specifically to persons diagnosed with high-functioning autism, or Asperger's syndrome. However, for brevity, we will keep the general term autism.

9 See Temple Grandin (1992, 1997, 1995); Temple Grandin and Margaret M. Scariano (1986); Lianne Holliday-Willeys (1999); David C. Miedzianik (1986); Edgar Schneider (1999); Jim Sinclair (1992, 1993); Donna Williams (1996, 1998, 1992, 1994).

10 See Holliday-Willeys (1999); Schneider (1999); Sinclair (1992); Williams (1996, 1998).

11 In line with Freeman and Brockmeier's conception of autobiographical narratives as consisting of both cohesive and fragmentary spoken and written, autobiographical material, we treat all of T's self-statements as self-narratives.

12 The first author (L.V.) has known T and his parents for five years. She has worked with him in different settings and roles: she has been his after-school program instructor, summer program inclusion facilitator, social skills group leader, therapist and tutor. She is currently working with him as a tutor and therapist and meets with him twice a week for two to three hours, at either his or her home. T is currently in a grade seven regular class in a public school in Toronto, Canada.

13 For a more in-depth of these writings and for a picture of the first essay as written see Vuletic and Ferrari (in press).

14 None of T's writings presented in this project were corrected for spelling mistakes.

15 It should be noted that, in our opinion, this is the only place where one might find any evidence of the researchers' life-story expectations to have had any impact on T's autobiographical writings.

16 There are also many variations on the theme. One of the well known is the Buddha's axiom "We are what we think." Buddha (1925).

17 It should be noted that descriptions by everyone who knows T are consistent with this description. For more details, see Vuletic and Ferrari (in press).

References

Allport, Gordon W. 1937. *Personality: A psychological interpretation*. New York: Henry Holt.

American Psychiatric Association. 1994. *Diagnostic and statistical manual of mental disorders*. 4th ed. Washington, DC: American Psychiatric Association.

Asperger, Hans. 1991. "Autistic psychopathy" in childhood. In *Autism and Asperger Syndrome*, ed. Uta Frith, 37–92. Cambridge, UK: Cambridge Univ. Press.

Attwood, Tony. 1998. *Asperger's Syndrome: A guide for parents and professionals*. London: Jessica Kingsley.

Baron-Cohen, Simon. 1989. Do autistic children have obsessions and compulsions? *British Journal of Clinical Psychology* 28(3): 193–200.

———. 1995. *Mindblindness: An essay on autism and Theory of Mind.* Cambridge, MA: MIT Press.

———. 2000. Theory of Mind and autism: A fifteen-year review. In *Understanding other minds: Perspectives from developmental cognitive neuroscience,* ed. Simon Baron-Cohen, Helen Tager-Flusberg and Donald J. Cohen, 3–20. Oxford: Oxford Univ. Press.

Baron-Cohen, Simon, Alan M. Leslie, and Uta Frith. 1985. Does the autistic child have a "Theory of Mind"? *Cognition* 21(1): 37–46.

Bruner, Jerome. 1990. *Acts of meaning.* Cambridge, MA: Harvard Univ. Press.

Buddha. 1925. *Some sayings of the Buddha according to the Pali Canon,* trans. Frank Lee Woodward. London: Milford.

Cytowic, Richard E. 1993. *The man who tasted shapes: A bizarre medical mystery offers revolutionary insights into emotions, reasoning and consciousness.* New York: Jeremy P. Tarcher/Putnam.

Ferrari, Michel, and Ram Mahalingam. 1998. Personal cognitive development and its implications for teaching and learning. *Educational Psychologist* 33(1): 35–44.

Freeman, Mark, and Jens Brockmeier. 2001. Narrative integrity: Autobiographical identity and the meaning of the "good life." In *Narrative and identity: Studies in autobiography, self and culture,* ed. Jens Brockmeier and Donal A. Carbaugh, 75–100. Amsterdam: John Benjamins.

Frith, Uta. 1989. *Autism: Explaining the enigma.* Oxford: Blackwell.

Grandin, Temple. 1992. An inside view of autism. In *High-functioning individuals with autism,* ed. Eric Schopler and Gary B. Mesibov, 105–26. New York: Plenum.

———. 1997. A Personal perspective on autism. In *Handbook of autism and pervasive developmental disorders,* ed. Donald J. Cohen and Fred R. Volkmar, 1032–42. New York: J. Wiley.

———. 1995. *Thinking in pictures: And other reports from my life with autism.* New York: Doubleday.

Grandin, Temple, and Margaret M. Scariano. 1986. *Emergence: Labeled autistic.* New York: Warner.

Happe, Francesca. 1994. Wechsler IQ profile and Theory of Mind in autism: A research note. *Journal of Child Psychology and Psychiatry* 35(8): 1461–71.

Hesse, Hermann. 1965. *Demian, the story of Emil Sinclair's youth,* trans. Michael Roloff and Michael Lebeck. New York: Harper and Row.

Holliday-Willeys, Liane. 1999. *Pretending to be normal: Living with Asperger's Syndrome.* London: Jessica Kingsley.

Kanner, Leo. 1943. Autistic disturbances of affective contact. *Nervous Child* 2: 217–50.

Langellier, Kristin M. 2001. You're marked: Breast cancer, tattoo, and the narrative performance of identity. In *Narrative and identity: Studies in autobiography, self and culture,* ed. Jens Brockmeier and Donal A. Carbaugh, 145–84. Amsterdam: John Benjamins.

Lewin, Kurt. 1951. *Field theory in social science: Selected theoretical papers.* New York: Harper.

Locke, John. 1690. *An essay concerning human understanding.* 6th revised ed., 2 vols. London: Penguin, 1997.

MacIntyre, Alasdair C. 1981. *After virtue: A study in moral theory.* Notre Dame, IN: Univ. of Notre Dame Press.

McAdams, Dan P. 1993. *The stories we live by: Personal myths and the making of the self.* New York: Guilford.

———. 1995. What do we know when we know a person? *Journal of Personality* 63(3): 365–97.

Miedzianik, David C. 1986. *My autobiography.* Nottingham, UK: Univ. of Nottingham.

Miller, Leon K. 1999. The savant syndrome: Intellectual impairment and exceptional skill. *Psychological Bulletin* 125(1): 31–46.

Nelson, Katherine. 1989. Introduction. In *Narratives from the crib*, ed. Katherine Nelson. Cambridge, MA: Harvard Univ. Press.

Nochi, Masahiro. 2000. Reconstructing self-narratives in coping with traumatic brain injury. *Social Science and Medicine* 51(12): 1795–804.

Oatley, Keith. 1992. Integrative action of narrative. In *Cognitive science and clinical disorders*, ed. Dan J. Stein and Jeffrey E. Young, 151–70. San Diego, CA: Academic, 1992.

O'Riordan, Michelle, and Kate Plaisted. 2001. Enhanced discrimination in autism. *The Quarterly Journal of Experimental Psychology* 54(4): 961–79.

Polkinghorne, Donald. 1988. *Narrative knowing and the human sciences.* Albany: State Univ. of New York Press.

Rimland, Bernard, and Deborah Fein. 1988. Special talents of autistic savants. In *The exceptional brain: Neuropsychology of talent and special abilities*, ed. Loraine K. Obler and Deborah Fein, 474–92. New York: Guilford.

Schneider, Edgar. 1999. *Discovering my autism: Apologia pro vita sua (with apologies to Cardinal Newman).* London: Jessica Kingsley.

Sinclair, Jim. 1992. Bridging the gaps: An inside-out view of autism (or, do you know what I don't know?). In *High-functioning individuals with autism*, ed. Eric Schopler and Gary B. Mesibov, 294–302. New York: Plenum.

———. 1993. Don't mourn for us. Our voice. *The newsletter of Autism Network International* 1(3). Online version is at < http://ani.autistics.org/dont_mourn .html >.

Tager-Flusberg, Helen, Robert Joseph, and Susan Folstein. 2001. Current directions in research on autism. *Mental Retardation and Developmental Disabilities Research Reviews* 7(1): 21–29.

Taylor, Charles. 1989. *Sources of the self: The making of the modern identity.* Cambridge, MA: Harvard Univ. Press.

Vuletic, Ljiljana, Michel Ferrari, and Mihail Teodor. 2005. *Transfer boy: Perspectives on Asperger syndrome.* London: Jessica Kingsley.

Vygotsky, Lev Semenovich. 1934. *Thought and language*, trans. Alex Kozulin. Cambridge, MA: MIT Press, 1986.

Williams, Donna. 1996. *Autism, an inside-out approach: An innovative look at the mechanics of "autism" and its developmental "cousins."* London: Jessica Kingsley.

———. 1998. *Autism and sensing: The unlost instinct.* London: Jessica Kingsley.

———. 1992. *Nobody nowhere: The extraordinary autobiography of an autistic.* New York: Times Books.

———. 1994. *Somebody somewhere: Breaking free from the world of autism.* New York: Times Books.

Creativity, Cultural Studies, and Potentially Fun Ways to Design and Produce Autobiographical Material from Subalterns' Locations

Creating, Cultivating, Celebrating, and Circulating Our Own Voices[1]

> I believe it is time to take on the most despised, even reviled, features of pro-
> letarian poetry, its commonality and shared cultural mission. I am therefore
> trying to reformulate a perceived weakness as a genuine strength. The uni-
> fying historical and rhetorical elements of progressive poetry give it special
> power and meaning. (Nelson 2001, 6)

Technology, such as email, fax machines, desktop publishing programs, affordable phone packages, and Priority Post, has made it possible for small, marginalized voices to design and distribute books, and to design and accomplish community in different ways. Cyberspace too, Dale Spender suggests, is changing the neighbourhood of writers' communities, with the potential for empowerment (1995). Writing circles are a form of personal and political activism and healing. While producing the final product of the book, we are also accomplishing the process of healing ourselves and each other. We are learning and hearing our own autobiographies into existence.

Finding Each Other, Finding Form, Finding Formats

Much has been written about how hard it is for women and other oppressed groups to publish their writing.[2] Social activists, or "subalterns," as Booker describes them (1998), designing books—and hanging onto the whole process from beginning to end? In this process, we who publish books ourselves are claiming our identities and reshaping each other's identities into something larger and braver. In this paper, using ideas from contributors to cultural studies,[3] from what might be called the "creativity for healing"[4] movement (Cameron 1996; Adams 1930), and from social workers/activists (Moran,[5] Goldman 1997), I will summarize observations that I have made from being a facilitator/writer in the centre of five self-publishing circles, and two more emerging self-publishing circles. The books that have been made are *Battle Chants* (2000), *Escaping Beauty* (2000), *Stress (Full) Sister (Hood)* (2000), *Groping Our Way Beyond Grief* (2001), and *Outlaw Social Work (the unsecret poems and stories)* (2002), *This Ain't Your Patriarchs' Poetry Book: Candles, Comrades, Connections* (2003). The seventh book, *Making Noise: Northern Women Caring and In/Visible Dis/Abilities*, will be published, we hope, in early 2006.

At different moments, these projects have invited us to become *spectacles* (Brooker 1999, 204), to toy with the carnivalesque (23–24), and to consider the performance of marketing. What these books have in common is that they are multi-genre (poetry, prose, diary, letter, testimony, qualitative interview), multidisciplinary (contributors had backgrounds in journalism, social work,[6] education, sociology, computer repair, and women's studies), and multi-themed (they are about grief, romance, disobedience, female relationships, social services, and family issues). We have been inventing some portions of our selves as we invent the books. We design the books and they redesign us. We have also had a lot of fun. Burnout and grief are commonly experienced phenomena among activists/professional helpers, especially if they are also from vulnerable populations (Transken 1997). Play is a necessary activity for health (Abrams 1997), and fun is a necessary activity and source of soul-replenishment for activists (Transken 2002b)!

During the production of these books, each author has had control over her[7] own section's shape, stance, and words. Each author has made a commitment to try to coach or encourage the other authors; in cyberspace, through phone calls, and often as persons in friendships, we have networked and raised each other's consciousness and self-confidence. Hundreds of hours have been shared in the process of accomplishing each project. Collectively, twenty authors/editors have contributed directly to five finished books, and another ten have designed quotes for the back of those texts; about thirty people will be directly or indirectly involved in the two newest projects.

These grassroots projects are especially important when they are considered in the context of the current state of Canadian publishing, where ever-larger publishing companies are taking over the industry. These takeovers and amalgamations not only steamroller over subaltern populations but minimize or erase Canadian voices. In a recent email, Darren Wershler-Henry comments on how a relatively small publishing company is feeling threatened by the biggest players on the field. He also emphasizes the necessity of keeping diversity growing in the publishing "ecosystem":

> Why does it matter if a few small poetry and literary fiction publishers go under? Because the small presses are the heart, the soul, and the guts of Canadian literary culture. Presses like Coach House, Talonbooks, Oberon, Mercury, Broken Jaw, Turnstone, TSAR, Brick, and Aresenal Pulp invest the most time and energy in author development. We're the farm teams: we find promising authors, edit their work, and otherwise help them develop their writing styles. And we get that work to market for the first time—usually in better quality editions than mass-market paperbacks, to boot. In other words, the editors of the small press are responsible for the stunning variety and high calibre of Canadian writing today. (2002)

Well said. If Wershler-Henry's level of publishers are the farm teams, then we subalterns are the backyard garden and composting teams! These self-publishing/self-help projects are ad hoc; they form and then dissolve; but the skills, insights, and confidence can later feed into the next level of publishing, for which Wershler-Henry is advocating more government protection and support. It is probable that the government will not substantively alter the terrain in the near future, so it becomes that much more vital for "free-range" voices to assert themselves, and to reinvigorate the spaces available to us in whichever small ways are possible for us. Artists in a variety of media have taught us these lessons.[8]

How do these innovative methods of grounded cultural artifact design and production invigorate the individual writers, many of whom have never published before? How do these playful, experimental, and mindful texts serve as rallying points for vulnerable populations to feel seen and heard—not just to outsiders, but to each other? How much fun can we have producing propaganda and promoting our own unique versions of reality? This paper will discuss how the writing circles began, where there have been uncomfortable moments, how these experiences have changed some people's sense of their own entitlement to voice, and how I am continuing to initiate and participate in these creative adventures in the future. My own paths with these projects might be useful for others to consider, so they might avoid some of the glitches we have encountered, and reproduce some of the successes we have accomplished.

Insights from Cultural Studies

There are four things that make many books dangerous to indigenous[9] readers: (1) they do not reinforce our values, actions, customs, culture and identity; (2) when they tell us only about others they are saying that we do not exist; (3) they may be writing about us but are writing things which are untrue; and (4) they are writing about us but saying negative and insensitive things which tell us that we are not good. (Smith 1999, 35)

Cultural studies (CS) is a body or flow of knowledge that provides analytical resources and tools which help us to expand our usefulness as social activists. Among other things, CS gives us guidance and permission to become "undisciplined discipline-jumpers and genre-jumpers"; this permission and guidance is vital to our future strength as activists. With new and expanded ways of thinking about the world, I am now conversing with a poet's ear; CS is assisting me to listen as an "organic intellectual" (Ng, Staton, and Scane 1995) or a "resisting intellectual."[10] These new[11] conversations are happening within a small but growing circle of lucid, creative conversationalists and change catalysts, who are evaluating practice/praxis competency while expanding the necessary inserts from multiple disciplines and multiple communities. We are creating words as we create ways to have conversation. In this world, as Appadurai (1993) suggests, almost everything and everyone is in motion within international flows of ethnoscapes, technoscapes, finanscapes, mediascapes, and ideoscapes. Our identities as social workers and our narratives must evolve as the wideness and intersectionality of the world's "scapes" evolve. As writers in these kinds of circles, we are creating our own wordscapes and meaningscapes.

With CS, we are understanding, and making permeable, barriers that we did not construct and which no longer serve us. We are learning to jump[12] through and forward and across patriarchal and capitalist fences. In the following pages, I allude to how the paths of being a student, a writer, a survivor, an activist, a therapist, a professor, a feminist, and a dreamer have led me to know myself as an "undisciplined discipline-jumping and genre-jumping social worker"—as a CS social worker. While facilitating the creation of these books, I have felt extremely useful as a social worker.

Multiple Disciplines and Multiple Boundaries

I hadn't yet recognized that as a woman I was alienated by both tradition and temperament from conventional argumentative discourse; I only vaguely sensed why it was an emotional struggle for me to read and write in what I later found out has been called the "male" or "logocentric" or even "phal-logocentric" mode. (Freedman 1992, 3)

A dominant Eurocentric/capitalist/patriarchal myth has been that we are rational, linear, and sequential in how we live, think, write, and need. A more realistic version of our experience is that humans always have multiple intersecting and mobile identities if we admit to them. These evolve in response to our natures, our environments, and the choices we make on our journey. While imagining worlds (inner and outer) of diversity and abundance—in contrast to the hegemonic scarcity model of life, where we're only allowed to belong to one ethnocultural group, one class location, and one sexuality—we can not only admit our multiple identities but situate them within multiple bodies of knowledge and within multiple contexts. We are untidy texts being read by others while we read the texts around us. Texts are the complex codes of the cultures we are located in: the conjunctures of our time and place. Necessarily, then, we are amalgamations and unique imprints—and the issues we confront are also contested intersections of the perceptions and wants of many.

Writer

Creative writing contributes to the profession of social work. Since I first encountered Dr. Seuss, I have thought of the processes and products of writing as being glorious accomplishments. I have always admired writers, and thought this activity was one of the most magnificent things for humans to do. Both the inner, private world and the outer, public world can be changed by writing. One writer can produce something that changes the minds and behaviors of millions of people! Freedman describes something about writing that has always enticed me:

I have discovered more and more personal, mixed-genre, metadiscursive writers published by more journals or presses. They challenge the critical canon with their "common" language and hybrid, alchemical forms as much as they do any other canon. I praise them for refusing to deny their personal histories or the process by which they come to know what they know or to believe what they believe. Combining poet with critic, they join private and public, writer and teacher, and past and present as they experiment with and announce a blending of traditional genres (poetry, autobiography, drama, fiction among them), subgenres (free-verse lyrics, fables, epigrams, diaries, exhortations), and disciplinary discourses. Mixed, crossed, or blurred genres is my shorthand way of referring to such anomalous, self-conscious blendings (1992, 4-5).

I propose that this kind of writing is also a wholesome and necessary way for social workers to dis-cover what needs to be dis-covered, and to try to bring about change on many levels with our clients in their process of learning about journaling, for example, or in our own processes as helping professionals doing self-care—and in many other forums and formats.

Hall (1993, 507–17) discusses the meaning of language and how we send, receive, code, and decode the texts of the world around us. Each community uses codes and decoding differently. For example, First Nations people are more inclined traditionally to use storytelling as a way of imparting knowledge. When we insist that our students in degree programs use a formal style of essay writing, we are, in a way, excluding some people from becoming organic intellectuals within the social work profession. Poetry and creative writing may be a more natural way for some communities to explicate the consciousness of their own centred perspectives, and to express their authenticity, analysis, solidarity, and resistance.

Survivor/Woman/Oppressed Person/Resisting

As Smith (1999) and so many others have proven to us, *where you stand and how you stand determine much of what you see, feel, know, and perceive*. It is important, then, to disclose and ponder our locations.

I know that I felt compelled to write some of the things that I have published in these forums. As a person who was sexually abused during childhood, the mother of a male child, and a person from a poverty-oppressed heritage, I have struggled to find ways to be healed, become stronger, figure it all out, pass the knowledge on, and then move on.

The journey I have been on begs to be summarized now and then into something coherent. Making things make their own sense and putting them out into the world like grown children ready to leave home seems to free up space in me for other things to enter my life. My sense is that this often happens to people who decide to write in self-publishing forums. We get to control what gets said or not said, and this is strengthening.

During this journey I discovered eclectic wisdom in Buddhism, feminism, creativity, and expressive arts. All of this is inside me and it informs my daily life; my praxis; my practice. What I have learned in my own heart is knowledge that becomes something I offer to clients, students, activists, and readers. From this field of knowledge production comes my belief in my intuition, and my trust in the knowledge clients offer to me. When a practitioner is regularly informed by her client group and her own community, how does that wisdom circle back into the profession's databases? It is to this that my quest always returns. Freud, for example, assumed too much; he did not know as much about healing from incest as most of my incest-recovering clients do. In our profession we must remain alert to various knowledgescapes so that we can continually bring in new and fortifying insights.

Most cultural studies scholars are also activists: they propose that we bring our wisdom to the street and the wisdom of the street to academia. This is the life and mission of organic intellectuals.

Listening to the Poets/Creative Writers on the Path

A case can be made that poetry/creative writing is a natural manifestation of social work, and vice versa—think of Jane Addams, Dorothy Livesay, Bridget Moran, and Emma Goldman—and it might be the discursive field in which insights from all the other disciplines can find ways to make themselves heard. In *Revolutionary Memory*, Cary Nelson (2001) makes many points that relate to this discussion. He talks about a sense of powerfulness that came from being connected to a group of writers who were also activists. He describes how that powerfulness was disrupted during the McCarthy era, when poets and others who tried to tell a subversive truth were erased by cowardly intellectuals in the universities. These poets imagined and spoke elegantly about an incomplete and disharmonious world, and about a potentially revolutionary future world.

Revolutions can be taken in tiny, ordinary steps by ordinary people. Below is a poem published in *Outlaw Social Work* (2002, 66). I realize now that it was a poem that I have been writing for years.

> To you, for community
> in a previous era/ a traditional context
> a casual range of smiling gestures
> created cohesion
> & unstranger-liness.
>
> then/ there:
> a handful of special
> seeds from my own garden;
> a bouquet of roses or lilies;
> pies, muffins, cookies
> from home-bred recipes;
> or something hand
> knitted or sewn—
>
> but i have no yard,
> no ripe food,

no oven,
no craft—only fresh
precious words—
portable, common,
nutritious, compostable
& un-store-bought.

so nodding, hand held out
i offer these small
poems in neighbourliness.

This process of writing, connecting, and publishing gives us new ways to be neighbours.

Coming to, Celebrating, Containing, Commodifying Voice

Through the writing and publishing of our own voices, many connections were made between activist women in two different provinces, even though we had never physically met. Through the magnificent technology of email, we were able to affirm something precious in each other long before we had our first face-to-face conversation. We were activists acting creatively, and making differences in each other's lives through the power of the word—the power of the text—with words and texts mediated minimally through the usual regimes of representation, which includes publishing houses and professional editors.

The six concluded books I am discussing here were produced between 1998 and 2003. They range from seventy-five to 229 pages and sell for between ten and twenty dollars CDN. Below I will describe the six projects individually, and discuss how each intellectual and pragmatic adventure advanced my knowledge. These experiences might be useful in other contexts and for other communities.

As I describe the finding of voice, I am noticing how my own voice has been found and lost and found and centred and decentred over the last four years. Joyously I celebrate what these privileged positions have given me. I recognize, too, that portions of who I am/who I was/who I am becoming have become commodified and contained in these pages. Further, as a therapist, I am aware of how slightly I can assert myself and thus shift someone's voice. It is probable that I have done that in millions of ways along the way with these authors and supporters of our projects. That is my responsibility to own. Influence is a magical and sometimes morose thing. Previously unpublished people, or people who haven't produced or published this kind of experiential, autobiographical, creative writing before, can be exquisitely tender and tentative. It has not escaped my consciousness that any of the people involved in these projects might have a radically different version of these stories to tell from the one that I am documenting here. Nonetheless, the only story I can offer is my own—and in this fragile moment this is it.

Battle Chants

The first book emerged in response to writing-for-healing circles that I was attending or co-facilitating in my private practice as a therapist, and while I too was on a personal trajectory towards expanding my creative writing skills. In 1998, a variety of practices, activities, and people just seemed to fall into place. I'd come across the writings of people like Cameron (1992, 1996), Ballenger and Lane (1996), Ealy (1995), Felman and Laub (1992), Fox (1995), Gere Lewis (1993), hooks (1994a, 1994b), and McNiff (1992). Deena Metzger's *Writing for Your Life: A Guide and Companion to the Inner Worlds* (1992) had influenced me significantly. The collective suggestions these writers made about finding the creative voice had made a profound impact upon me. Many of these resources I regularly lent out to clients, and used in our work together.

Julia Cameron (1992, 63), quoting Shakti Gawain's dictum "The universe will reward you for taking risks on its behalf," devotes a whole chapter in her book to using journaling and creative writing as a way to recover our sense of power. Poetry and prose can feel like very risky ways to express ourselves because our vulnerabilities and our own lives are displayed. Cameron encourages us to find circles of supporters for our re-emerging creative child. The five books that have emerged from our subaltern voices display our authenticity and our contradictions. We are innocents evolving.

A pattern of regulars at the first writing circle began to form. A circle of women had been attending regularly, and in some subtle ways we were co-facilitating some aspects of the process. Each session had a theme: body image, anger, depression, etc. We were increasingly amazed by our creativity and writing talent, and also by both the distinctiveness and the universality of some aspects of our stories. We began playfully chatting about some day putting these pieces of writing into a book. Then one day we said, Why not now? And we actually did it: we produced *Battle Chants*.

The women in this first circle included two who had been involved semi-professionally in desktop publishing and the production of texts. Other women had other talents that they brought to the ad hoc project: their ability to edit, their design skills, their stamina and ability to keep us focused, and their computer skills. This was all quite informal, hectic, and delightful, and somehow it all just manifested in this wonderful experience and this wonderful (to our eyes) product. We were encouraged when the community welcomed us to do readings, and we were invited to speak at a women's centre and at a Chapters bookstore. Our creativity was embraced and celebrated by many gazes and voices. All of this came together rapidly, too, so our enchantment with the process and with each other wasn't lost.

The glitches in the experience manifested after the book was published. Then we had complications within the group over how best to promote and distribute it. Should we all do readings all of the time? Should the women who did the most readings get the most returns from the sales? Should we have a joint bank account and do monthly statements and have meetings? Marketing and money management was not fun. It was all quite disenchanting compared to the original circle's intentions. My present assessment of this phase is that a group is better advised to keep everything as simple as humanly possible. All production costs should be equally divided. All writers should contribute approximately the same number of pages of text to the book. All writers should get their share of the print run when it is finished being printed. No joint accounts. Maintaining the elements of play, adventure, and spontaneity is more conducive to comfort for all. *Battle Chants* taught me about the enormous potential inside most women; it also taught me about the practicalities involved in the financial and organizational process of producing a book. The subsequent projects affirmed these lessons.

Escaping Beauty

This project was the most disappointing of the ones I've been involved in. I embarked upon it too soon after *Battle Chants*, when I was too drained psychically and financially to be the leading voice in such an intensive experience. *Escaping Beauty* attempted to make a spectacle of heterosexuality, to authentically document some of the dimensions of obsessive affections for another person, and to explore issues around non-monogamy and women's desire. These are volatile and potentially troubling topics that I was examining in my own life, as were some of the women in the healing circles and many of my clients. The voice that is explicitly presented in the book is my own, but the implicit understanding was that the book would be the portal through which many women's voices would be expressed. In some ways, I was acting as a ghost writer without fully knowing the consequences that might arise from that role and task. The other women in the circles often (understandably) wanted their confidentiality protected, and I was so positioned that I could be the ghost writer for their curiosity, their confusions, and their contradictions—and my own. A lot of raw emotional messiness was present in this whole experience. In some ways, our innocence made us potentially incoherent to a reader of the text.

A major lesson that I took from the *Escaping Beauty* experience is that people will read your material in ways that you hadn't expected. The extreme subordinations that are displayed in the pages of *Escaping Beauty* are renditions of what a woman in that location might feel; at the same time, some of the lines are also mocking the phenomenon. Some aspects of being human are just so silly—and we tried to communicate that in some of the pages of *Escaping Beauty*. As tortured lovers, we can see ourselves as ridiculous and infected with all of Hollywood's dumb lies while at the same moment feeling totally distracted and lost because our loved person hasn't returned our phone call. As a therapist and a writer, I know that a lovesick woman can feel a hundred emotions all in the same day. The majority of readers of the text, though, are not therapists—and neither are they creative writers. The average reader's gaze has been conditioned to respond to text in a certain way. As we wrote and published *Escaping Beauty*, I hadn't fully realized the monodimensionality that most readers were likely to bring to such a document.

There were professional peers who felt shocked and puritanical about what I'd written. There were clients who thought every single word was totally true and that I'd lived every word of *Escaping Beauty* myself. They felt worried and sorry for me, which certainly complicated my role as a therapist. There were feminists in the community who thought I'd lost all my political scruples and militant enlightenment. Almost everyone I encountered made some reference to it. It was a tidy coincidence that I was leaving town.

Escaping Beauty taught me to be much more overt about every single dimension of what we are doing with our process, our product, and our promotions of the material. The organic, diffuse connections to each other, to the project, and to the theme can benefit from being made vigorously explicit. Who is doing what, for what reasons, and for how long? What is motivating each person to stay with the activity and what is her need? How will we speak to each other and shift if there are conflicts, evolutions, or exits? Pre-existing relationships that did not get fully renegotiated and reclarified became awkward. For example, some of the people involved in *Escaping Beauty* had been involved in *Battle Chants*, and they may have been semi-consciously inclined to reproduce the same relationships and responsibilities that had been in place within that first writing circle. However, they were now "employees" for the project, as opposed to the *Battle Chants* experience, in which we had all been equally responsible for paying for the production of the book. Each circle is a brand new circle, even if people have done things together before. Start fresh. Start clear. Speak it all through.

Stress (Full) Sister (Hood)

Stress (Full) Sister (Hood) brought together women from my old geographical community and women in my new community. This text became a bridging experience for me between my past and my present/future. The process of pulling this book together also made profoundly clear to me how important cyberspace could be as a resourced geography for women.

Dale Spender (1995) describes many of the ambiguities and complexities of cyberspace, but she recognizes its potential to liberate women in rural or isolated communities (isolated geographically or intellectually). Even though the authors were in different geographical locations, we could be in touch every day, and affordably. Often, one of us would compose a poem or prose piece in the middle of the night, go to bed, and wake up to find fresh comments from those at the other end of the nation Also, someone could drop out of the process for a long time and then hop in where she had left off, because she could read her backlog of emails. No problems with childcare expenses. No meetings had to be harmonized among all of us. This process was liberating.

Stress (Full) Sister (Hood) was different in that the roles women took up were more clearly defined, and became even more vividly articulated toward the end. I assumed control of many dimensions of the process, and the others seemed to be comfortable with that. I initially felt ambiguous about the control factor, however, because it was quite a different ethic from the emergent-organic flow that had been characteristic of the first experience.

Pragmatically (and accidentally), I had some time for facilitation, and the other contributors did not. In a common-sense way, I moved forward chunk by chunk with the process and sought feedback from the other four authors, from the people who might give quotes for the back, and from the designer of the cover. Among feminists and other social activists, there have been many conversations about the "tyranny of structurelessness." I tried to not be a tyrant against the tyranny, but I did want to see the book come out, and so I took the reins. This quickly became satisfying for everyone, and the book did get done.

Groping Our Way beyond Grief

Margaret Atwood recently talked about the meaning of writing about our shadows. "Possibly, then, writing has to do with darkness, and a desire or perhaps a compulsion to enter it, and, with luck, to illuminate it, and to bring something back out to the light" (2002, xxiv). This bookspace became a grieving ground, and a location from which to rise up again. There were many women around me at the time who were very disenchanted and depressed.

In *Groping Our Way beyond Grief*, our fourth book, I took a very central role in identifying the theme, recruiting the authors, and providing them with text to brainstorm or dance around with. It was known from the beginning what the financial costs would be, which we hadn't had enough experience among us in the first three writing/publishing adventures to accurately predict, so people didn't always know what they were consenting to. The cybercircle was more fluent in that all of the participants were able to keep their offerings gracefully moving around and moving forward. The process was much tidier, much more predictable. Timelines were expressed right up front.

In *Groping Our Way beyond Grief*, three women left the circle during the process. Their entrances and exits were cleaner and less disruptive than the leavings during *Stress (Full) Sister (Hood)*, and they were, this time, anticipated losses. After the experience with *Stress (Full) Sister (Hood)*, I knew there would inevitably be exits, and respected that pattern as one of the unavoidable manifestations of patriarchy/capitalism's interferences with the well-being of vulnerable populations' lives. Someone would leave, I knew, because of a loss of financial support, because of the illness of a loved one, because of job stress, and so on. I recognized that the exits were gentle, and conducive to future reconnecting on other projects. Thus, exit was normalized and politicized rather than problematized and psychologized.

The response we received from the community for *Groping Our Way beyond Grief* was just as I had hoped. We'd timed its publication so it could be available for the December 6 mourning ceremonies commemorating the women killed at the L'École Polytechnique de Montréal in 1989. We read from it on December 6 at the University of Northern British Columbia, and at a First Nations Friendship Centre. The local radio station interviewed us, and I was able to read a poem that spoke specifically to the sentiments we had about violence against women. Clearly, by this, the fourth book, the multiple political intentions were fulfilling themselves. Also, the personal dimensions of healing, promotion of self-esteem, and validation of our powerful potential for creative resistance have been achieved in the book.

Outlaw Social Work (The Unsecret Poems and Stories)

In this project, a vivid theme-cluster was there for me right from the beginning, and I recruited participants who I knew had an organic and powerful alliance to the themes. The topics needed to be focused enough for the product to make sense to an outside reader, and for us to feel a sense of cohesion and solidarity as writers. The topics also needed to be flexible enough for each unique contribution to emerge, remain authentic, and connect soulfully with a reader.

Educating the potential contributors about those themes was vital, but how do you communicate an emerging and organic theme? How do you facilitate the vibrancy and intensity while maintaining some coherence and sustained, focused flow? My experience of all this was almost like that of facilitating a therapy group. A lot of cyber-writing and phone calls can be necessary. However, these could also be seen as a subtle form of coercion. Our ethics and integrity challenge us.

It now seems to me that there also needs to be a *ripeness* for the theme area. The timing and the resonance of a topic are central to the successful fruition of these books. Having a soulful ear to the wind and letting your fingers dabble in the stream for a long time before the beginning of the construction of a theme area is important. Finding appropriately stimulating, but not overwhelming, guide quotes, poems, or newspaper articles can be a sign that a readiness exists in your community and in your circles of conversation.

Trust seems to be a complex and central dimension to these book-creation stories. People need to trust that the product will make them proud. They need to feel they can trust the facilitator and the other authors to enhance their writing, deepen their thoughts, and enrich their creative forces. They need to trust that they will be respected and honoured. They need to feel that they are in the right circle of creativity, at the right time in their lives, doing the right things. *Outlaw Social Work* has been very successful in every way possible. I feel that it has been as smooth, memorable, and productive as any project like this could be.

This Ain't Your Patriarchs' Poetry Book:
Candles, Comrades, Connections

Originally this was going to be two books, one in which men offered their thoughts on resisting patriarchy and a second book of women's voices resisting patriarchy. Eventually they morphed into one book.

One-third of the pages in *This Ain't* are the words of men sharing their stories, poems, prose, and testimony of how they are connecting differently with female energy. My initial hope had been that eight to ten men would volunteer to be part of this project—but there wasn't a large enough cohort to make the project viable. My request to those writers was that they speak broadly to how feminism has made a difference in their lives, in regard to how they love their partners, students, daughters, mothers, sisters, Mother Nature, and so on. As a feminist therapist/activist, I m interested to see how progressive men are contributing postiively to the well-being of our world through these relationships. So much of the material I read is about how men have done the wrong things, displayed the wrong attitudes, and hurt us. though these are accurate renditions of what happens in many women's lives and experiences, my clients (and friends, comrades, and peers) also often want to see some positive material that they can feel uplifted by.

Two-thirds of the pages in This Ain't are devoted to the "Candles, Comrades, Connections" women have found and forged in resistance to patriarchy. Eight women share how other women have mentored them. They speak about how they've been reconnected through their relationships with other women. Some of the women from the previous projects have grown the theme for this book with men.

We have read from this book at various events. We have raised funds for cancer treatment and for women's organizations. We have had guest readings in all kinds of contexts from Northern Ontario to Fort St. John to Vancouver. We have read individually or in small clusters. Even the president of the University of Northern British Columbia has sent us a letter congratulating us on the book. From this project I leaned more about flexibility. We had begun as two circles of voices and when I opened my mind to preparing the circles to merge, they did so with grace and positivity. By merging the two groups, both projects were enhanced in regards to the availability of more text, more resources, more diversity, and more speakers to promote the book's ideas in various forums. The technology used in this production was also different. for this book we used print-on-demand to produce the book. This means the up-front costs that each author adds to the "pot" are much lower but that the end cost of each book is three times higher. I would add a word of caution for potential writers wanting to use this technology: "print on-demand" actually means "print-whenever-someone gets around to it." We have been ordering books in boxes of forty and find that it takes up to ten weeks to receive them. On the other hand, the advantage of this production method is that the books can be produced forever and that they are distributed through Amazon.com. this means we can sell the ones we order at our events, but people anywhere in the world also have access to our voice.

Making Noise: Northern Women Caring and In/Visible Dis/Ability

This book is still in process and it is teaching me about patience. Given that all of the women in the project have moderate to sever health issues (including myself) and/or are caring for others with these health issues, we must all be very gentle in our process. We have chosen to leave the deadlines and the conclusion of the book entirely in the air—when it accomplishes enough pages of text we will bring it to the next stage (final editing, design, and publication). At this moment there are twenty-two participants who range in age from twenty-four to seventy. We come from a variety of enthnocultural heritages, alliances, identity pegs, and geographical locations. We are living with issues like high blood pressure, cancer, depression, migraines, the death of a loved one, asthma, fibromayalgia, MS. Again this book was originally going to be a forum for three different "clusters" of health concerns but it morphed into one. I feel uplifted and joyous to witness it having its own organic unfolding and "birthing." We have applied for grants to assist with the publication of this one and it may be a blended project between "self publishing" and being published by the University of Northern British Columbia Press. Given the health concerns and the poverty that many of these women face we don't want to be a burden on them in the production process if we can find another way to get their voices out into the wider world. Making Noise may form itself to manifest in some other way than the previous books did. None of us feels an urge to pressure the process or the outcome.

This most recent book will go forward more smoothly than any of the others. The potential contributors can all see examples of the previous books, and they can judge how they might contribute best to those kinds of conversations. Also, given that this next book already has a larger circle of committed participants than previous projects, the costs will be decreased for each author. This facilitates participation.

What have these experiences meant for my own autobiographical writing process?

Atwood describes her shift from being "not a writer to being one" as "instantaneous" (2002, 14). Although I have been publishing poetry and other forms of writing for fifteen years, I would rarely call myself a "writer." It is only in the last year, and because of these collective projects, that I can feel myself moving closer to truly owning that word.

My sense of immediacy has become more validated and solidified. The usual turnaround time for publishing a book of poetry might be two years or longer. In my own writing process, I am invigorated by the feeling of "now-writing"—writing done in an almost "foreign journalistic" way. Enormous satisfaction comes to me from seeing the material out there, and being read while it still feels fresh. If the process forces me to wait more than a year, then I usually do not feel like seeing the piece published. It no longer feels accurate. It no longer feels appropriate. Instead of publishing it, I want to revise it, reshape it, and reconsider all of the parts of it. The style, the intention, the philosophical assumptions are always shifting slightly. I like to write while the pulse is most intense and then see the piece of writing claim its own independent, unpredictable life—separate from my own evolved-again life. Organic intellectuals doing this kind of writing must be served fresh and be serving freshness.

My judgments around what I approve of in my own writing have changed. I now ask myself if I have really told the truth—as opposed to reproducing that which is fed into our minds from the dominant cultures—about the version of my world that is precisely centred in/voiced from my own incomparable location. That is always shifting and morphing. This is also how I am more likely to assess other people's writing for inclusion in the next books. Have they expressed their own authentic, complex world view and experiences with an accuracy that impels? Even if that world view is contrary to my own, I'm most interested in the authentically nuanced voice. I do not want to be judged by the rules of pre-existing genres that were formed without my consideration and consent.

My mind is increasingly located to question the tiniest components of the process. I recognize that we have all been subconsciously (and consciously) positioned to engage with text according to far-away-designed formulas that have existed for generations. Even our vocabularies and baseline assumptions have a million minds, colonies, gender roles, racist assumptions, and so forth, carved right into them. We must aerobically engage with our imaginations to hope to extricate the things we desire to be free from or to express and experience differently.

The majestic in the ordinary has been enhanced for me. These group writing projects have been somewhat like group diary entries. These are moody tourists in a neighbourhood that is, perhaps, my own. These writers are kindred and comrades and leaders. These are ordinary folks who are sharing their ordinary perceptions, and trying to refine them into something extraordinary in writing that is precise and carries an explosion of insights. The process of actually writing and sharing the drafts has educated me about how something that ends up being intense and memorable began with just a minor rumbling of a question or a concern. These are cyberspace consciousness-raising groups. I now feel that the splendid and mesmerizing lurks and lingers unavoidably nearby. Everyone has something special to say.

Spreading the non-news that writing and reading are incredibly powerful resources for personal change and healing has become a blessing and a cause for me. These writing circles are sometimes like therapy groups in that the writers explore and share their sentiments and perceptions, and find new ways to reframe what may have been old problems for them. For some of us, this writing could be the thing we do instead of creatively cutting our own forearms, binge eating, or drinking. Our problems continue to find some kind of orderliness from the chaos in our minds/spirits/practices. And even after the original author of a thought has left the room or the conversation in cyberspace, there are others who may pick up the themes and take them where they need to go next. Further, there is a glory in how eventual readers will touch up against a theme or idea again in a book, and experiment further with it. In some ways, through these writing projects, we have all become therapists for each other. And we continue to do so, whether through direct contact or through the stability of the writing.

Some of this writing is just casual bathroom graffiti. Its intention is to leave a small mark that notes a name or a passage of some experience. These writings can be promises from our present selves to some imagined future selves. No refund is possible on our past or our present, but we can exchange bits of our flawed or flailing selves for a stronger, more grounded future self. Some of this is the bathroom graffiti that we didn't get to compose somewhere along the way because we were not allowed to bring a pen, didn't know to bring a pen, or were too afraid to declare our inner thoughts.

Most of the writers in these circles have also used this space as a type of counter-judiciary. It is a place in which we can bring forth our own version of the unfolding world and make our judgments. This is our court. These writings are our exhibits. And we publicize the proceedings—that is, we read our poetry in all kinds of community forums such as Take Back the Night marches, International Women's Day events, union rallies, and anti-poverty marches. Smith Tuhiwai insists that organic intellectuals (although she doesn't use that precise label) have an obligation to bring their insights to the community—and to bring that information forward in comfortable, accessible ways:

> Sharing contains views about knowledge being a collective benefit and knowledge being a form of resistance. Like networking, sharing is a process which is responsive to the marginalized contexts in which indigenous communities exist.... It is important for keeping people informed about issues and events which will impact upon them. It is a form of oral literacy, which

connects with the story telling and formal occasions that feature indigenous life.

Sharing is a responsibility of research. The technical term for this is the dissemination of results, usually very boring to non-researchers, very technical and very cold. For indigenous researchers sharing is about demystifying knowledge and information and speaking in plain terms to the community. (1999, 161)

Most of the participants in each of the books have done a variety of readings in a variety of community forums. Our jury is composed of the communities we want to connect with and believe we have comradeship with. In a mainstream courtroom, our cases might be thrown out. Our dramas would be assessed as mundane or wrongly scripted. Sometimes, in mainstream courtrooms, we organic intellectuals often believe criminals are running the system. In forums such as the seven books discussed in this paper, using our creativity, our insights from cultural studies, our kindness, and comradeship, we can potentially have fun *and* heal. We can produce pedagogical resources, propaganda, and pride-full-ness. We can heal and we can help others heal. We can accomplish this through our own authentic ways and means.

Notes

1 There are many people who have made these books and this specific paper possible. This is a list of some of them: Ken Belford, Julia Emberly, Cathy Denby, Karen Thistle, Judith Lapadat, Kate Tilleczek, Jacqueline Baldwin, Glen Schmidt, Marianne Gosztonyi Ainley, Tamar Eylon, Dina Ripsman Eylon, Soni B., Dawn Hemingway, Kwong-Leung Tang, Rob Budde, Catherine Baylis, Andrew Burton, Chuck Fraser, Vicky Bryant, Paulette Dahl, Louise Lane, Melanie Marttila, Carole Trepanier, Barry Wong, David Mah, Melanie Robitaille, Julie LeBreton, Teena Lacoste, Roxana Ng, and Kathleen Adams.

2 Some of these commentators include Clark and Ivanic (1997), Nelson (2001), Ortiz (1998), and Spender (1983).

3 My influences in cultural studies include Norman Denzin, Stuart Hall, Lawrence Grossberg, Irving Goffman, bell hooks, Cary Nelson, Edward Soja, and Trinh T. Min-ha. See also the constitution of the Association for Cultural Studies (2002) at < http://www.tam perereconference.fi/crossroads/constitution.htm >.

4 When I use the word *healing* in this paper I mean healing in its widest ways. We live in a capitalist, patriarchal, racist, homophobic, multiply oppressive world, and the need for healing exists in all of us. I've often said that I am more concerned about those who never reach out for therapy than those who are always in therapy.

5 This paper links to a paper I presented at the 2002 Bridget Moran Conference at the University of Northern British Columbia, which celebrated Moran's writing of five books, her work as a cultural studies-oriented social worker, and her creative social activism.

6 Social work might be defined as my mother discipline in that it is the one that has given me a paycheque for the last ten years or so. There are many other disciplines that I feel I have an affinity with. For the purposes of this paper, I want to say that I believe social work-

ers are not particularly connected to the scholars from cultural studies. I have inferred a disconnection between these two bodies of scholarship and activism for several reasons. My research assistant emailed all of the schools of social work in Canada on my behalf to ask if any of the professors used cs in their courses and whether they would be interested in dialoguing about this topic, and only four responded with a yes. All four of them made reference to teaching anti-racist courses or to being Aboriginal, or they had program titles that suggested they came from this kind of location. Also, I emailed Dr. Lawrence Grossberg, one of the central thinkers in cs, and asked if he knew of any social workers or anyone engaging with social workers who used cs. His answer was no. Further, for more than six months I have been on the cs listserve and I have never seen the words *social worker* in any of the hundreds of comments and calls for papers. At this time, my personal library has about one hundred books which could be identified with cs, but none of them has the words *social worker* in their contents or indexes. I am amazed at how these two disciplines have been living in parallel worlds but have not intersected with each other. Many social workers are familiar with some of the central speakers in cs but don't seem to identify these authors as falling into this group of thinkers. For example, bell hooks is a cultural studies scholar whose ideas many social workers use to guide their practice and whose books many social work professors use in their courses.

7 The majority of people involved have been women. This has been largely because those are the circles I travel in and because, as seen in the discussion below, the writings initially grew out of healing circles that I was involved in as a therapist/community activist. For the sake of simplicity I will use the female pronoun throughout most of this paper.

8 Some of these artists include Cabico and Swift (1998), Chicago and Lucie-Smith (1999), Felshin (1996), Lacy (1995), Marino (1997), and Ryan (1999).

9 Of course, Smith Tuhiwai is speaking specifically about First Nations/Maori peoples and their dynamics, but so much of the wisdom about patterns of oppression is relevant to other contexts (class issues, gender issues). I value her wisdom and believe she would feel comfortable with the way I am connecting to her discussions and insights.

10 Giroux, Shumway, Smith, and Sosnoski (2001) and Hall (1993) take up a discussion of the "resisting organic intellectual." These are advocates for the oppressed who position themselves in the space between the streets and academia; between the concrete and the abstract analysis; who hold the tension of the two locations with the intention of informing both locations and bringing about social change that enhances the lives of vulnerable populations.

11 I am defining these conversations as new although cs has been an evolving conversation for over two decades in England and the us. My sense is that it is a new conversation in Canadian social work schools—I infer this because I have been unable to find any courses or books that have the words cultural studies and social work in the same title or sentence.

12 While reconceptualizing and reconstructing our worlds (interior and exterior), language that has been ivory tower-centred and male-created often doesn't serve us. The word *jump* has come to me—and I'm using it here in a transitional, temporary, experimental way—because it expresses memories of the vibrant spontaneous energy of robust girls playing double skip rope while bright summer sun shines on us. We jumped into and out of the centre of the ropes while other girls took turns at the ends spinning the ropes. Those in the location of spinning, those girls watching, and those jumping were always changing positions in a minute-to-minute way. This was a playful, healthy, accessible (working-class girls could afford a rope), and shared activity. I like the image of us now as adults vibrantly jumping in and out of places that we want to experience and centre our view from within.

References

Abrams, Rebecca. 1997. *The playful self: Why women need play in their lives.* London: Fourth Estate.

Acker, Sandra. 1996. Equity with strings attached: Experiences and concerns of women academics in faculties of education. *Ontario Confederation of Faculty Association Forum.* Toronto.

Addams, Jane. 1930. *The second twenty years at Hull House.* New York: Macmillan.

Appadurai, Arjun. 1993. Disjuncture and difference in the global cultural economy. In *The cultural studies reader.* 2nd ed, ed. Simon During, 220–32. London and New York: Routledge.

Arrien, Angeles. 1992. *The four-fold way: Walking the paths of the warrior, teacher, healer, and visionary.* San Francisco: Harper Collins.

Atwood, Margaret. 2002. *Negotiating with the dead: A writer on writing.* Cambridge: Cambridge Univ. Press.

Ballenger, Bruce, and Barry Lane. 1996. *Discovering the writer within: Forty days to more imaginative writing.* Cincinnati, OH: Writer's Digest.

Bane, Rosanne. 1999. *Dancing in the dragon's den: Rekindling the creative fire in your shadow.* York Beach, ME: Nicolas Hays.

Bannerji, Himani. 1991. *Unsettling relations: The university as a site of feminist struggles.* Toronto: Women's Press.

Bannerji, Himani, ed. 1993. *Returning the gaze: Essays on racism, feminism and politics.* Toronto: Sister Vision Press.

Bender, Sheila. 1998. *Writing personal poetry: Creating poems from your life experiences.* Cincinnati, OH: Writer's Digest.

Boles, Janet K., and Diane Long Hoeveler. 1996. *From the Goddess to the glass ceiling: A dictionary of feminism.* London: Madison.

Breathnach, Sarah Ban. 1999. *The illustrated discovery journal: Creating a visual autobiography of your authentic self.* New York: Warner.

Brooker, P. 1999. *A concise dictionary of cultural theory.* Oxford: Oxford Univ. Press.

Brown, Laura S. 1994. *Subversive dialogues: Theory in feminist therapy.* New York: Basic.

Bunch, Charlotte. 1987. *Passionate politics: Essays on feminist theory and action.* New York: St Martin's.

Burstow, Bonnie. 1992. *Radical feminist therapy: Working in the context of violence.* Newbury Park, CA: Sage.

Cabico, R., and T. Swift, eds. 1998. *Poetry nation: The North American anthology of fusion poetry.* Montreal: Véhicule.

Cameron, Julia. 1992. *The artist's way: A spiritual path to higher creativity.* New York: Putnam.

———. 1996. *The vein of gold: A journey to your creative heart.* New York: Putnam.

Caplan, Paula. 1993. *Lifting a ton of feathers: A woman's guide to surviving in the academic world.* Toronto: Univ. of Toronto Press.

Chesler, Phyllis, Esther D. Rothblum, and Ellen Cole, eds. 1995. *Feminist foremothers in women's studies, psychology, and mental health.* Binghamton, NY: Harrington Park.

Chicago, J., and E. Lucie-Smith. 1999. *Women and art: Contested territory.* Vancouver: Raincoast.

Clark, Romy, and Roz Ivanic. 1997. *The politics of writing.* London and New York: Routledge.

Clark, VeVe, Shirley Nelson Garner, Margaret Higonnet, and Ketu Katrak. 1996. *Antifeminism in the academy.* London and New York: Routledge.

Corey, Gerald. 1996. *Theory and practice of counseling and psychotherapy.* 5th ed. Pacific Grove, CA: Brooks/Cole.

Crossley, Michele L. 2000. *Introducing narrative psychology: Self, trauma, and the construction of meaning.* Buckingham, UK: Open Univ. Press.

Dagg, Anne Innis, and Patricia J. Thompson. 1988. *MisEducation: Women and Canadian universities.* Toronto: OISE Press.

Ealy, C. Diane. 1995. *The woman's book of creativity.* Berkeley, CA: Celestial Arts.

Ernst, Sheila, and Lucy Goodison. 1981. *In our own hands: A book of self-help therapy.* London: The Women's Press.

Felman, Shoshana, and Dori Laub. 1992. *Testimony: Crises of witnessing in literature, psychoanalysis, and history.* London and New York: Routledge.

Felshin, Nina, ed. 1996. *But is it art? The spirit of art as activism.* Seattle, WA: Bay.

Fox, John. 1995. *Finding what you didn't lose: Expressing your creativity through poem-making.* New York: Penguin Putnam.

Freedman, Diane P. 1992. *An alchemy of genres; Cross-genre writing by American feminist poet-critics.* Charlottesville, VA: Univ. Press of Virginia.

Friedman, Marilyn, and Penny A. Weiss, eds. 1995. *Feminism & community.* Philadelphia: Temple Univ. Press.

Garber, Marjorie. 2001. *Academic instincts.* Princeton, NJ: Princeton Univ. Press.

Garfield, Charles, Cindy Spring, and Sedonia Cahill. 1998. *Wisdom circles: A guide to self-discovery and community building in small groups.* New York: Hyperion.

Gere Lewis, Magda. 1993. *Without a word: Teaching beyond women's silence.* London and New York: Routledge.

Giroux, Henry, David Shumway, Paul Smith, and James Sosnoski. 2001. The need for cultural studies: Resisting intellectuals and oppositional public spheres. < http://eserver.org/theory/need/html >.

Goldman, Emma. 1969. *Anarchism and other essays.* New York: Dover.

———. 1977. *Living my life.* Scarborough: New American Library.

———. 1983. *Vision on fire.* New Paltz, NY: Commonground.

Goffman, Erving. 1959. *The presentation of self in everyday life.* New York: Anchor.

———. 1964. *Stigma: Notes on the management of spoiled identity.* Englewood Cliffs, NJ: Prentice Hall.

Hall, Stuart. 1993. Cultural studies and its theoretical legacies. In *The cultural studies reader.* 2nd ed., ed. Simon During, 97–112. London and New York: Routledge.

———. 1996. The problem of ideology: Marxism without guarantees. In *Stuart Hall: Critical dialogues in cultural studies,* ed. David Morley and Kuan-Hsing Chen, 25–46. London and New York: Routledge.

Hanmer, Jalna, and Daphne Statham. 1989. *Women and social work: Towards a woman-centered practice.* Chicago: Lyceum.

Hayakawa, S.I., and A.R. Hayakawa. 1992. *Language in thought and action.* 5th ed. San Diego, CA: Harvest.

Hill, Marcia, and Esther D. Rothblum, eds. 1996. *Classism and feminist therapy: Counting costs.* New York: Harrington Park.

Hogan, Susan, ed. 1997. *Feminist approaches to art therapy.* London and New York: Routledge.

Holly, Mary Louise. 1989. *Writing to grow: Keeping a personal-professional journal.* Portsmouth, NH: Heinemann Educational.

Holzman, Lois, and John Morss, eds. 2000. *Postmodern psychologies, societal practice, and political life.* London and New York: Routledge.

hooks, bell. 1994a. *Outlaw culture: resisting representations.* London and New York: Routledge.

———. 1994b. *Teaching to transgress: Education as the practice of freedom.* London and New York: Routledge.

———. 1995. *Art on my mind.* New York: The New Press.

Horsman, Jenny. 1999. *Too scared to learn: Women, violence, and education.* Toronto: McGilligan.

Imber-Black, Evan, and Janine Roberts. 1993. *Rituals for our times: Celebrating, healing, and changing our lives and our relationships.* New York: Harper Collins.

Jordan, Judith V., ed. 1997. *Women's growth in diversity: More writings from the Stone Center.* New York: Guilford.

Kadi, Joanna. 1996. *Thinking class: Sketches from a cultural worker.* Boston: South End.

Lacy, S., ed. 1995. *Mapping the terrain: New genre public art.* Seattle, WA: Bay.

Langer, Ellen J. 1997. *The power of mindful learning.* New York: Merloyd Lawrence.

Laxer, James. 2002. Turn the page on publishing. *Globe and Mail,* 22 May, A17.

Livesay, Dorothy. 1977. *Right hand, left hand. A true story of the thirties: Paris, Toronto, Montreal, the West and Vancouver. Love, politics, the Depression, and feminism.* Don Mills, ON: Musson.

———. 1998. *Archive for our times: Previously uncollected and unpublished poems of Dorothy Livesay.* Vancouver: Arsenal Pulp Press.

———. 1991. *Journey with my selves: A memoir 1909–1963.* Vancouver: Douglas and McIntyre.

Logan, Carolyn. 1997. *Counter balance: Gendered perspectives for writing and language.* Peterborough, ON: Broadview.

Long, Elizabeth. 1996. Feminism and cultural studies. In *What is cultural studies?* ed. John Storey, 197–206. New York: St Martin's.

Luke, Carmen, ed. 1996. *Feminism and pedagogies of everyday life.* Albany, NY: State Univ. of New York Press.

Maisel, Eric. 1999. *Deep writing: Seven principles that bring ideas to life.* New York: Jeremy P. Tarcher/Putnam.

Malmo, Cheryl, and Toni Suzuki Laidlaw, eds. 1999. *Consciousness rising: Women's stories of connection and transformation.* Charlottetown, PEI: Gynergy.

Marino, Dian. 1997. *Wild garden: Art, education, and the culture of resistance.* Toronto: Between the Lines.

Marx Ferree, Myra, Judith Lorber, and Beth B. Hess, eds. 1999. *Revisioning gender.* Thousand Oaks, CA: Sage.

Marx Ferree, Myra, and Patricia Yancey Martin. 1995. *Feminist organizations: Harvest of the new women's movement.* Philadelphia: Temple Univ. Press.

Mayberry, Maralee, and Ellen Cronan Rose. 1999. *Meeting the challenge: Innovative feminist pedagogies in action.* London and New York: Routledge.

McAllister, Pam. 1991. *This river of courage: Generations of women's resistance and action.* Philadelphia: New Society.

McClanahan, Rebecca. 1999. *Word painting: A guide to writing more descriptively.* Cincinnati, OH: Writer's Digest.

McLeod, Eileen. 1994. *Women's experience of feminist therapy and counseling.* Philadelphia: Open Univ. Press.

McNiff, Shaun. 1992. *Arts as medicine: Creating therapy of the imagination.* Boston: Shambhala.

Metzger, Deena. 1992. *Writing for your life: A guide and companion to the inner worlds.* New York: Harper Collins.

Miller, Jean Baker, and Irene Pierce Stiver. 1997. *The healing connection: How women form relationships in therapy and in life.* Boston: Beacon.

Moran, Bridget. 1988. *Stoney Creek woman: The story of Mary John.* Vancouver: Tillacum Library.

———. 1992. *A little rebellion.* Vancouver: Arsenal Pulp Press.

———. 1994. *Justa: A First Nations leader.* Vancouver: Arsenal Pulp Press.

———. 1998. *Judgement at Stoney Creek.* Vancouver: Arsenal Pulp Press.

Morley, David, and Kuan-Hsing Chen, eds. 1996. *Stuart Hall: Critical dialogues in cultural studies.* London and New York: Routledge.

Myers-Avis, Judith. 1998. Workshop handout. Intensive training institute in narrative therapy. Maritime School of Social Work, Continuing Education Program, Dalhousie University.

Nelson, Cary. 2001. *Revolutionary memory: Recovering the poetry of the American Left.* London and New York: Routledge.

Neysmith, Sheila M., ed. 2000. *Restructuring caring labour: Discourse, state practice, and everyday life.* New York: Oxford Univ. Press.

Ng, Roxana, Pat Staton, and Joyce Scane, eds. 1995. *Anti-racism, feminism, and critical approaches to education.* Toronto: OISE Press.

NurrieStearns, Rick, Mary NurrieStearns, and Melissa West, eds. 1999. *Soulful living: The process of personal transformation.* Deerfield Beach, FL: Health Communications.

Ortiz, Simon J., ed. 1998. *Speaking for the generations: Native writers on writing.* Tucson, AZ: Univ. of Arizona Press.

Osho. 1999a. *Courage: The joy of living dangerously.* New York: St Martin's / Griffin.

———. 1999b. *Creativity: Unleashing the forces within.* New York: St Martin's / Griffin.

Overall, Christine. 1998. *A feminist I: Reflections from academia.* Peterborough, ON: Broadview.

Palmer, Bryan D. 1992. *Working-class experience: Rethinking the history of Canadian labour, 1800–1991.* Toronto: McClelland and Stewart.

Parameswaran, Uma, ed. 1996. *Quilting a new canon: Stitching women's words.* Toronto: Sister Vision / Black Women and Women of Colour Press.

Perkins-Reed, Marcia. 1996. *Thriving in transition: Effective living in times of change.* New York: Touchstone.

Putnam, Dana, Dorothy Kidd, Elaine Dornan, and Patty Moore, eds. 1995. *The journal project: Dialogues and conversations inside women's studies.* Toronto: Second Story.

Rich, Adrienne. 1979. Claiming an education. In *On lies, secrets, and silence: Selected prose 1966–1978,* 231–35. New York: W.W. Norton.

Richards, Dick. 1995. *Artful work: Awakening joy, meaning, and commitment in the workplace.* New York: Berkley.

Rooney, Ellen. 1996. Discipline and vanish: Feminism, the resistance to theory, and the politics of cultural studies. In *What is cultural studies?* ed. John Storey, 208–20. New York: St Martin's.

Scales-Trent, Judy. 2000. On statutes and dogs, poems and "regs," and life inside the classroom. In *Wise women, reflections of teachers at midlife,* ed. Phyllis R. Freeman and Jan Zlotnick Schmidt, 191–96. London and New York: Routledge.

Sinetar, Marsha. 1998. *The mentor's spirit: Life lessons on leadership and the art of encouragement.* New York: St Martin's / Griffin.

Smith, Dorothy E. 1999. *Writing the social: Critique, theory, and investigations.* Toronto: Univ. of Toronto Press.

Smith Tuhiwai, Linda. 1999. *Decolonizing methodologies: Research and indigenous peoples.* London: Zed.

Soja, Edward W. 1996. *Thirdspace: Journeys to Los Angeles and other real-and-imagined places.* Oxford, UK: Blackwell.

Spender, Dale, ed. 1983. *Feminist theorists: Three centuries of women's intellectual traditions.* London: The Women's Press.

———. 1995. *Nattering on the Net: Women, power and cyberspace.* Toronto: Garamond.

Stalker, Jacqueline, and Susan Prentice, eds. 1998. *The illusion of inclusion: Women in post-secondary education.* Halifax, NS: Fernwood.

Stimpson, Catherine R. 1988. Nancy Reagan wears a hat: Feminism and its cultural consensus. In *Feminist cultural studies.* Vol. 2, ed. Terry Lovell. Camberley, UK: Edward Elgar.

Tator, Carol, Frances Henry, and Winston Mattis. 1998. *Challenging racism in the arts: Case studies of controversy and conflict.* Toronto: Univ. of Toronto Press.

Taylor, Ella. 1989. *Prime-time families: Television culture in postwar America.* Berkeley and Los Angeles: Univ. of California Press.

Terr, Lenore. 1999. *Beyond love and work: Why adults need to play.* New York: Touchstone.

Transken, Si. 1997. Personal, professional, and political roles: Struggling with empowerment and burnout. In *Equity and justice,* ed. Dana Hearne, 84–96. Montreal: John Abbott College Press, Canadian Women's Studies Association and Université du Québec à Montréal.

———. 2000a. *Escaping beauty.* Sudbury, ON: Women's Circle.

———. 2000b. How budget cut backs to services for sexual assault victims are dissolving, dividing, and distressing. In *Care and consequences*, ed. Diana Gustafson, 127–53. Halifax, NS: Fernwood.

———. 2002a. Creativity, cultural studies, and potentially fun ways to produce pedagogical resources, propaganda, and pride-fullness. Paper presented at the Canadian Women's Studies Association Conference, University of Toronto.

———. 2002b. Creativity/healing/writing: Bridget Moran as a cultural studies-oriented social worker. Paper presented at the Bridget Moran Little Rebellions Conference, University of Northern British Columbia.

———. 2002c. Expressive arts for political purposes and processes. *Feminist Utopias: Re-Visioning Our Futures*, ed. Sheila Neysmith and Margrit Eichler. Toronto: York University, University of Toronto, and the Institute for Women's Studies and Gender Studies. 213–32.

———. 2002d. Poetically teaching/doing the profession of social work as a joyful undisciplined discipline-jumper and genre-jumper (AND as if the world mattered). Paper presented at the Canadian Society for the Study of Higher Education Conference, University of Toronto.

Transken, Si, ed. *This ain't your patriarchs' poetry book: Candles, connections, comrades.* Prince George, BC: Transformative Services.

Transken, Si, Catherine Baylis, Andrew Burton, and Chuck Fraser. 2002. *Outlaw social work (The unsecret poems and stories)*. Prince George, BC: Transformative Collectives.

Transken, Si, Jacqueline Baldwin, Kate Tillechek, Karen Thistle, and Judith Lapadat. 2001. *Groping our way beyond grief*. Prince George, BC: Transformative Collectives.

Transken, Si, Tamar Eylon, Kate Tilleczek, Dina Ripsman Eylon, and Soni B. 2000. *Stress (Full) Sister (Hood)*. Prince George, BC: Self-Publishing Collective.

Transken, Si, Vicky Bryant, Paulette Dahl, Louise Lane, Melanie Marttila, and Carole Trepanier. 2000. *Battle chant*. Sudbury, ON: Battle Chant Ink.

Trinh, Min-ha T. 1991. *When the moon waxes red. Representation, gender and cultural politics*. London and New York: Routledge.

———. 1992. *Framer framed*. London and New York: Routledge.

Turner, Joan, and Carole Rose, eds. 1999. *Spider women: A tapestry of creativity and healing*. Winnipeg, MB: Gordon Shillingford.

Van Den Bergh, Nan, ed. 1995. *Feminist practice in the twenty-first century*. Washington, DC: The National Association Of Social Workers.

Virshup, Evelyn, ed. 1993. *California art therapy trends*. Chicago: Magnolia Street.

Walters, Suzanna Danuta. 1995. *Material girls: Making sense of feminist cultural theory*. Berkeley and Los Angeles: Univ. of California Press.

Warner, Sally. 1991. *Encouraging the artist in yourself (Even if it's been a long, long time). Dozens of failure-proof projects to rekindle the joy of making art*. New York: St Martin's.

Weiss, Penny A., and Marilyn Friedman, eds. 1995. *Feminism and community*. Philadelphia: Temple Univ. Press.

Wells, Valerie. 1990. *The joy of visualization: Seventy-five creative ways to enhance your life.* San Francisco: Chronicle.

Wershler-Henry, Darren. 2002, May 8. The national literature we deserve. Available from < www.rabble.ca >.

Wisechild, Louise, ed. 1991. *She who was lost is remembered: Healing from incest through creativity.* Vancouver: Raincoast.

ANDREW LESK 🦋

Camp, Kitsch, Queer:
Carole Pope and Toller Cranston
Perform on the Page

THE DEARTH OF CANADIAN LESBIAN AND GAY AUTOBIOGRAPHIES might lead some to believe that the field is neither rich nor worth exploring. However, the recently published memoirs of two Canadian performers—Anti Diva by Carole Pope, and Zero Tollerance: An Intimate Memoir by the Man Who Revolutionized Figure Skating, and When Hell Freezes Over, Should I Bring My Skates? by Toller Cranston—suggest that there is worth and interest to be to be found in Canadian gay and lesbian autobiography.

The memoirs of Pope, the former lead singer of the then-controversial 1980s band Rough Trade, and Cranston, a one-time Canadian Olympic skating bronze medalist and self-described roué and painter, both recall an earlier autobiography memoirist John Glassco. Glassco's rather libidinal evocation of a Canadian in late-1920s Paris, Memoirs of Montparnasse, was more about the act of literary self-creation as performance than it was about the truth.[1] Unlike Glassco, neither Pope nor Cranston are fiction writers, but they share with him notions of self-creation as performance, and so make the kind of autobiography that Shirley Neuman says "is being produced in many other media other than publication." Neuman correctly speculates that "we need to give attention to these alternative manifestations of the autobiographical impulse" (1996, 9).

I read "impulse" as a performative act when discussing Pope and Cranston, since both, on their respective public stages, are consummate actors. They differ quite significantly, however, in their revelations, or lack of them, of lesbian and gay matters in their books and elsewhere. Pope, never shy about sexual disclosures in her lyrics first and, later, her memoirs, makes her status as a lesbian icon clear. Cranston, however, although as outré as Pope, steadfastly avoids mention of his sexual orientation and its invariable relation to his obvious kitschy persona. Regardless of Cranston's reticence, I want to locate how their recent literary exploits emphasize the machinations of a performative lesbian and gay subjectivity in the Canadian cultural arena.

More specifically, I will argue that Pope and Cranston, by using the shaping power of narrative, wish to situate and define their respective positions as public performers, with an eye to (re)affirming their status as cultural icons. Pope uses her lesbian subjectivity as a catalyst in order to explore her role in the transformation of Canadian music culture, but Cranston eschews any gay self-identification. Instead, he prefers to endorse a view of himself as a misunderstood aesthete, whose self-aggrandizing in the realms of skating and visual art is not merely a role but a responsibility. Additionally, where Pope sees her sexuality as a foundational wellspring of her creativity, closely wedded to an essentialist notion of innate homosexuality, Cranston asserts a professedly inborn, intuitive, and (again) misinterpreted eccentricity as the source of his apparently asexual creative passions.

These autobiographies function as entries into the shaping of a Canadian public consciousness in that they are deeply occupied with a cultural criticism that discloses the stakes involved in personal political (in)action concomitantly with lesbian and gay rights. In their distinct ways, Pope and Cranston demonstrate how different arts—music, skating, song lyrics, painting—can be put to use in order to express the imbricated relationship of work and culture. Each utilizes a variant of camp or kitsch aesthetic, whereby subcultural forms often allied with "trash" or dissent evolve into symbols of popular (dis)identification. Moreover, unwittingly self-parodic narrative performances like Cranston's expose how his lack of sexual self-exposure is nevertheless revealed through the kitschy markings of fetishized celebrity and the veneration of consumerism and commodification. Deliberately, unlike Cranston, Pope plays both to a campy "trash" aesthetic and the spirit of monied glam, though she promotes the awareness that political engagement has saved her from the more dispiriting forms of gauche stardom and celebrity.

If autobiography is a field of cultural production, and if self-authorship represents an attempt not only to shape the public self but also the reception of that self, then the struggles to either differentiate or conform to homogenous productions of autobiography are, if not crucial, then paramount. In discussing the avant-garde nature of new cultural products, Pierre Bourdieu writes that

> On one side are the dominant figures, who want continuity, identity, reproduction; on the other, the newcomers, who seek discontinuity, rupture, dif-

ference, revolution. To "make one's name" means making one's mark, achieving recognition (in both senses) of one's *difference* from other producers, especially the most consecrated of them; at the same time, it means *creating a new position* beyond the positions presently occupied, *ahead of them*, in the *avant-garde*. (1993, 106)

But how does queer autobiography, particularly Pope's and Cranston's, contribute to the elastic nature of the genre as a whole? Or do Pope and Cranston establish something different and avant-garde?

In ascertaining just what each writer sets out to do, I discuss, in part, the respective aims of the memoirs. As minority models, they necessarily shift the often prescribed discussion of public life, which is a contribution to the heterosexual imaginary. In his discussion of such marginal genres, Brian Loftus writes, "The problem with trying to develop a set of claims about queer autobiography is that it is a tradition without a base of reference." Moreover, he asks, "How can a text consolidate a subject on the grounds of sexuality when that sexuality has no history to document, no proper cultural space and no symbolic categories?" (1997, 31). Loftus bases his contentions on the notion that an engagement with majority/minority forms of writing will simply reaffirm the binary straight/queer. In its place, he proposes a plural "I" that will deny solidification of any circulating master discourses.

Yet, invariably, we return to the prison house of language, as it were. It should be noted that Loftus might have achieved the same thing with available "master" discourses. Furthermore, the base of reference for the history of queer autobiography is heterosexual autobiography, regardless of contrary dissidence. That said, what Pope and Cranston might each have hoped to achieve with these memoirs is to create—or, to enact through the recollections of their performances—their own respective *cultural spaces*, with or without recourse to historical precedence or symbolic categories which might collude with heteronormativity, in all its prescribing forms.

The constitution and revelation of any self-ascribed "alternative" performance is always a fragile proposal, since any performance is at least initially beholden to what has come before. How can Pope and Cranston think that their cultural creations might be any different, and how might their reminiscences of them either accede to or deviate from heteronormative forms of public self-revelation? Pope's lyrics to her song "All Touch" suggest, perhaps, that the caresses of language, either written or spoken, homosexual or heterosexual, are at best glancing. She writes and sings: "Splintering fragments of conversation / Never got down to cold hard facts / All touch but no contact" (Rough Trade 1981). "All Touch," a song about the dangers of miscommunication, sexual and otherwise, reveal that communication is often, at best, a unstable endeavour.

So, too, might Pope's lyrics serve, perversely, to critique Cranston's rather glaring omission of a discussion of his own sexuality and how it may or may not have influenced his career path. Although Cranston's first auto-biographical venture, *Zero Tollerance*, is subtitled *An Intimate Memoir by the Man Who Revolutionized Figure Skating*, little is revealed, unlike Pope's straight-forward narrative of personal, and sexual, intimacies. Of course, Cranston simply may not have experienced much in the romantic and sexual arenas. Deirdre Kelly, in her review of the book, writes that "Cranston's reticence stems from a deep-rooted wish to appear inscrutable.... But maybe there was never much sex to talk about" (1997, D11). However, Cranston's omission of such an obvious "cold hard fact" calls attention to what might have brought about his evasive autobiographical verve. As he writes of one debat-able skating statistic, "I'm not absolutely certain that was true, but it was the truth we knew at the time" (1997, 13). His dissimulation here, a kind of dis-ingenuous bravado, sets the tone for the rest of his memoirs: truths which offer surface touches and glances, which in turn reveal that autobiogra-phies—especially queer ones—are invariably truncated affairs with varying degrees of dissimulation.

Cranston's entries in the public arena of autobiographical disclosure are like the arenas in which he has skated, he implies: the performances will be under his control, of his making. But there are obvious omissions which allow the reader room for pause. The unstated reasoning for Cranston's lapses is, conversely, central to Pope's own political credo. She writes that, upon getting over her disillusionment with her increasingly commodified lifestyle, she was:

> upset by the indifference of gays who didn't use their political power to instigate change. That indifference eroded any power we had as voters. We were still the niggers in this scenario. I was sick of the stigma and self-loathing attached to our sexuality, as if sexuality defines what kind of per-son you are. That thought process is so dangerous and wrong. (2000, 156–57)

Pope's "warts-and-all" approach, by turns cutting and sharply droll, suggests that public lives essayed in letters bear the responsibility of owning up to the truth, or at least as near to the truth as one might get. The result is that Pope's writings are meant to show how artistic performances that are trans-parently different are also inevitably political, since they invariably go against the grain.

Yet, perhaps unwittingly, Pope suggests here that one should *not* be defined by one's sexuality, though it would appear that she really meant to call attention to the kind of pathologized homosexuality, such as internalized homophobia, that she says is embraced by those lacking positive self-esteem. Pope echoes the kind of discourses which call attention to homosexual difference as sexual deviation, which demand that gays and lesbians account for their marginality while somehow simultaneously shutting up about it. Cranston, whose apparently cataleptic circumlocutions highlight his distaste with his (homo) sexuality, professions of difference notwithstanding, allow him to be co-opted by these very homophobic discourses Pope points to.

Yet Cranston's dissimulations reveal him to be, ironically, more mainstream than he might imagine. With his abjuration of things sexual, he is left with a discussion of his artistic differences, which have now been co-opted and refined by others. But have such performances really escaped a cultural reading that would, nevertheless, ascribe homosexuality to him? In writing of Roland Barthes's *Le plaisir du texte*, Robert K. Martin observes that, "A text will be 'homosexual' to the extent that it presents itself as both subject and object of desire, a text in the act of beholding itself, often through the mirror of the other, and loving itself" (1993, 293). Cranston certainly positions himself as the fount of his own creation, as an original who needs to guard his novelty from the encroachment of the misunderstandings of others. To that end, his memoirs forcefully constitute the act of beholding himself; the analogous exchange of text with context here at least suggests that a kind of homosexual sensibility underscores Cranston's musings, if one borrows, as Martin does, from the notion of homosexuality as, in part, a kind of narcissism.

With his clearly expressed self-importance, Cranston presents his own (self) creation as a spontaneous, innate thing. "Whatever I became later in life, the seeds were planted from birth, and there never any change of persona or vision. I had an understanding of the child that I was and a sense of my own destiny" (1996, 2). It would appear that Cranston's difference, marked virtually from birth, would naturally give rise to the "revolution" that is the hallmark of his skating career, and which is part of the title of his first book. He repeats that he is misunderstood in different forms throughout the memoirs. This is at once a real plaint and an embraced public characteristic: it allows him to place himself ahead of his field as wholly original. "Everything I did was new, different, and shocking to the Old Guard, and I was punished for it" (1996, 10). But although he presents himself as different, Cranston uses such uniqueness not to rupture the establishment he feels has wronged him, but to retrospectively position himself as an *agent provocateur*, a marginalized but not marginal aesthete.

His cultivation of the outcast role places his performative concerns second to his veneration of what such "bad boy" poses might allow him to acquire materially. Cranston's narrative is neither the boldly forthcoming document he thinks it to be nor much of a challenge to the established order he so longs to be part of. His textual closeting ironically enables us to observe Cranston himself as both the subject—the lover—and the object of that love. This kind of homoerotic self-absorption reveals what he himself will not, namely that his text, in thrall with its very exploitation, is as homotextual as he is homosexual.[2]

Pope understands very well the kind of celebrity cult that Cranston nutured, although her uncloseted persona expresses a greater awareness of her own motives than Cranston might admit to. She writes that "in the eighties, when it was all about me, the cult of me loomed large on the horizon and life was one big, trendy party" (2000, 153). Whereas Cranston simply encourages celebrity worship, Pope understands that her celebrity is an outgrowth of being a cultural producer and that the "outsider" performances that concretized her reputation both have a certain shelf-life and entail a personal and political accounting. Of her first performance, she notes that she "was driven to do it. I had to release all my pent-up anger, and the sexuality that was the core of my music, or I would explode" (22–23). Pope does not encourage sympathetic notice for the ways in which her theatricality may have been misunderstood, since she seems aware that her sexual and artistic impulses, intimately *interconnected* and therefore not conventional, would certainly guarantee her notoriety and recognition, for good or ill. In *Anti Diva*, she challenges homogenizing models of literary/sexual narrative which are usually found in the "coming out" or "progress to a vocation" accounts of various writers. Whereas Cranston tends towards the spiritual, pious, and often to the sanctimonious, which altogether disdain the sexual body politic, Pope reveals a life engaged in visceral corporeality and wedded to an astute political sensibility.

Pope appears to have anticipated that writing a memoir like Cranston's, which leaves out so much, would be far less than truthful; she therefore highlights her homosexuality not because it was necessary to do so, but because it was unavoidable. Margaretta Jolly writes that in life writing, the subject of the self is held out but cannot be fully known, since *desire* cannot be wholly comprehended. In queer life writing, the paradoxes of the self as a fictive construct, as perhaps parodic or performative, are "even more emphatic. For here, we are dealing not only with a form based on the impossibility of identity, but the destabilizing effects of identity and desire" (2001, 475). It may seem problematic that Cranston has largely avoided a discussion of these very things, though to anyone with a glancing acquaintance of Cranston's career knows that his gay identity and desires are rather obvious. It might be argued, however, that what Cranston *writes* is destabilizing since it is still, in part, secretive and demands decoding in a manner similar to how his public performances deny easy or comfortable interpretation. Witness, for example, his admiration for a Nijinsky-like androgyny, which all but collapses the distinction between a gender-bending aesthetics and a concomitant homosexual sensibility.

Pope herself writes that "Artists who are androgynous, wanton, twisted and/or satanic appeal to the dark side of our id" (2000, 242), and it is not a stretch to suggest that such a "dark side" has often been ascribed to the presumed marginal realm of homosexuality and its more historically "deviant" associations. The name of Pope's band, Rough Trade, is derived, as she says, from her obsession "with [male] homosexuals and their lifestyles" (35), though the term itself may have originated with male street prostitutes. As an affirmation of the band's fringe sensibilities, the New York *Daily News* stated that the band "work out out of the basement of the psyche ... [and] celebrated and satirized those regions of carnal knowledge that society prefers to keep underground" (92). Their performances, which include the breakthrough song "High School Confidential," may have been subcultural and threatening in their day, but much of what was once underground has now become more conventional, and it would appear that, at least in urban centres, this is also true of queer sexualities. What queer autobiography possibility accomplishes, then, is to foreground the shifting nature of what one may think of as a stable desire. Queer self-exposure shapes the practice of autobiography by "shaking the foundations" (as Rough Trade might have put it) of homogenous, linear, and largely heterosexual narratives of normative self-discovery, and to reveal that being in *and* out of the closet continues to carry the freight of personal cost, and of repressed or expressed subjectivity.

Part of this cost of an engagement with marginalia is courting a camp or kitsch persona, one often associated with a homosexual rhetorical style. Andrew Ross discusses the camp effect as being created "not simply by a change in the mode of cultural production ... but rather when the products ... of a much earlier mode of production, which has lost its power to produce and dominate cultural meanings, become available, in the present, for redefinition according to contemporary codes of taste" (1993, 58). For example, while Pope has made much of her large 1980s hair, she understands that it was an intentional part of an act that was very much of-the-moment and anti-normative. She suggests that it was camp at that time, as part of a theatricality of excess. Cranston, on the other hand, appears not to understand that what may have been *arriviste* in 1968 is no longer so. He makes a brave attempt to act as though he is and was master of his environments.

In writing of his experience with the troupe Holiday on Ice, Cranston states that "I like gourmet trash. I enjoy the bad much more than the almost good" (1997, 116). But rather than take this for the daring and outrageous comment it is meant to be, the reader likely senses that there have been many times where the misunderstood Cranston has had to settle for trash instead of the gourmet; his rhetoric here merely covers his tracks for his failure to achieve more than those misunderstanding critics would let him. Similarly, his *outré* performances, once indeed gourmet figure skating, are now merely mainstream, and his instances of addressing his public as if he is still cutting-edge relegate him to not the camp but the kitsch.

Ross, in his reading of Susan Sontag's seminal work on camp, addresses distinction between the two. He writes

> The producer or consumer of kitsch either is unaware of the extent to which his or her intentions or pretensions are alienated in the kitsch text, or else is made to feel painfully aware of this alienation in some way. Camp, on the other hand, involves a celebration, on part of cognoscenti [the knowing], of the alienation, distance, and incongruity reflected in the very process by which it locates hitherto unexpected value in a popular or obscure text. Camp would thus be reserved for those with a high degree of cultural capital. It belongs to those who have the accredited confidence to be able to devote their idiosyncratic attention to the practice of cultural slumming in places where others would feel less comfortable. (Ross 1993, 63)

Cranston's pretensions to slumming and campy self-awareness are undone by his continuing promulgation of his alienation from both the mainstream—he is still misunderstood—and by his increasing marginalization in the world of figure skating. His fringe sensibility, accompanied by a diminished cultural capital, is redolent of kitsch more so than camp, since his self-promotion, which he hopes might place him amongst the "knowing," is simply an empty boast.

His notable accomplishments in both skating and painting are overshadowed by his unwillingness to recognize that he either has been surpassed by other skaters or has been merely imitative (of the British Aubrey Beardsley and the Canadian Gary Slipper). As a result, he lacks the claim to being, as Pope does, self-consciously campy. If camp sensibility is in part mocking and is infused with an awareness of the duality of that gesture, Cranston's eager overcompensation indicates his alienation from camp. His memoirs, which concern his reasons why he is alienated from society, become unwittingly campy themselves. Though he eschews the kinds of gestures by which one might read his life as gay, Cranston's incongruous writing—a gay man trying to hide the open secret of his gayness—nevertheless engages what Jack Babuscio terms as "the idea of gayness as a moral deviation" (1993, 21).

This incongruity—gayness as a mark of deviancy while perhaps passing as normal—suggests that Cranston's deviation is understood as a deliberate courting of normalcy while not appearing to be aware that no one might ever "mistake" him for heterosexual. His overriding efforts to downplay this awareness overshadow his attempts to play the camp card, and so he becomes the dupe of his own cynical energies. In playing to an audience of his own creation, he effectively creates a self-serving autobiography whose readers he believes he controls. This unawareness, that he cannot ever fully anticipate what his readers might infer, leads to kitsch, and not camp. As Eve Sedgwick writes, "unlike kitsch-attribution, the sensibility of camp-recognition always sees that it is in dealing in reader relations and in projective fantasy ... about the spaces and practices of cultural production" (1990, 156). Cranston's inability to sense how what he writes might be perceived—that the reader should believe his memoirs to be genuine artistic and cultural contributions—renders his efforts as kitschy and his memoirs as merely camp artifacts.

As an illustration of Cranston's slide into kitsch, he writes of meeting Liberace, noting that the pianist's "greatest fear ... [was] that his fans would think he was gay. Was there anyone who could have thought otherwise?" (2000, 126). This line of questioning positions Cranston, as a self-presumed arbiter of things gay, as somehow not beholden to such scrutiny. It is quite amusing that Cranston might demand accountability from an unwilling object of camp derision who publicly renounced his homosexuality, since his own memoirs are so rife with a tacit repudiation of his own queerness. Cranston's fancy for over-the-top outfits and wildly elaborate home décor furthermore recall Liberace's kitschy stylings. Cranston's aspirations to dramatic flair—"I have the theatrical sense" (105)—underscore his courting of the image of the aesthete and dandy, while he simultaneously wishes that people would see through his façade so that he might be understood—yet only on his terms.

Barbara Klinger writes that "camp operates as an aggressive metamorphosizing operation, attaching norms of behaviour, appearance, and art to revel in their inherent artifice. Camp taste is thus distinctly antinatural, eschewing beauty and realism in favour of the patently gilded" (1994, 134). Again, the notion of "antinatural" allies itself with other (social) forms of the non-normative, such as homosexuality, and it is not unsurprising that many homosexuals have actively embraced camp as a way, as Klinger comments further, to "assert their marginality and difference through theatrical style" (135). Cranston's hedonism, however, eschews the gay sensibility often associated with camp. For him, the exposure of this one "difference" is truly akin to bad taste. In his theatre of marginality, he fails to consider how he might use camp to mock those who think this to be the case. As a result, his autobiographical engagement with artifice suffers from the burden that he is being purposefully evasive.

Oddly enough, Cranston seems to be aware of the limits of his embracing of kitsch and camp, when in concluding his first memoir he writes, "Artifice, fabrication, the creation of images are all wonderful to behold, but in the final analysis, facing up to the truth about oneself is what matters" (1997, 340). This confession of the shortcomings of his memoir only exacerbates his unwillingness to communicate with his readers the reasons for either his glib rationales or self-absorbed defenses. Cranston's acknowledgement of the contradictions in his approach is likely the result of his insularity. In positioning himself as an original, he shuns the type of group identification which might give him broader insight as to what might constitute camp boundaries. As Klinger notes, for many homosexuals "camp emerges as a means of celebrating group solidarity through the exercise of shared aesthetic codes.... It also offers the potential to materialize an alternative voice through the willful conversion of mainstream standards and ideals" (1994, 135). For Cranston, the problem occurs when he espouses the beliefs he holds as not emanating from or shared by others.

As a result, his appeals to honesty fall flat. When he decides to sell all of his belongings in order to "reinvent" himself, he says that "it might have been among the more courageous things I've ever done. If not courageous, then it was my most unconsciously brilliant move" (1997, 233). His move to divest himself of camp and artifice, however, and "reveal the honesty underneath" (233) does not obviously extend to later years when he retrospectively reassesses his earlier behaviour. His memoirs clearly reveal that his bouts with "honesty" are subsumed by the tightly controlled artifice that is the memoir itself.

Pope own engagements with theatricality, camp and artifice are prefaced with an admission, similar to Cranston's desire to be "honest." Yet, she avoids his forms of insincerity by admitting her duplicity: "I crave all the trappings of success, and yet I'm so disdainful of them. I admit it: I'm a hypocrite" (2000, xii). Of course, such simple declarations might be construed as a rhetorical move to avoid accusations of disingenuity, but Pope's very centred attitude to what she perceives as necessary to relate with and *without* artifice is affirmed throughout the memoir. In other words, she is frank: "This book deals with my denial and discovery of my true sexuality, and how all that has affected my life and art," she says (2000, xii).

Unlike Cranston, Pope recognizes that her sense of the stage and camp works in tandem with her sexuality and her flirting with androgyny. She writes that she and her band mate, Kevan Staples, as constituting Rough Trade,

> ended up pushing musical and sexual envelopes. We morphed androgyny, humour and various musical genres into one twisted freakish phenomena. We became a myth, a cult, something for people to cling to: an echo of a blip in time that encompassed the late seventies and the eighties, when we thought we were invincible. Some people are nostalgic for those days. I'm not, but it was a trip going back there and reliving how driven and naïve we were. (2000, xi–xii)

As a result, Pope achieves a kind of coming-to-terms with a persona which has had its uses. Her sense of what Jolly calls "the destabilizing effects of sexuality and desire" in autobiography (2001, 475) embraces the understanding that what was once "destabilizing"[3] and *outré* may not withstand the passing of time.

In her critique of the late 1990s phenomenon Lilith Fair, from which she and many other rock divas were excluded, she understands that her reputation may have precluded involvement. She asserts, "If it wasn't for me there wouldn't be any blatantly sexual chick singers in Canada, but fine, I can live with that [exclusion]," but adds, "no, my ego isn't that big; it's just that I think I made a somewhat warped contribution to music in Canada by throwing the love that dare not speak its name in people's uncomprehending faces" (2000, 233). Being a lesbian is not "dated," but breaking ground in announcing that one is, on stage, certainly *was*. The appeals to androgyny and homosexuality that underscored the theatre of Rough Trade may not play well in certain quarters even today, yet Pope recognizes that they once played well to only very few.

Of the band's early beginnings, when they did play to the few, Pope writes that she "wasn't your typical non-threatening girl singer. My voice and sexual androgyny were powerful" (2000, 39). Later in the 1970s, she and Staples "had morphed into queens of androgyny. We were a combination of punk, bondage and glam" (49). Their self-promotion as theatrical artists, rather than simply a rock band, lead to camp, as their involvement in 1984's Art Gallery of Ontario show "Going Through the Motions," assembled by General Idea, demonstrated. Pope writes that, "It was such a high to camp it up at the AGO. Under the guise of art, people will tolerate almost anything" (66). Pope peels the seriousness from much performance art, intimating that it is the enjoyment of the artifice and the paradox of the guise itself which might be better appreciated.

Pope's androgyny as a camp act highlights how Cranston's attempt to explain his own forays falls short of the camp standard. He says that he "was an exotic creature. Although it is out of fashion today, I wore that extreme make-up...that was *de rigueur* at the time. It made sense because the whole [skating] production was exotic, flamboyant, and unworldly—and so was I" (1997, 105). Unlike Pope's sense of journey and mature resolution, Cranston's reliving of the denial that his exoticism was quite campy keeps his autobiography temporally mired in the past and not open to the *knowing* incongruity required by camp.

His admission of androgyny, something that he "cultivated to the max" (1997, 105), is puzzling given his shunning of the binary's feminine aspects. Although he insists that he "had an entirely original way of putting myself together," he depended on emulating Rudolf Nureyev's "androgynous (but never feminine) glitter suits that were gas to my fire" (1997, 61). Lest anyone think that such femininity signal homosexuality, Cranston is sure to stamp out that fire in advance. Whereas Pope is open about how her lesbianism worked in partnership with her camp performances, Cranston treats camp as a serious matter separate from his Liberace-like lavishness, when in fact the two are often intimately related. In the end, his evasiveness about certain aspects of his life leaves the reader with a series of self-aggrandized events that speak of disingenuity rather than artifice, of absorbed self-reflection rather than frank self-exposure, thereby undercutting the very idea of autobiographical self-knowing outrageousness he hopes to project.

Problems with veracity aside, both Pope and Cranston contribute to expanding the understanding of the Canadian social and cultural fabric by reminding us that their contributions were important, as indeed they were. Pope, in reflecting upon her calculated performances, shows that her contribution changed things; her memoir reveals that the change she nurtured was significant and influential and, now, concluded. Cranston reminds us that remaining in the closet results in the perpetuation of the very misunderstanding that he thinks his autobiographies might clear up. His books are instructive in that they reveal how being beholden to a selectively remembered past in which one was a formative and creative artist courts kitschy sentiment rather than accolades. Both performers continue the dialogue of the personal-as-(a)political and demonstrate its necessity even in today's age of queer ambivalence and postmodern cultural theatricality.

Notes

1 See my essay "Having a Gay Old Time in Paris: John Glassco's Not So Queer Adventures" (2001).

2 I draw on Jacob Stockinger's "Homotextuality: A Proposal," to define the homotext as one in which there exists "a dialectical tension with a hostile envirnoment" (Stockinger 1978, 139), regardless of what one might make of authorial intentionality. This environment's tension is derived from the concurrent resistance to and acceptance of (literary) heterosexual normative discourses; concomitantly, the notion of a character's (possible) homosexual subjectivity may be assumed. Homotextuality might be, for example, revealed as (but not restricted to) a text's ambiguity.

3 In a recent interview with Pope, Lauren Keegan writes that "I always knew the 80s looked and acted like they did, but I don't think I ever fully believed it. Judging by the pictures found the middle of the book [Anti Diva], both Carole and her hair really lived it up in that decade" (2000, 17).

References

Babuscio, Jack. 1993. Camp and the gay sensibility. In Camp grounds: Style and homosexuality, ed. David Bergman. 19–38. Amherst: Univ. of Massachusetts Press.

Bourdieu, Pierre. 1993. The field of cultural production: Essays on art and literature. Trans. by Richard Nice et al. New York: Columbia Univ. Press.

Cranston, Toller, with Martha Lowder Kimball. 1997. Zero tollerance: An intimate memoir by the man who revolutionized figure skating. Toronto: McClelland and Stewart.

———. When hell freezes over, should I bring my skates? 2000. Toronto: McClelland and Stewart.

Jolly, Margaretta. 2001. Coming out of the coming out story: Writing queer lives. Sexualities 4(4): 474–96.

Keegan, Laren. 2002. Pray to the Pope. Trade Queer Things 3(3): 17–19.

Kelly, Deirdre. 1997. Toller Cranston and the search for love." Globe and Mail 8 Nov.: D11.

Klinger, Barbara. 1994. Melodrama and meaning: History, culture, and the films of Douglas Sirk. Bloomington: Indiana Univ. Press.

Lesk, Andrew. 2001. Having a gay old time in Paris: John Glassco's not so queer adventures. In Queer nation: Gay and lesbian studies in the Canadian Context, ed. Terry Goldie. 175–87. Vancouver: Arsenal Pulp Press.

Loftus, Brian. 1997. Speaking silence: The strategies and structures of queer autobiography. College Literature 24(1): 28–44.

Martin, Robert K. 1993. Roland Barthes: Towards an 'ecriture gaie.' In Camp grounds: Style and homosexuality, ed. David Bergman. 282–98. Amherst: Univ. of Massachusets Press.

Neuman, Shirley. 1996. Introduction: Reading Canadian autobiography. *Essays on Canadian Writing* 60: 1–13.

Pope, Carole. 2000. *Anti diva.* Toronto: Random House.

Ross, Andrew. 1993. Uses of camp. In *Camp grounds: Style and homosexuality,* ed. David Bergman. 54–77. Amherst: Univ. of Massachusetts Press.

Rough Trade. 1981. All touch. *(for those who think young).* True North. TN–48.

Sedgwick, Eve Kosofsky. 1990. *Epistemology of the closet.* Berkeley and Los Angeles: Univ. of California Press.

Sontag, Susan. 1966. *Against interpretation.* New York: Farrar, Straus and Giroux.

Stockinger, Joseph. 1978. Homotextuality: A proposal." In *The gay academic,* ed. Ellen M. Barrett and Louie Crew. 135–51. Palm Springs: ETC.

LAURIE MCNEILL 🦋

Writing Lives in Death:
Canadian Death Notices
as Auto/biography

Years ago I belonged to a small writing group, and the
leader of our group ... advised us to read obituaries because
they carry, like genes packed tight in their separate chro-
mosomes, tiny kernels of narrative.
                                —Carol Shields, *Unless*

IN THE 1990S THE OBITUARY FORM EXPE-
rienced a major revival, appearing with renewed vigour in the pages of many
dailies and magazines. Citing the newspaper obituary as one of the decade's
"most satisfying rediscoveries," an article in the *Economist* noted that the
obituary was becoming "something of a cult: we are seeing the advent of the
obituary as entertainment" ("The Obituarist's Art" 1994-95, 64). The overwhelming success of the *Globe and Mail*'s "Lives Lived" column, which features obituaries of "regular" people (that is, individuals who were not public
figures) written by their family, friends, or colleagues, indicates that this
entertainment value has not been limited only to tributes to the famous.
Readers take an active interest in the personal as well as public lives of their
contemporaries: private citizens, often like themselves. Through the act of
reading, audiences create a temporary community with the obituary subject
based on shared experience, age, or values. They identify with the deceased,
take on his or her stories, experience a sense of collective history, identity,
or memory, even, or perhaps even more so, if the deceased has not been a
public figure but an "ordinary" person.

The majority of Canadians, however, will never be celebrated in a newspaper obituary. Instead, their lives will be publicly chronicled and com-

memorated in death notices, which take the form of family-written paid announcements. Borrowing the newspaper obituary's evaluative, eulogistic language and formulae, death notices reflect on and attempt to represent the lives of the loved one as an individual and as a meaningful member of society. The public venue requires family obituarists to justify the value of the deceased to the community at large, and argue that the bereavement will be felt not only by the immediate family but also by the general public. "Though the loss is personal," Luis Roniger notes, "the mourners nonetheless announce the death of their loved ones in terms that stress his or her significance to society in general" (1992, 152). This public expression of private sorrow shapes how (and which) individuals are remembered. Condensing lives into newspaper columns, restricted by grief, time, and economy, family obituaries by necessity produce narrative fragments, the "tiny kernels" Shields describes. These combine to create texts that represent not only the deceased but also the mourners, who take on the collective identity of "survived by." The paid obituary, then, is a family and a community auto/biography that incorporates spouses, children and grandchildren, friends, the predeceased, and the imagined readers into a life story of personal and public relevance. By telling their loved ones' lives and stories for the reading public, family obituarists craft texts that intersect personal and public spheres, histories, and functions, situating their subjects as simultaneously individual and representative.

The contemporary hunger for intimate personal detail that fosters the consumption of tell-all talk shows, revealing Internet journals, and confessional memoirs can be satiated in the death notice's "tiny kernels of narrative" that give the subject life after death. As another site of personal narratives for a reading public "obsessed" with "consuming" other people's lives (Smith and Watson 1996, 3), death notices function as what Smith and Watson call "everyday autobiographies," autobiographical practices that take place in daily life and that shape individual self-performances. Through these everyday practices, they argue, "autobiographical narrators move out of isolation and into a social context in which their stories resonate with the stories of others in a group" (15); the individual life/story takes on meaning through this ongoing collaborative narrative of self and/in community. Addressing communities with whom they share experiences, values, interests, and knowledge, auto/biographical performers link their individual self-constructions to communal narratives and acceptable subject positions. Simultaneously producers and products of these acts, individuals in contemporary society consume and rearticulate the stories they see and hear around them, incorporating others' performances into their own.

The complex interplay of personal and public auto/biographical acts inherent in everyday practices makes them a rich site for unpacking the narrative structures of contemporary culture—the chromosomal strands that link individual and collective identities. Death notices contribute to this collective gene pool of autobiographical experience in which identities circulate and particular kinds of experience and subjects become dominant: the norms against which all self-constructions are assessed. As part of the "conservative social process" (Eid 2002, 75) of death rituals, these notices, as Mushira Eid theorizes, "conform to a certain format and reflect aspects of the social context in which they are written" (14). Within this conservative genre, the possibilities for auto/biographical constructions are continuously foreclosed by the formulae and expectations of the genre and the culture it both creates and is created by. These notices therefore impose "legible subjectivit[ies]" (Smith and Watson 1996, 11) on practitioners, setting limits on whose lives count in death and what experiences and subjects merit public grief, meaning that the "ordinary" people who are commemorated must already fit, or be made to fit, into acceptable subjectivities. Reinforcing cultural norms through generic practices, the death notice gives insight into how such norms operate, and are reiterated in the particular time and place of its production.

Contemporary death notices therefore function as life-writing on multiple levels, creating auto/biographical identities that are both personal and communal, and that claim to speak for and to "Canadians" as a community. Focussing on death notices in daily English-language newspapers from major urban centres across Canada since the year 2000, I will examine how these public announcements of personal grief and loss incorporate and construct individual and collective identities for the writers, the deceased, and their communities. Although differences in style and content are apparent between newspapers and across regions, the texts draw on and replicate similar generic models and inscribe comparable public identities for the deceased, suggesting an institutionalized form that sets a nation-wide standard for death writing and its subjects. Consequently, these notices provide examples of how Canadians perform their own identities, as well as create identities for others, in a public forum overwritten by ritual and sanction, formulaic languages and institutionalized elements. In tracing what Canadians have to say at the beginning of the twenty-first century about the value of a life and about what experiences, mores, and individuals are worthy of commemoration across generations, I will chart the kinds of auto/biographical performances Canadians enact, and the cultural institutions they evoke, when they write lives in death.

Last Writes: Constructing Subjects in Death

A "traditional text-type" associated with "various ceremonies" marking major public and personal events that require or invite public celebration or commemoration, such as births, marriages, and deaths (Fries 1990, 539),[1] the death notice in Canada has evolved to suit the changing needs of Canadian society. As MaryEllen Gillan notes in *Obits: The Way We Say Goodbye*, over the last thirty years Canadians have with increasing regularity, combined the informational aspects of the death notice with the narratives of obituaries, those "more detailed accounts of a person's life ... often prepared by the newspaper" (1995, x). This conflation of genres reflects changing death rites in Canada, where many people request no formal funeral or memorial service. In such cases, these texts provide the only public tribute to the deceased. Since social norms require the family to "mak[e] some public declaration of death" (Prior 1989, 146) as part of traditional grieving rituals, announcements thereby perform personal and communal tasks by alerting the community to respond in appropriate ways. Additionally, death notices act to reaffirm and reestablish communities that may become geographically dispersed, a reality of contemporary Canadian living. Once published, these announcements provide "important means of connecting far-flung distanced communities; they enable people to keep track of the movements of acquaintances, and facilitate the expression of sympathy even across nations and continents" (Roniger 1992, 163). Since many among the bereaved will be spread out across the country and may not be able to attend a service in person, the family obituary allows such individuals to participate in this rite of mourning and confirm their part in a community.

These texts are generally the products of non-professional writers working under extreme emotional pressure and against the newspaper's submissions deadline and rates, to accommodate the potentially conflicting desires of the "survived by" group whom they represent. These circumstances of production, along with the genre's often inelegant pairing of the funeral announcement and the obituary, have caused the death notice to be dismissed as a "gray expanse of pallid prose" (Singer 2002, 28), an inferior cousin to the newspaper-written tribute. While staff-written obituaries are considered news items and are therefore included in the newspaper's front sections (Eid 2002, 22), death notices as paid announcements are often relegated to the back pages of the newspaper where they may be paired, rather incongruously, with the comics. This placement demonstrates the low value attached to this genre and, by extension, to the subjects whose lives it seeks to memorialize. Such generic and media snobbery masks a more significant elitism about whose lives, and whose deaths, count in the public sphere. By paying, often substantially, to publish the death notice of their loved one, family obituarists insist on the value of the deceased's life and on his or her significance to society at large.

Literally framed by the newspaper column, or in some newspapers by an actual text box, the subjects of death notices are also framed, contained, and shaped by generic codes in concert with social prescriptions. Highly intertextual, death notices exhibit recurring characteristics that have become familiar generic markers, such as the name of the deceased and the date of death. They may also give details of the upcoming funeral or memorial service, thereby performing their role as community notices. Place and date of birth, cause of death, and the names of those identified as "left to mourn" are often included, but are not obligatory. Birth and death dates, grouped together headstone-style, illustrate the limits of the deceased's story; the narratives that follow these dates fill in the life suggested by the hyphen. Some newspapers, such as the *Ottawa Citizen*, allow writers to incorporate a subtitle under the deceased's name, a phrase that identifies, or perhaps summarizes, the deceased, delineating how readers will interpret the subsequent biographical details. James McGinley is presented as "Veteran—w.w. II" (*Ottawa Citizen* 6 June 2001, B15); Darlene Pollock's memorialists describe her as "Employee at Andy's Foodland, Winchester" (*OC* 2 Oct. 2001, C17). These subtitles highlight the deceased's contributions or connections to public life, and in the latter case, her geographic as well as professional community. Although both notices go on to describe other aspects of these individuals' lives, these subtitles define how the deceased are seen by the family and how they will be read by the public, identifying up front the particular communities they address, and positioning these subjects in very particular social identities.

In addition to text, notices may also include photographs and graphics such as symbols for clubs (the Masons, Order of the Evening Star), employers, or military organizations, elements that visually frame the subjects and signal to members of the deceased's communities. The choice of photograph in particular represents an idealized vision of the deceased for the public and, like the subtitles, suggests the ways in which, or for what, he or she should be remembered. Esther Hallam and Jenny Hockey note a similar impulse at work when families include photographs on gravestones. They argue that "displaying a living likeness at the grave sustains a publicly visible face that has been selected as the preferred memory form by those involved in the rituals surrounding death.... The now departed are 're-embodied' in that their physical disappearance gives way to a replacement image fixed at a previous time in their lives" (2001, 147). Fixing the public image of the deceased in the past allows the survivors to focus their memories as well as public knowledge on how the deceased was in the prime of his or her life; frequently, family members choose pictures of the deceased in youth or mid-life, even when he or she has lived long past that stage. Through such choices, Hallam and Hockey posit, "the healthy, active and often happy looking person is brought into the present, obscuring the painful phases of dying and death" (147), reflecting contemporary Western's society's fear of aging and mortality. The selection of photographs to stand in for the deceased thus reflects the obituarists' ideal images of the loved one whose passing they celebrate and announce. Additionally, pictures of the deceased from decades past, often clearly dated by dress or hairstyle, will alert other members of that generation to read the notice. Some obituarists juxtapose two photographs of the deceased, one as a younger person and one as he or she looked nearer to death. Such montages give a nod toward the multiple identities the deceased has occupied, and reflect the differing ways in which the survivors, who often span several generations, have known this person.

Death notices further enclose their subjects by inscribing them within life histories that position the deceased as an embodiment or exemplar of social norms. The flexibility of the contemporary death notice allows its writers to incorporate substantial personal detail about the deceased, crafting biographies that range from a few sentences to multiple columns that shift the focus of the text away from announcing death to celebrating life. Since most readers will not know the deceased intimately, if at all, family obituarists must negotiate personal and public concepts of the well-lived life and the worthy citizen, creating texts and subjects that are edifying as well as engaging. Commemorative writing, as Hume notes, "reflects what society values and wants to remember about a person's history" (2000, 12). Playing out private grief on this public stage, survivors must address in part why the individual mattered to the greater community, and why too this life in particular should be remembered and mourned. As public documents circulated in commercial space, death notices contribute and conform to "society's shared memory and collective values," and thus must also show "an individual's adherence to the social norm" (14); for "ordinary" people, an individual's claim to public commemoration lies in his or her compliance with received models for behaviour. This genre upholds socially prescribed attitudes towards and concepts of dying and death, gender roles, community participation, service to family and nation, and the "well-lived" life. In these most quotidian texts, then, we can trace the re-inscription of traditional codes—

for gender, morality, citizenship—as well as the conservation of existing dominant hierarchies of power, value, and voice.

Even though the survivors often do not belong to the same generation as the deceased, they uphold that generation's values and social structures when they inscribe the deceased in ways that conform to those patterns for public and personal behaviour. Thus, the death notices of older men represent the deceased as successful professionals who were also devoted family patriarchs. Such subjects, well-established within their fields, are the type of individuals who could well be the subject of formal obituaries, and indeed their death announcements closely resemble the newspaper obituary's content and organization, with professional and public contributions coming before private life. The style of these announcements indicates that public and professional service is still a defining feature for men's lives: that is, for men of the middle to upper class, usually white and heterosexual. Though these men have also been husbands, fathers, and grandfathers, their roles as executives and professionals continue to be weighted more heavily, as indicated by the foregrounding of the career over family involvement. The bereaved's choice of traditional obituary language, content, and organization demonstrates that this ideal of manhood still carries cultural currency in Canada, even in the twenty-first century. These death notices uphold the public image of the man, crafting a legacy built on dominant norms for gendered behavior and professional success as determined by economic well-being.

Seventy-one-year-old G. Peter Cunningham's death announcement, set off by a text box from the other notices on the page and preceded by a formal portrait of the deceased, chronicles his career and public honours from high school until retirement, before turning briefly to his marriage and family (*Globe and Mail* 19 Sept. 2001, s8). The death notice of Donald C. Archibald, who died at age ninety-three in the year 2000, succinctly lists his survivors in seven lines, then outlines his stellar service in the meteorological field from the 1930s onwards, his education, honours, innovations, and contributions to the war effort. Though he too was a "beloved husband" and "greatly loved grandfather," his public legacy remains his professional not personal life (GM 20 Jan. 2000, A18). Such notices, like newspaper obituaries, conflate personal virtue with professional acumen; in both forms, as Hume observes, the "listing of the deceased's associations or accomplishments" (2000, 131) are accepted and acceptable demonstrations of individual merit, admissible evidence of worthwhile lives and experiences. In these cases, the survivors' familial and personal values are in tune with perceived community values, and the writers address like-minded readers who will also appreciate the value of the deceased's occupation and affiliations, as well as his success as a "family man."

Women of Cunningham's and Archibald's generations receive similarly conventionalized treatments, with survivors casting their mothers and grandmothers as models of femininity, even in the face of daunting circumstances. The children of Marjory Schofield (1912–2002) write that she was "very adventurous and a risk taker in her early years but she was also a tower of strength and support for her children when adversity later arose" (Winnipeg Free Press 24 Aug. 2002, C13). Schofield's early "risky" behaviour, worth noting if not explaining, remains appropriately contained by her solid service as a mother and wife and, the notice adds, as a contributing member of "the local PEO chapter, the Selkirk United Church and later the Gordon Howard Seniors Centre." The family's selection of these attributes and affiliations reflects both their sense of what their mother would want to be remembered for, and what they themselves found admirable and noteworthy in her ninety-one years. Lillian Blackwell's family summed up her ninety-four years of life by noting that she was "a loving mother who never demanded anything for herself" (Vancouver Sun 6 Feb. 2002, G10). Reflecting the values and perceptions of her "beloved sons," this phrase conveys the admiration of the younger generation for a woman who, in their opinion, upheld conventions of women as selfless, totally devoted to family and others, and consequently was a model mother and citizen. Carrying over into the next generation such norms of the "good" woman/wife/mother, the death notice of Jo-Anne Elaine Stevens-Purtill, who died in 2002 at forty-three, celebrates its subject for her devotion to family, her "love of gardening," and her volunteer service to school and neighborhood activities (WFP 24 Aug. 2002, C13). Although the deceased's hyphenated last name indicates some changing conventions across generations, her death notice constructs her public identity with traditional codes for the acceptable female subject.

Holding their rendition of the deceased up for public inspection pressures obituarists into socially ordained, institutionally backed subject positions, "universally" recognizable to the death notice's imagined communities. When Anne McKibin died in June 2001, her family memorialized her as "Beloved wife," "Loving mother," and "Cherished grandmother" (OC 6 June 2001, B15). Robert Buist was similarly commemorated in September 2001 as "Dearly beloved husband," "loving father," and "dear grandfather" (GM 17 Sept. 2001, S6). The survivors, similarly cast as adoring, loving, and honoured, are also contained by this language, which performs and regulates appropriate ways in which to mourn publicly, thereby maintaining social order even in the midst of crisis. Cast in these positions, the deceased temporarily lose individualized identity and take on social roles that are seen as universal; the obituarists imagine audiences that would all have and/or value mothers, spouses, and brothers, and that would conceive of them in similar ways. The recitation of formulaic adjectives surrounding the deceased's death correspondingly limits the possibilities for self-construction. If obituarists describe the death at all, they inevitably evoke current acceptable standards for dying, for "good deaths": "peacefully;" "at home, after a good day;" "after a courageous battle" or a "long struggle;" "surrounded by." "Good" subjects do not die "cowardly," or "give up" in the face of illness or adversity, going gently into that good night. The clichéd adjectives—beloved, loving, cherished, proud, devoted, dear, peaceful, courageous—construct particular identities for the deceased and the bereaved, suggesting the sanctioned roles that contemporary society expects for men and women, husbands and wives, parents and siblings, the living and the dead.

The absence of negativity in these notices, in which "hated fathers," "unfit mothers," and "abusive grandfathers" never appear, indicates that only lives that fit into the "already provided narratives of identity" (Smith and Watson 1996, 11) will be publicly remembered. Pairing the conservative nature of the death notice genre with the homogenizing impulses of the institution of the newspaper means that the unacceptable, the unruly, and the unbeloved will be filtered out before becoming part of the larger narrative the "announcements" pages create. Only families that meet the current definition of happy, functional, and loving—or those willing to masquerade as such—need apply. Death notices, then, are conservative in the sense not only of attempting to hold on to what has been lost, to preserve a life now extinguished, but also of conforming, upholding institutions and public mores.

Death notices perform such socio-cultural conservation through sequestered codes that maintain certain social boundaries by ignoring "deviant behavior or attributes that were socially unacceptable" (Hume 2000, 14). For example, while death notices may acknowledge the deceased's flaws, they avoid critical comment. Although "skeletons in the closet" may be hinted at, these secrets are rarely explicitly named. When Laura Ann Demerais died in Vancouver at age thirty-nine, her obituarists first listed her career accomplishments and personal virtues, before referring obliquely to the "trials and tribulations of later life" and the "whispers of evil" to which she eventually "succumbed" (VS 5 Sept. 2001, D14). These latter references suggest mental illness, substance abuse, and even suicide, but her obituarists avoid any such explicit public confession or critique. Even the most untraditional announcements, those that include humour or whimsical content, adhere to these unwritten and constantly changing codes of decorum, of what can and cannot be said, which reflect and reify the values and power structures of the society that uses them. In obeying the social etiquette of the genre, users align their principles to mesh with the institutionalized codes for generic behaviour safeguarded by the newspaper itself. Sheila Adams notes that "the newspaper may refuse to print a notice which is seen as inappropriate or likely to cause offence to readers; therefore the notices are standardized" (2002, 139). In order to avoid being excluded, then, obituarists must toe the generic lines. But the ambiguity of these guidelines leaves the nature of these boundaries largely unspoken and left up to the discretion of newspapers' editorial policy boards, and driven by the commercial interests which finance the publications. While explicitly racist, sexist, homophobic, or libelous content would likely be considered "offensive," what other narrative elements—or subjects—are "inappropriate"? Such unarticulated codes, which assume that the newspapers and obituarists share a definition of "offensive," limit the possibilities for the kinds of subjects and life stories that death notices can construct.

These codes, however, are not fixed but instead change over time to reflect what Canadians will tolerate as public auto/biographical performances, as well as to institute social norms. The entry of the formerly transgressive into the conservative narrative of death notices provides a textual barometer of social change, a weather map of the unstable boundaries of intelligibility that inscribe and prescribe subjectivities. The permissible definition of "family" in death notices is one site of ongoing evolution; the survivors—those with the social sanction to mourn—have expanded to include same-sex partners, ex-spouses, paid caretakers, mothers/fathers of the deceased's children: even pets. Once considered "disenfranchised" mourners whose grief lacked legitimacy, these individuals are now publicly "acknowledged ... and socially supported" (Northcott and Wilson 2001, 94), inscribed into the community by the conservative social patterns of the death notice. Taboos surrounding cause of death show similar fluctuations in accordance with public values and norms, and changing concepts of a "good" death. For instance, in the 1980s and 1990s, deaths from AIDS-related illnesses could not be publicly announced but only hinted at by coded references that fellow community members could unpack. Codes such as these included references to young men, unmarried, dying of pneumonia, and in particular hospitals, for example. At the present time such subjects, at least in large cities, may be fully disclosed, part of a political and health revolution that resisted such stereotyping and silencing. Death by suicide, however, remains problematic for many mourners, as the death notice for Demerais may illustrate. Obituarists in these cases cannot shoehorn their subject into the received formulae that sanctions subjects in and after death. Instead, writers may mask this situation under the euphemistic "at home, suddenly," a safely nondescript cause of death that avoids social abjection. Leaving readers in many cases to read between the lines, obituarists carefully negotiate these prohibitions based on constantly shifting definitions of the "good life" and, more to the point, the "good death."

But even though the death notice in Canada appears more inclusive now than in previous decades (Gillan 1995, xxii), the genre still polices the norms for acceptable subjects through exclusive practices. Given that hundreds of people die each day in Canada's major cities, but that only an average of twenty death notices appear daily in the papers, not every individual is commemorated in a death announcement. Their absences in English-language papers may reflect communities that speak other languages, or that are predominately based outside of cities and therefore would read death notices in smaller, regional papers; they may also indicate that, for some mourners, the costs of publishing a notice are prohibitive. But what happens to the subjects whose lives do not confirm the status quo? Or to those who lack the kin or community connections that indicate membership in a public community? Such individuals may become the "excluded dead," including those "to whom only the Coroner will pay any attention" (Prior 1989, 151–52). The lack of notices for transients, prostitutes, single men and women without families or friends, prisoners, criminals, or drug addicts who have not been in treatment suggests that such individuals fall outside not only the social safety net, but also the limits of collective auto/biographical narratives. In this commemorative genre, which eulogizes its subjects and minimizes any negative traits—if it acknowledges them at all—and seeks to confirm the deceased's place within the dominant social order, cultural subjects who cannot be redeemed in death may not be inscribed. If they have survivors but are not "beloved," they may never be publicly mourned, meaning that they will leave no formal legacy, no mark of their presence to disturb the homogenous and homogenizing ritual space of the obituary pages.

Even with such received models in circulation, though, transgressions do occur, and their presence in the face of the death notice's formidably conservative formulae makes them significant, underscoring the limits of these generic practices to contain subjects. Subjects who should not, according to generic and cultural criteria, be remembered, let alone mourned, can be textually rehabilitated through their family's use of the death notice, turning its codes to their advantage. On Monday, June 24, 2002, Manjinder

(Robbie) Kandola was killed in front of his Vancouver home in what police called a "gang-style execution" (Bolan and Richards 2002, A1). The latest slaying in an escalating Indo-Canadian gang war, Kandola's death was front page news in the city, with headlines in the *Vancouver Sun* trumpeting "Gangster shot dead on city street" (24 June 2002, A1). Follow-up stories proclaimed "Cocaine dealers were his friends" (Bolan 2002, A2) and quoted police to confirm Kandola's "extensive involvement" with "high-profile" Indo-Canadian gangs (Bolan and Richards, A2); they also revealed that Kandola had separated from his wife earlier in the year. On Wednesday, however, Kandola's family wrote back, placing a brief notice on the paper's "Births & Deaths" page to announce the "sudden" death of Kandola, and give information about the upcoming funeral services (VS 26 June 2002, F7). His wife and grandmother were listed as his survivors. By Friday, this nondescript mortuary announcement had been replaced by a longer notice, accompanied by a handsome photograph of the deceased. This version extolled Kandola's virtues, adding to his short list of mourners "many loving family and friends," and celebrating the deceased for his "unique sense of charm, his extraordinary sense of humour, his wide range of knowledge and intelligence, as well as his drive to succeed, but most of all his profound generosity and loyalty" (VS 28 June 2002, B8).

Published immediately after the media blitz that painted Kandola as a career criminal, flashy gangster, and failed family man, these notices added "damage control" to the death announcement's list of generic functions. Writing against this wealth of information, Kandola's survivors portrayed the personal side of a man known for his (alleged) public exploits. Both notices, and particularly the second, are remarkable for their insistently positive construction of the deceased, using the socially sanctioned method of the death announcement, including its language and capacity for eulogy and euphemism: the man whom the media reported was killed in a "hail of gunfire" (Bolan and Richards 2002, A1) merely died "suddenly." Their adherence to the death notice formulae ensures that Kandola will have at least one public memorial to stand in his defense in the court of public opinion. The death notice lends legitimacy to Kandola's life and death, and to his obituarists' identity as mourners with the right to grieve publicly, a right usually denied when the death is seen as somehow unacceptable, as is the case with "deaths by murder, suicide, and accident" (Northcott and Wilson 2001, 92–93). His mourners' decision to run not one but two notices, the second a corrective, perhaps, of the first's lack of eulogy, indicates the ways in which the death notice allows the socially excluded to be written back into the community through commemoration, an act that presumes the worthiness of its subject. Calling on the traditional language and tone of the death notice, Kandola's obituarists assume the same general communities as the Buists and McKibins, addressing readers who are willing to believe in the value of the deceased's life and consequently regret the loss. In this case, the genre's rigid subjectivities have been hijacked by a subject whose public identity would normally preclude the commemoration of a death notice. Though the success of this auto/biographical performance may be questionable, given the context within which it appeared, its production as a part of sanctioned public mourning rituals indicates the legitimizing authority of this seemingly innocuous genre, which has flown so long beneath the radar of cultural perception.

Dulce Et Decorum Est: Inscribing National Identities

At the same time that death notices limit auto/biographical performances by producing and adhering to dominant ideologies and norms, they also contribute to an evolving social history of Canada, charting the otherwise unsung contributions of private citizens to the public history of cities, provinces, and the nation. The version of history that the death announcement fashions, however, is ultimately a conservative one that does not question the exclusions and misprisions of official history, but instead tacks individual stories onto the existing institutionalized narrative. The types of public experience that survivors choose to highlight, often in great detail, from the life of the deceased give some sense of what concepts of "Canada" and "Canadian" are in circulation in this contemporary moment. In particular, since death notices are texts that are created in the present but that celebrate the past, they construct and disseminate "Canadian history" on both macro- and micro-levels. Through chronicling their loved ones' contributions to public life, obituarists construct particularly Canadian identities for these deceased and, by extension, for their readers. As Prior argues, "the publication of death notices serves, at least in part, as a mechanism whereby kinship, community and political groups can reaffirm and reassert their solidarity" (1989, 150).

Since the majority of the dead commemorated through family obituaries are not major public figures but private citizens, whose lives may have intersected with some element of public life or history, their death notices represent the one opportunity for their stories to be told outside of the immediate family. The public venue of the death announcement allows obituarists to write the deceased into public history by publicizing his or her role, however small, in recognizable historic moments or sites. Charting encounters with powerful figures and local celebrities, listing buildings named after the deceased, or chronicling his or her part in a public works project, writers emphasize moments in which the individual became part of local or national "history." Bert Nonnweiler's obituarist, for example, tells readers to "Think of my Dad when you travel the Fraser Canyon as he worked on the tunnels you travel through, plus the Hell's Gate Tram System" (VS 27 Oct. 2001, B6), inscribing the deceased into the pioneering history of British Columbia. Obituarists therefore narrate the history not only of their beloved but also of the places in which they lived. Clearly connecting the deceased's life to the "greater good," such death notices indicate that the worth of the ordinary citizen can be justified through their inscription into public stories. Even in the cases where the deceased has been the victim of state-sponsored injustices, the death notice may mention this experience but will still maintain generic decorum by not commenting on it, protecting the official history and the collective identity produced by and invested in it. Imagining readers who will correctly interpret coded references, obituarists can hail particular communities who have shared the experiences of the deceased without disrupting the commemorative tone of the death notice. Thus the survivors of Takeyo Akizuki (1908–2001) remark that their mother immigrated from Japan to Steveston, BC, where she lived until 1942, "when the family went to Lethbridge, AB. She returned with her family in 1950" (VS 23 May 2001, C8). Similarly, Kenji Nishikihama's obituarists note that their father was born in Vancouver but "spent the war years in Minto, BC" (VS 16 May 2001, D16). Through these elliptical references, both sets of survivors record their loved one's involuntary participation in the ugly chapter of Canadian history during which Japanese Canadians were interned. Their decision to include this item, however obliquely, indicates the significance of this event in the deceased's life and in the lives and identities of the survivors. However, their refusal to make this statement fully, concealing the deceased's lack of choice and agency, suggests perhaps a lingering sense of shame, as well as a refusal to directly indict either the Canadian government or their fellow Canadians, many of whom would have been complicit in the internment scenario. Though both obituarists gesture to the deceased's "contribution" to this particular historical moment, they do not adopt the public forum of the death notice to offer resistant narratives of that time and place. Using the death notice to assign blame or to voice political views may be seen as indecorous, disrespectful, and possibly "offensive." Even after death, then, the subjects of Canadian death notices, and the survivors who represent them, must conform to "normative concepts of national subjectivity" (Smith and Watson 1996, 5).

Based on the overwhelming number of citations in death notices, one of the most significant contributions to public life and history in the twentieth century has been military service in World War II, an event and experience that defined a generation and a nation, and whose cultural currency has remained high almost sixty years after its conclusion. The wide-reaching and long-lasting effects of this conflict meant that it became for many individuals and their families the defining experience of their lifetimes. Consequently, the death notices of people who were young men and women during World War II typically mention contributions to or service in the war. For women, the announcements might cite factory work, nursing, or involvement with the WRENS; less directly, a woman's connections to the war may have been her role as a war bride, an experience that combines personal with public history. The death notices of former soldiers often give quite detailed information, including branch of service, regiment, rank, citations, and campaigns, and include photographs of the deceased from the war years, dressed in their military uniforms, freezing and framing them in that era and identity. To their obituarists and their imagined readers, the lives of these "old soldiers" have merit—are even exemplary—because of their experiences in fighting for Canada or her allies.

World War II, as Canada's first war as a sovereign nation free of Britain's governance, played a central role in the country's national history and identity. Consequently, service in any aspect of the Canadian war effort takes on additional value as service in the birth of the nation as a legitimate international presence. The perceived undervaluing of Canada's role in the war, both at home and abroad, throughout much of the twentieth century has led to renewed interest in Canadian veterans and their stories, an interest fuelled no doubt by the fact that the generation who lived through and fought in the conflict are now aged and dying. The recent flurry of publications of personal war narratives demonstrates that war service has retained, if not increased, its cultural value across generations. Arguably the last international conflict fully supported by a majority of Canadians (outside of Quebec), World War II also stands as the final "worthy" war, one that history has not (yet) recast in terms other than "good" versus "evil." Obituarists can therefore feel confident that any contributions made by the deceased, however overshadowed these may have been by years of civilian life, will be met with acclaim by the "Canadian" reading public.

Several death notices of war veterans recount at length stories of the deceased's survival or heroism, ensuring that these narratives of war pass beyond the family history and into communal or public memory. Bob Rogers's death notice provides this detailed account: "On December 29,

1944, during his nineteenth mission, Bob's Lancaster 'L for Love' was hit by flak and exploded during the bomb run; he was blown clear and regained consciousness in time to safely deploy his parachute. He was the sole survivor of the crew of seven and spend the rest of the war as a POW" (VS 8 Sept. 2001, C10). Similarly, Ian Bell's lengthy (108 line) announcement commits one-tenth of his notice to his service in the Royal Canadian Navy. In addition to chronicling his military career, his obituarists paused on the following story about "One of the Corvettes...he commanded...until it was torpedoed in August 1944 in the Atlantic. Although the captain went down with his ship, which sank in twenty seconds, an air bubble carried him to the surface where another serviceman, Frank (Sock) Williams, grabbed at his clothing and hung on until they were rescued forty-five minutes later" (VS 19 Dec. 2001, B13). The weight given these military vitae overshadows the details of these men's pre- and post-war lives, including marriage, family, and career, suggesting that their obituarists see this service as the deceased's real legacy.

Marie de Chastelain, who was born in the United States but who married a British petroleum engineer and lived in Canada after 1955, aided the war effort by "working for Sir William Stephenson in British Security Coordination" and with the "Secret Intelligence Service" (GM 19 Jan. 2000, S11). These prestigious jobs on the international front merited lengthy exposition in her death notice, which inscribes her otherwise only through a chronological listing of her places of residence and the obligatory roll call of her survivors. Future Canadian Victoria Wasilewski, born in Poland in 1917, survived the Soviet Gulag, where her first husband and two infant children died, before fighting with the Polish Free Forces and immigrating to Canada (VS 8 June 2002, C7). Half of this short death notice chronicles Wasilewski's war years, shaping her as a war veteran as well as a mother: two roles that demonstrate her public value to a Canadian collective identity. Though these women's war service preceded their Canadian citizenship, they served honourably on the "right" side of the conflict and thus merit public commemoration.

By narrating in such detail the war stories of their loved ones, obituary writers ensure that these tales will survive them, an effort that becomes increasingly urgent as more and more veterans die. In marking the deceased as a war veteran, obituarists mourn the passing not only of their particular relative or friend, but also of a generation and a dwindling community whose narratives must now become part of their own. Such attention to war service points to the high value still accorded that generation's sacrifices and contributions. The largely Anglo-European ethnicity of many of the war veterans' names, though, should remind us that, in Canada, the death notice continues to reserve this admiration for the men and women who fought for the Allies. Pride of place remains for the victors alone, and thus death notices construct a collective, even national, auto/biography that upholds the World War II generation's concepts of heroism, nationalism, and history. A very different story would emerge, for example, from the death notice of the German veteran who moved to Canada after the war, or for the Japanese Canadian interned on the West Coast, or for Chinese Canadians, who fought for Canada but were initially forbidden to serve, and who were historically the kind of veterans who did not count. These variations on "acceptable" war narratives draw attention to the norms—of World War II history, Canadian identity, nationalism—that death notices reinstitute and rearticulate.

What counts as suitably historic, just like who counts as family, will certainly change over time as competing ideas about Canada and its history become "official." Then as now, though, only subjects of the "right" history, that is, the version of history currently enjoying institutional status, can claim that experience for commemorative purposes and use it for credit in the public's assessment of "good" citizens: those who have represented themselves, their families, and their country well. Such death notices address an imagined—or, more accurately, an imaginary—"Canadian" audience who share cultural ideals, espouse the same values, and understand what obituarists mean when they apply another formulaic phrase to the deceased: "a true Canadian."

Backed by commercial and institutional investments in the status quo, death notices over the last decade have become a more recognizable institution and a received auto/biograpical form, part of an active industry of commemoration that banks—literally—on the genre's appearance of stability. Even on the Internet, the next frontier of commemoration, print standards have been reinstituted, directing obituarists down standard routes for writing lives and constructing subjects. A how-to guide on Obituaries Today, a Canadian online memorial service, tells obituarists that the second paragraph, for example, should list the survivors and the third should describe employment, military service, "memberships," and "accomplishments or great passions" (Obituaries Today), re-establishing in cyberspace the norms of experience worthy of public record.

Despite the textual and commemorative innovations possible online—hypertext narratives, for instance, or notices that could remain permanently available—this medium at present simply provides a new staging ground for traditional performances. Changing technologies, both of writing and of the self, may well bring about changes to the death notice and the cultural identities it advocates, but the genre's reliance on existing models for texts and subjects suggests that the evolutionary pace will be slow. Since narrative resistance or innovation in this genre could easily be misread as dishonouring the dead, such generic standards offer obituarists safe patterns to follow, using another's (exemplary) life as a sanctioned template and rewriting new subjects into old subject positions. In death as in life, then, the twenty-first century Canadian looks remarkably like those of the last millennium.

Notes

Author's Note: I would like to thank Eva-Marie Kröller for bringing the passage from *Unless* to my attention.

1 What constitutes such a worthwhile event demonstrates the dominant, typically conservative public values that major newspapers institutionalize. For example, Canadian papers do not—yet—include "divorce announcements" in their announcement pages. However, as mainstream society, i.e., the reading and consuming public, changes its definitions of the "acceptable" marriage and family, newspaper notices will likely offer these categories.

References

Adams, Sheila. 2001. Death notices. In *Encyclopedia of death and dying*, ed. Glenys Howarth and Oliver Leaman, 139–40. London and New York: Routledge.

Bolan, Kim. 2002. The short, brutal life of Robbie Kandola. *Vancouver Sun*, final ed. 24 June, A1–2.

Bolan, Kim, and Gwendolyn Richards. 2002. Indo-Canadian gang war erupts again. *Vancouver Sun*, final ed. 24 June, A1–2.

Eid, Mushira. 2002. *The world of obituaries: Gender across cultures and over time*. Detroit: Wayne State Univ. Press.

Fries, Udo. 1990. "A contrastive analysis of German and English death notices." In *Further insights into contrastive analysis*, ed. Jacek Fisiak, 593–60. Amsterdam and Philadelphia: John Benjamins.

Gillan, MaryEllen. 1995. *Obits: The way we say goodbye*. Vancouver: Serious Publishing.

Hallam, Esther, and Jenny Hockey. 2001. *Death, memory and material culture*. New York: Oxford Univ. Press.

Hume, Janice. 2000. *Obituaries in American culture*. Jackson: Univ. Press of Mississippi.

Northcott, Herbert C., and Donna M. Wilson. 2001. *Dying and death in Canada*. Aurora, ON: Garamond.

Obituaries Today. 14 May 2003. Online memorial service. http://www.obituariestoday.com.

"The obituarist's art: Lives after death." 1994–95. *Economist*, 24 Dec.–6 Jan., 64–66.

Prior, Lindsay. 1989. *The social organization of death*. New York: St. Martin's.

Roniger, Luis. 1992. From eulogy to announcement: Death notices in the Jewish press since the late eighteenth century." *Omega* 25(2): 133–68.

Shields, Carol. 2002. *Unless*. Toronto: Random House.

Singer, Mark. 2002. The death beat." *New Yorker*. 8 July, 28–32.

Smith, Sidonie, and Julia Watson. 1996. *Getting a life*. Minneapolis: Univ. of Minnesota Press.

BARBARA HAVERCROFT 🥀

(Un)tying the Knot of Patriarchy: Agency and Subjectivity in the Autobiographical Writings of France Théoret and Nelly Arcan[1]

Pour celle qui écrit, se saisir comme "noeud," c'est avoir l'acuité de regard du clinicien, sans en avoir la froideur, c'est aussi appréhender un noyau de résistance, se donner un moyen de défense. (Suzanne Lamy 1983, 145)

ALTHOUGH WOMEN HAVE BEEN ENGAGED in autobiographical writing in Quebec for well over a century,[2] it is only in recent years that they have started publishing an unprecedented number of texts belonging to the entire range of personal genres: diaries, memoirs, autobiographical narratives, correspondence, and autofictions.[3] Significantly, many of these texts have been penned by noted feminist writers such as Nicole Brossard, Madeleine Gagnon, France Théoret, and Denise Desautels, or by those who have expressed an overt concern with women's issues, particularly with questions of subjectivity and agency. As Mary Jean Green (1983, 124–36) has demonstrated in an oft-cited article analyzing autobiographical narratives by Claire Martin and Marie-Claire Blais, there exists an underlying pattern common to certain Québécois women's life writing, a pattern which traces the protagonist's arduous search for subjectivity. This quest frequently commences with the initial rejection of familial, religious, and social constraints, continues with a revolt against the patriarchal norms endemic to these three types of institutions, and concludes with the emancipation of the heroine. It is, in the cases of Martin, Blais, and numerous others, the coming to writing, the performative gesture of chronicling this quest for liberation, that constitutes the last, most decisive stage of the acquisition of subjectivity and agency. Thirty years after the publication of these texts by Martin and Blais, similar concerns still haunt the autobio-graphical writings of certain Québécois women authors, despite the social and cultural gains made during and since the Quiet Revolution, and espe-cially by the feminist movements of the 1970s and the 1980s. Indeed, access to the status of subjecthood and the exercise of agency remain fraught with obstacles, and life writing continues to play a major role in the representa-tion and enactment of these processes.

This quest for subjectivity and agency is precisely what is at stake in two recent Québécois women's autobiographical texts: France Théoret's diary-narrative, *Journal pour mémoire* [*Journal/Diary for Memory*] (1993), and Nelly Arcan's autofiction, simply and provocatively entitled *Putain* [*Whore*] (2001). While both writers refer to their exodus from a stifling, religious, rural milieu to the more tolerant urban setting of Montreal, they speak from very different subject positions.[4] Théoret is a seasoned, much-published and well-respected writer long associated with the feminist movement in Que-bec, whereas Arcan belongs to a younger generation of women writers much less concerned with voicing an explicit feminist agenda. In *Journal pour mémoire*, Théoret intercalates her current reflections on her writing, reading, and activities while writing, with a non-linear, retrospective narration of her youth, emphasizing the difficult struggle required to find her voice in order for her to become the agentified subject she is today. In *Putain*, it is the ongoing, agonizing search for her voice and identity which preoccupies the young Arcan, whose text addresses sexually explicit matters that are totally absent from Théoret's journal. Indeed, the "shocking" revelation of the nar-rator's double life as a student in literary studies and as a part-time, high-class prostitute caused a veritable media and critical sensation upon its publication by the prestigious French publishing house, Éditions du Seuil.[5] What ties these two different texts together is not merely their common emphasis on the search for identity, but also their conception of writing: more specifically, of life writing as a performative gesture that mobilizes specific discursive strategies which both repeat and question the very norms that condition agency and subjectivity. If both writers use the image of the knot (*le noeud*) to express a similar entanglement in patriarchal ideology and oppression, only Théoret succeeds in untying her knot—*Journal pour mémoire* is in fact the story of this disentanglement—while Arcan, although acutely conscious of hers, remains bound up within it, perpetually untying and retying it through repetitive discursive and behavioural patterns, and oscillating in the contradictory aporia of a life-death/active-passive oppo-sition that Théoret has evoked in her journal and elsewhere, but has man-aged to escape.

Agency and the Discursive Subject

During the past decade, theoreticians of autobiography and feminism have turned their attention to the complex question of agency, exploring its intricate social, political, ethical, and discursive dimensions.[6] The inextricable relationship between agency and subjectivity has been formulated in diverse ways by numerous different theorists, including Helga Druxes, for whom agency is the subject's modus operandi (1996, 9), and Shirley Neuman, who defines agency as "the capacity to act in autonomous ways, to affect the social construction of one's subjectivity and one's place and representation within the social order" (1993, 10). But to what extent is the subject actually able to act in "autonomous ways"? The response to this crucial question obviously depends upon the particular conception of subjectivity and agency espoused by the theorist. For the purposes of this paper, the theoretical writings of Judith Butler and Susan Hekman, in which they conceive of agency as a possible reconfiguration or reiteration of the discourse in which the subject is enmeshed, will provide the basis for the analysis of specific discursive strategies in Théoret's and Arcan's texts, strategies which depict, enact, and inscribe agency as a discursive repetition.

Exploring the various feminist responses to the male subject of modernity, Susan Hekman (1995, 194–207) claims that the latter remain trapped within the rigid dichotomy of the constituting subject (transcendental, agentified, equipped with free will and the liberty to determine and forge its own destiny) versus the constituted subject, the always already determined "product of social forces rather than their creator, a social dupe" (202), passive and incapable of action. Drawing on Foucault's observations concerning the necessary, inevitable situatedness of the subject within a multiplicity of institutional discourses and ideologies that are historically and socially specific and that infringe upon the subject's freedom of action, Hekman insists upon the deconstruction of the constituting/constituted dichotomy, displacing it to a different epistemological plane with the recognition that subjects are always both constituting and constituted at once, in varying degrees and configurations. According to Hekman, this heterogeneous, "discursive subject" is non-hierarchical, plural, mutable, and non-essentialist, based on differences, and produced by "fluctuating, changing, and often conflictual historical and social influences" (201). Subjectivities are thus both produced and bounded by the multiple and contradictory discourses surrounding them, and do not exist prior to such discourses. In a manner which recalls Judith Butler's ongoing engagement with formulating a theory of agency, Hekman contends that agency and construction do not coexist in an oxymoric coupling, but that agency is a "product of discourse, a capacity that flows from discursive formations" (202), inseparable from creativity and resistance. In Hekman's view, then, agency consists in the reconfiguration of existing, enabling, non-hegemonic discourses, thereby creating transitory, mobile sites of resistance.[7]

This intricate nexus of discourse, ideology, and potential sites of agency has also been addressed by France Théoret, who has consistently evoked "l'usage du langage [qui lui] est apparu marqué par les idéologies" [the use of language which seemed to her to be marked by ideologies] (1987, 99).[8] In a chiasmic gesture that underlies all of her writing, Théoret has never ceased to investigate our use of discourse, and of that which discourse makes of us. In several of her texts, she has brilliantly illustrated how one can be a subject of enunciation without being an agent, without any claim or capacity to effect social change, however minimal. In *Journal pour mémoire*, Théoret comments upon the distinction between subjects and agents, using these terms at the point in her own development at which she attained the status of a subject who could not as yet act upon surrounding social limitations: "À l'écoute des discours, je n'étais plus dans un rapport passif, j'étais dans un rapport de sujet. Le sujet que j'étais se révélait faible et malhabile, incapable de dépasser la négation" [Listening to discourse, I was no longer in a passive relationship; I was in a subject relationship. The subject that I was revealed itself to be weak and awkward, incapable of going beyond negation] (1993, 171). The difference between subject and agent is also evident in Théoret's notion of *la mère patriarcale* [the patriarchal mother], who uses her status as an enunciating subject merely to repeat worn, oppressive clichés intended to inculcate her dutiful daughter with the paternal status quo,[9] thus ensuring her entry into the awaiting patriarchal mould of expected, docile behaviour. In this instance, the subject reaffirms its constituted status, simply by parroting oppressive, hegemonic discourse in the manner of a ventriloquist, thereby reconstituting a subjugated state. Here, discursive interaction is but the repetition of the same discourse which institutes and maintains originary subjection: a reuse of institutional norms and utterances that is devoid of discernment and intervention. In contradistinction to this pessimistic portrait of the uncritical repetition of the same, there exist other instances where the subject, constituted but simultaneously constituting with a view to altering its own constitution, stakes a claim on agency by means of critical re-enunciation and reiteration: restating, creatively combining, and borrowing existing discourse, figures, and images to disrupt, subvert, and act on this very discourse. It is precisely at this juncture where Judith Butler's writings on agency as a repetition with variation prove exceedingly pertinent, as the following analysis of Théoret's and Arcan's texts will indicate.

France Théoret's *Journal pour mémoire*: (Un)Tying the Knot

A number of critics have previously remarked upon the autobiographical character of Théoret's entire oeuvre, even if her texts do not correspond to the habitual characteristics of any of the subgenres of life writing.[10] In *Journal pour mémoire*, however, the autobiographical underpinnings of Théoret's work become more explicit, as she uses her own proper name for self-reference and, in so doing, effects the referential coincidence, typical of life writing, of the text's three principal discursive instances: author, narrator, and main character.[11] In *Journal pour mémoire*, as in her previous publications, Théoret analyzes what Karen Gould describes as "relations of family, class, culture and history in the formation of female subjectivity and the female writing subject" (1993, 83), but her journal differs from her earlier texts in that she overtly and explicitly presents her *own* story of becoming a subject who exercises agency.

Composed of descriptions of daily activities temporally situated at the moment of writing, literary and philosophical reflections, memories of her working-class childhood and adolescence during what is now termed "la grande noirceur" [the great darkness] of the conservative, religious Duplessis era in Quebec, as well as of musings on existential and analytical questions, Théoret's journal distances itself from the typical traits of the *journal intime*,[12] especially since it does not consist solely of a day-to-day recording of events. In a revealing metatextual comment, Théoret (11) rejects the very term *journal intime*, choosing instead to describe her text as a "journal littéraire" [literary journal], or as a "projet d'écriture" [writing project] (8).[13] Indeed, the journal could perhaps most judiciously be termed the testimony of a *parcours* [her personal itinerary or evolution], a word which Théoret employs repeatedly in the text, given that she is primarily concerned with her own coming to subjectivity and writing as well as with the search for an identity and a language which would enable her to go beyond the initial, oppressive phase of her existence where "habitée par une angoisse, [elle] n'avai[t] que des mots venus d'une éducation religieuse" [inhabited by anguish, she had only the words of her religious education] (Théoret 1988, 180). At times, her journal resembles a fragmentary autobiographical narrative, as Théoret recounts her college and university studies, her employment as a teacher in a poor, working-class district of Montreal, her urgent quest for knowledge, and the evolution of her writing and its primordial role in her life, in addition to her personal development and her attempts to claim agency, despite her membership in a "triple ghetto of sex, culture [and] class" (Gould 1990, 232). Théoret's narration is largely non-chronological, and features numerous intertextual references; it is based more on the associative and multi-temporal functioning of memory than on any sort of faithful correspondence to the unfolding of extratextual events. What is paramount in this journal is the long and arduous road travelled to become the feminist, writer, and intellectual she is today: a tortuous process often associated in her oeuvre with the metaphor of the knot (le noeud).

Knots, Subjection, and Writing

Especially in the 1980s, textile metaphors—weaving, knotting, quilt-piecing, and the like—have repeatedly been linked to women's writing, both in specific literary texts and in feminist critical studies of such works.[14] Théoret pursues this tradition of tying memories and knots together as the knot is a repeated and important image that figures prominently in her work, where it is tightly bound up with recollections of a difficult past. Featured particularly in the prose poem "Noeud" ["Knot"] in the volume entitled Nécessairement putain (1980, 28–32), and in the autobiographical novel Nous parlerons comme on écrit (1982), the knot is a polysemic image for Théoret, heavily invested with negative connotations. This complex metaphor simultaneously denotes the patriarchal clichés, ideological and institutional constraints, and the social myths that resulted in Québécois women's subjection, passivity, immobility, and silence. Hence Théoret's contiguous combination of the metaphor of the knot with the term "generations" to convey the stranglehold of this oppressive knot, passed down from one generation to the next: "Il y a dans ce noeud le nom des générations.... Elle sait le noeud des générations" [There is in this knot the name of generations.... She knows the knot of generations] (1982, 29, 31). In addition, the knot also refers to the female subject's own tortured state, seen as the result of the above-mentioned norms that subjugate her: "Je suis un noeud bloqué dur, tourné, vissé, sûr de la solitude" [I am a tightly tied knot, stuck in a stranglehold that won't come undone, certain of my solitude] (1982, 17).[15] The knot itself, a reiterated, recycled image, also suggests sterile repetition, the act of bequeathing, from mother to daughter, the same stereotypical, androcentric norms, and the ongoing transmission of this gloomy inheritance to successive generations. Nonetheless, the very use of the knot as a metaphor, and the narrator's awareness of her own existence as a knot provide Théoret not merely with a main thread [un fil conducteur] in certain of her texts, but also with a means of resistance, as the reiteration of the sinewy threads composing the knot enables its undoing, its untying. In this sense, the untying of the knot goes well beyond the explicit occurrences of the actual metaphor itself; this process necessitates the weaving into the text of the knot's multiple discursive threads, simultaneously recycling the oppressive discourse that once imprisoned the narrator and undoing their complex grip on her. Nowhere is this process of discursive repetition with a claim to agency more apparent than in *Journal pour mémoire*, which is in part a retrospective recounting of the knot's undoing, of how Théoret gradually extricated herself from the paralysis it inflicted upon her. While the concrete image of the knot itself is absent from the pages of *Journal pour mémoire*, perhaps to signify Théoret's ultimate release from it, the multiple threads which compose it are ubiquitous, as the adult narrator recycles them yet again in the form of specific narrative strategies which illustrate her contention that writing "tente d'*agir* sur le langage" [attempts to *act* on language] (Théoret 1987, 122; my emphasis), so that women's writing is a form of discursive agency.

Discursive Threads: Repetition and Resistance

Théoret mobilizes a number of different discursive strategies in order to re-figure and untie the knot in *Journal pour mémoire*, three of which will be considered here: the re-enunciation of patriarchal clichés, snippets of stereotypical discourse that debase women; the reuse of the Antigone figure; and metatextual discourse foregrounding the performative potential of writing as a form of resistance. In all of these discursive instances, the iterability of the sign is essential to the creation of a counter-discourse. Accordingly, in *Journal pour mémoire*, Théoret reiterates existing figures and utterances in order to counter them, to resituate them within a different context in which they are open to new meanings. This is an act that recalls Judith Butler's conception of agency as a resignification resulting from a performative repetition, originally formulated in *Gender Trouble*: "In a sense, all signification takes place within the orbit of the compulsion to repeat; 'agency,' then, is to be located within the possibility of a variation on that repetition" (1990, 143). Whereas writing and speaking obviously constitute forms of action in themselves, the mere repetition of existing discourse or images without any critical recontextualization or response, as in the case of the patriarchal mother, produces no evident ameliorative effects on the social context in question but simply the maintenance of the status quo. The thrust of Butler's argument is that the repetition of offending discourse has the potential for contestation, as in parody, for example, and this critical repetition can subsequently lead to a reversal of its original, harmful effects: "the repetition of an originary subordination for another purpose, one whose future is partially open" (1997a, 38). Integral to this theory is Butler's conception of the subject as a discursive site that individuals "come to occupy" (1997b, 10), and her insistence on the subject's originary, founding subjection, which paradoxically must be reiterated in order to oppose subordination.[16] The implications of this theory of performative discursive agency for the analysis of women's autobiographical writing have yet to be fully explored, and the present study of specific enunciative instances in Théoret's and Arcan's texts represents a step in this direction.[17]

In her journal, Théoret uses two specific types of discursive repetition: the citation of certain patriarchal clichés and commonplaces, and the portrayal of stereotypical attitudes, a description that often takes the form of a metatextual representation, a paraphrase, or indirect discourse. These two forms of textual repetition accentuate the insidious nature of the negative term of a particular binary opposition that threads its way throughout the entire journal. This opposition expresses the ongoing conflict between, on the one hand, passivity and the perpetuation of outdated patriarchal norms, and on the other, movement, activity, and the difficult but gradual emergence of the female subject. Furthermore, the stereotypical utterances, whether they are quoted or paraphrased, emanate principally from one specific group of individuals, which Théoret baptizes les velléitaires [the indecisive ones, the irresolute]. The members of this group, whose discourse serves solely to oppress women, have different faces in Théoret's journal: the family, voices of tradition, familiar religious beliefs, or simply anonymous voices reiterating the same dispiriting, misogynist attitudes.

One such occurrence of recycled discourse is Théoret's citation of discouraging words uttered by her aunt, whose resistance to her niece's desire to pursue her studies typifies the entire family's attitude in this respect. A true incarnation of the patriarchal mother, the aunt laments: "À quoi bon tous les efforts, on n'y arrive jamais!" [What's the use of all of these efforts, one never succeeds anyway!] (1993, 170). By resituating this utterance within the context of her journal, many years after its original enunciation—and the completion of her university studies, for that matter—the narrator responds indirectly to her aunt, through autobiographical writing. This quotation, followed by Théoret's response, enables her to refute her aunt's pessimism, relating how she refused to abandon her education: "Mais si on fait aucun effort, on ne saura jamais. Ce sera pire encore.... Je n'allais pas céder à la tentation de m'arrêter. Je parvenais à formuler positivement ce que ma parente exprimait dans une double negation." [But if one makes no effort, one will never know. It will even be worse.... I wasn't going to give into to the temptation to stop [my studies]. I succeeded in formulating positively that which my relative expressed in a double negation] (Théoret 1993, 170). In this passage, Théoret effects a noteworthy pronominal slippage: to the anonymous *on* [one], tainted with negativity in her aunt's remark, Théoret responds with a personal, pugnacious *je* [I] to mark her difference from the destiny of the other women in her family. The pronominal slippage is accompanied by the passage from the general to the individual, which itself contains another movement, that from a passive pessimism to an optimistic, active determination that motivates the author's actions, accomplished despite familial opposition. In this manner, the author's "I" and her refusal of defeatist ideology replace her aunt's affirmation of resignation and the latter's acceptance of inactivity. But to reject the quotation, the discursive, foreign graft[18] knotted into her text, to construct her own counter-discourse, Théoret must first incorporate her aunt's words into the body of her own text. For it is only in making the voice of the other, the voice of the norm, re-sound that the narrator can subsequently reformulate and resist it. This strategy of quotation is, then, a double-voiced discourse, the tying together or conflation of two enunciating subjects within the aunt's utterance, which, when cited, is at once "un énoncé répété et une énonciation répétante" [a repeated utterance and a repeating enunciation] (Compagnon 1979, 56).

Recalling Antigone: Onomastic Repetition and the Counter-Exemplum

With the purpose of countering the presence of the *velléitaires*, be they fathers or mothers, Théoret turns to yet another form of discursive repetition by recycling the onomastic signifier "Antigone," which for Théoret represents the very model of agency itself. In this case, discursive reiteration takes on an intertextual dimension, recalling not merely Sophocles's tragedy but also, implicitly, the chorus of various rewritings and theoretical discussions of this famous figure.[19] As Théoret explains, this tragic character has been a major source of inspiration for her since childhood: "Sa figure de personnage solitaire m'accompagne depuis des décennies.... Nul autre personnage n'a aussi longue histoire dans mon imagination" [Her figure of a solitary character has accompanied me for decades.... No other character has such a long history in my imagination] (1993, 194, 195). So crucial is Antigone to her own personal development that Théoret devotes several pages of her journal to a consideration of her character and actions, in an attempt to elucidate the precise influence of this heroic figure on her own quest for subjectivity. This onomastic repetition allows Théoret to focus on a female figure worthy of respect, as opposed to the male and female *velléitaires*, whose lethargy inspires no emulation whatsoever. Repeating this proper name, weaving it into her journal in the form of a retrospective recollection of its contribution to the untying of her knot, Théoret reminds us of the positive connotations engendered by the original text. By naming certain qualities represented by the Antigone figure, traits forever attached to this proper name, Théoret draws our attention to those which are essential to agency: intelligence, solidarity, wisdom, rationality, generosity, dignity, courage, and so on. In addition, Théoret affirms the significance of Antigone's courageous action in burying her brother, noting her "adhésion à une logique différente" [support of a different logic] (1993, 196).[20] Indeed, the constellation of connotations clustered about the proper name "Antigone" constructs a paradigm of features common to those who claim agency, who act in a manner contrary to the passivity and pessimism of the *velléitaires*.

The proper name is consequently transformed into an *exemplum*—the heroic figure becomes a rhetorical one—and Théoret's use of the latter mobilizes all of the meanings of this term:[21] the idea of a model or example to be imitated, and that of a lesson and learned repeated by subsequent generations.[22] What is striking here is that Théoret's reiteration of the Antigone figure and the transformation of the proper name into an *exemplum* repeat the well-known but now outdated conception of autobiography as the site of the exemplary male figure (see Gusdorf 1956), the model worthy of admiration and emulation. Recalling this function of life writing, however, affords Théoret the opportunity to reverse it—to deconstruct it—to perform a variation on it: in *Journal pour mémoire*, the autobiographical subject does not present *herself* as the example to be followed, but substitutes a legendary, fictive other (woman) in the place of the self, thereby undoing the androcentric connection between the autobiographical text and the representative, unified, bourgeois subject.

Although mindful of certain contradictions in Antigone's behaviour, Théoret is concerned above all with the latter's belief in "son propre jugement intellectuel et moral" [her own intellectual and moral judgement] (1993, 195), with the generosity and love to which her actions testify. Appropriately, this section of the journal concludes with Antigone's words, taken from the eponymous play: "Je suis de ceux qui aiment, non de ceux qui haïssent, dit Antigone" [I am of those who love, not those who hate, says

Antigone] (196). In quoting Antigone's self-referring speech, Théoret creates an enunciative overlapping of two feminine voices—her own and that of the Greek heroine—and in so doing, makes the exemplary values of Jocasta's daughter, an agentified subject, her own. This re-citation consequently ties the narration of her own experiences to the legendary life of this intertextual *exemplum*, knotting together autobiograpical and fictive voices in an attempt to oppose those of the *velléitaires*.

Metatextual Reflections

A further discursive strategy, the use of metatextual commentary, also contributes to the untying of Théoret's knot. Concentrated in the initial section of the text (entitled "Liminaire"), metatextual discourse is also scattered throughout the entire journal. Metatextual remarks perform a number of diverse functions in *Journal pour mémoire*, but perhaps the most striking of these is that of a reflection upon writing as a means of claiming and exercising agency.[23] As this discourse comments on the very text that Théoret is in the process of writing, it constitutes a form of discursive agency in the second degree. Emphasizing how writing itself has assisted her in unravelling the knot of patriarchy—and how it continues to do so—these metatextual fragments describe and embody writing as a performative strategy. Numerous sentences place the first-person pronoun *je* in close, contiguous contact with the verb *écrire* [to write] or with the noun *écriture* [writing], as in the following passage: "L'écriture, je ne peux la concevoir autrement qu'en rapport avec un cheminement, jamais dans sa globalité" [I could never conceive of writing otherwise than in relation to an itinerary, an evolution, never in its globality] (1993, 57). Indeed, from the very beginning of the text, Théoret employs metatextual discourse to highlight the necessary relationship between writing and agency: "Source d'énergie psychique, l'écriture du journal recrée la distance essentielle à l'oeuvre littéraire" [A source of psychic energy, the writing of the journal creates the distance essential to the literary work] (7).[24] Like the claim to agency itself, writing is often a difficult, hesitant process for Théoret that foregrounds her self-doubt and uncertainty: "Je me sens maudite. Ma façon d'approcher l'écriture, dans le tremblement, le doute. L'écriture me dépasse ... je m'y inscris trop.... Je ne me fais guère confiance.... Écrire de façon cohérente semble au-dessus de mes forces" [I feel damned. My way of approaching writing, trembling and in doubt. Writing is beyond me.... I put too much of myself into it. I hardly have any confidence in myself.... To write in a coherent manner seems beyond my capabilities] (1993, 14, 15, 16). For Théoret, the discussion of the text she is in the process of writing is also to speak of herself, of her relationship to writing and, in a chiasmic posture, of the reciprocal effects of self upon writing and of writing upon the self.[25] The quest for subjectivity and agency is thus ineluctably, and inextricably, bound to writing; for this reason, *Journal pour mémoire* is a text which continually ties together the fragmentary, autobiographical narration of the narrator's life and the story of the evolution of her writing: the two are quite simply inseparable.

Nelly Arcan's *Putain*: (Re)Tying the Knot

Where *Journal pour mémoire* focuses on the untying of the knot of patriarchy, chronicling and re-enacting the gradual emergence of an agentified subject, Nelly Arcan's *Putain* presents the portrait of a young woman's perpetual entanglement in an archetypal scenario of subjection. As in Théoret's writing, the metaphor of the knot in *Putain* is polysemic, referring to the subject's agonized state and her awareness thereof, to the psychic stranglehold of destructive family relationships, and to the act of writing the text itself, for the narrative itself resembles the situation it depicts. Where is agency to be located in this repetitive, sorrowful lament, in this hybrid combination of testimony, confession, and autofiction?

Putain features the paradoxical story of an educated woman who acts, but in so doing, adopts a highly stereotypical role of objectification while being critically aware of the negative consequences of her choice. The narrator recounts her departure from a suffocating family situation in a small Québécois village—her father is a religious fanatic and her mother, chronically depressed, spends her life wallowing in bed—and her subsequent move to Montreal, where she devotes her time to three principal activities: literary studies at university, employment as a high-class prostitute, and frequent appointments with her psychoanalyst, which unfortunately do not alleviate her distress. Never revealing her true name, the narrator adopts that of her deceased sister, Cynthia, as her professional name, forging a connotative link between a death-like state and her prostitution. Indeed, death and hate accompany her constantly in her search for her own identity, an identity which would free her from the gloomy spectre of her parents, their disdain for each other, and their total lack of mutual love and communication. In a significant contrast, the mother remains silent, prostrated in bed, while the daughter, also in bed but engaged in remunerative activities, gives free rein to her voice in her breathless autobiographical lamentation.

Completely devoid of linear chronology, *Putain* is more akin to a long monologue, a veritable outpouring of words reminiscent of the repeated ejaculations of the narrator's numerous clients. Constructed of lengthy sentences lacking in periods—except at the conclusion of each paragraph—the text unfolds in a breathtaking rhythm, punctuated solely by commas. Like the serpent that bites its tail, this obsessive narrative continually turns back upon itself, reiterating the same details, the same images, and repeating the same suffering over and over again. Prefaced by a short, italicized, metatextual introduction in which the narrator relates the basic circumstances of her predicament, the text then follows a twisted, winding path, described by the narrator as "construit par associations, [par] le ressassement et l'absence de progression" [constructed of associations, repetitions, and the absence of progression] (2001, 17). Numerous discursive threads compose the knot that is this text: the frequent address to the narratee/reader [*vous*], testifying to the narrator's urgent need of a listener; short passages of reported discourse, some of which are imagined, and all of which are woven into the text's fabric; and a paradoxical oscillation between a number of different binary oppositions, including life/death, true/false, masculine/feminine, pleasure/pain, and subject/object.

Just as Théoret's *Journal pour mémoire* does not adhere to the canonical criteria of the *journal intime*, Arcan's *Putain* does not strictly correspond to the characteristics associated with any subgenre of life writing. Since the author's name does not appear within the text itself, the latter cannot be definitively classified as an autobiography or as an autofiction.[26] Arcan's text bears only the description "récit," a rather equivocal indicator of genre, given the French expressions *récit autobiographique* [autobiographical narrative] and *récit de vie* [life narrative]. Despite the absence of a "real" proper name in the text, which would provide a direct link to the extratextual author Arcan, thereby sealing the autobiographical pact, extratextual discourse such as interviews and book reviews has succeeded in arousing great curiosity and suspicion as to "Cynthia's" true identity, especially as Nelly Arcan was enrolled in the master's program in literary studies at the Université du Québec à Montréal.[27] Stéphane Baillargeon claims that Arcan has succeeded in resisting media pressure to reveal the truth value of her utterances, that she "n'a jamais consenti à démêler le vrai du faux de sa 'fiction autobiographique,' soi-disant pour protéger sa famille et pour se distancier du personnage de son roman" [has never consented to distinguish the true from the false in her 'autobiographical fiction,' supposedly to protect her family and to distance herself from the character in her novel] (2002, 38). Perhaps the most fitting generic characterization of this text is that of an equivocal autofictive space,[28] in which past events, many of which are possibly true, are filtered through the poetic and necessarily subjective vision of the narrator, without the promise of a faithful reconstruction of extratextual events, and despite the absence of the author's proper name within the text.

Recalling the "Call Girl"

In her portrayal of a prostitute's life, Arcan revisits one of the most powerful representations of women as powerless objects; the marginalized, collaborating victims of a commodified, misogynist society; women with no status or prestige. Located outside of the borders of "polite society" (Kappeler 1986, 155), the prostitute is an archetypal feminine figure to which numerous negative connotations are attached, ranging from indecent, immoral behaviour; lasciviousness or obsession with sexual success, physical appearance, and money; and finally, to secrecy and silence.[29] Interestingly, in Nécessairement putain, France Théoret also recycles this reviled figure with the purpose of reversing the pejorative portrait of the "whore," providing her with a voice with which to attack the patriarchal underpinnings of society, and its representations and treatment of women. For Théoret, then, the prostitute's existence is emblematic of the general oppression of all women, who are all "necessarily whores" in a male-dominated culture, a parallel that Arcan also draws. Putain, like Nécessairement putain, allows the previously mute prostitute figure to speak of and from her own experience, although the political import of Arcan's text is not as explicitly articulated as Théoret's.

As in Théoret's journal, specific discursive strategies are used in Putain to convey the narrator's attempts to become an agentified subject. Both descriptive passages and rhetorical imagery contribute to a sustained critique of her profession, bringing its positive and negative aspects to light. In this respect, a number of the narrator's introspective comments detail the advantages of her life as a prostitute, not the least of which is the distance it affords her from her noxious family situation, her religious upbringing and schooling,[30] and her former rural milieu, "cette campagne de fervents catholiques où ... on renvoie les schizophrènes aux prêtres pour qu'on les soigne par exorcismes" [that countryside of fervent Catholics ... where one sends schizophrenics to priests so that they can be cured by exorcisms] (Arcan 2001, 7). The protagonist's exodus to the city, and her revolt against her parents, are seen as possible paths leading to her emancipation. Prostitution also provides her with financial independence, with a certain degree of paradoxical self-esteem as she "performs" the work with great success (21), and with a most fitting means—a sinful profession—of pursuing her rebellion against her father and his religious fanaticism. The prostitute figure which she adopts forms an integral part of her search for identity, and differentiates her markedly from her conservative parents; she claims it as her own, as her only possession: "ma putasserie, [c'est] la seule chose que j'aie en propre, salement propre" [my "whore-ness," that's the only thing I have of my own/that's the only thing I have that is "clean"; that's really my own/that's dirtily clean] (27).[31] The narrator admits that, occasionally, she even takes pleasure in her work, although these moments are rather rare: "j'ai parfois du plaisir, je ne peux pas dire le contraire, j'en ai toujours lorsque ma voix parvient à me convaincre, lorsque mes cris percent ça et là du naturel, du spontané..., l'impression d'être là pour du vrai, pour du bon" [I sometimes take pleasure in this, I can't deny it, I always do when my voice succeeds in convincing me, when my cries convey something natural and spontaneous..., the impression of being there for real, of really being there] (20). This gratifying sense of self-presence, these fleeting and furtive moments of pleasure, the knowledge of her father's shock and horror were he to discover her activities—all of the above testify to a certain agency on "Cynthia's" part, to actions that bespeak her responsibility for her own situation.

Nonetheless, the narrator also devotes considerable space to a critique of various aspects of her profession, and the very fact that she is simply unable to quit, to pry herself free from a commerce that has transformed her into a commodity, evinces a negative agency on her part whereby acts of "emancipation" are revealed to be self-destructive in nature. Knotted into her narrative are numerous textual devices reiterating the negative, dark side of her job as a prostitute and its devastating effects upon her. This discursive critique of prostitution includes, for example, a number of metaphors which represent the narrating subject as an object. In one such instance, where the sexual and culinary registers combine, the narrator asks her employer to put her on the "menu du jour" (26), hoping that clients will select her as their "putain du jour" [whore of the day] (26), a "dish" to be "eaten" according to the appetites in question. Elsewhere, her own lack of identity is expressed in a series of synecdoches, in which her entire being is reduced to specific body parts: "une bouche fardée qui s'ouvre et qui se referme, des seins sur le point de jaillir d'un corset, des cheveux qui font voler leurs boucles..., des épaules et un dos qui offre la promesse d'un envers, une poitrine corsetée dont le surgissement est sans cesse reporté" [a made-up mouth that opens and closes, breasts about to spill forth from a corset, hair with flying curls..., the back and shoulders of a body that offers the promise of what's on the other side, a corseted chest whose liberation is constantly delayed] (24). This list of synecdoches, composed of sexual body parts, expresses the narrator's "broken," disassembled state, indicating her desperate search for subjectivity and identity. These diverse parts never reassemble themselves into a "whole"; each is substituted for the entire person, producing the portrait of a sexed body in disparate pieces. Moreover, the manner in which these parts are described seems to mimic or repeat the same representation they might receive, had it been engendered by the male gaze; it is as if the narrator sees herself through her clients' eyes.

Canine Metaphors and Subject (Con)figurations

It is perhaps the pejorative image of the dog [la chienne], repeated like a recurring refrain throughout the text, which best communicates and critiques the subject as object in Putain. A term heavily laden with negative connotations, "la chienne" evokes the representation of a trained, domesticated animal, thereby stripping the narrator of her humanity and reducing her to a position decidedly inferior to that of her male clients.[32] As she reveals, "Cynthia" prefers the "dog position" ["le petit chien"] during sexual encounters with her clients, during which she is "agenouillé[e] ... ou béant[e] sur le dos, [s]on corps réduit à un lieu de résonance" [kneeling... or sprawled on her back, her body reduced to a space of resonance] (2001, 20), in a posture of complete submission and obedience to the other. But this same position enables the narrator to maintain a certain distance between herself and her client, to avoid personal contact with him: "et quand je baise c'est le petit chien que je préfère, le petit chien bien sage fixant un mur sale tandis que là derrière s'unissent deux organes..., comme s'ils n'avaient rien à voir ... avec moi, avec ma tête qui se tient aussi loin que possible de cette rencontre qui ne me concerne pas, enfin pas personnellement" [and when I have sex, I prefer the little dog position, the well-behaved little dog staring at a dirty wall while behind me, two organs are joining together..., as if they had nothing to do ... with me, with my head that I hold as far as possible from this encounter that doesn't involve me, at least not personally] (45). The canine metaphor is thus a predominantly negative image, whereby the woman as animal offers herself as an object to fulfill men's needs, but Arcan tempers this harsh self-critique somewhat, rendering the posture of subjection more polysemic than it would first appear. Adopting the posture of the dog affords the narrator a certain measure of self-protection from the other who invades her corporal and psychic space; it allows her to keep an emotional distance from him, avoiding that crucial face-to-face and eye-to-eye contact which would render the encounter more intimate.

The bestial register reappears elsewhere in the text, in certain passages where servile connotations are linked to the critique of prostitution as a repetitive, exhausting profession. In one such instance, the narrator describes herself as she believes her client sees her, "à ce que je vois de moi dans son regard" [what I see of myself in his glance] (63): "cette bête rampante et servile qui n'a de force que pour se pencher et fermer les yeux" [this crawling and servile animal that has only the strength to lean over and close its eyes] (63). The animal metaphor is seen to originate in the eyes of the male other, reflecting a negative self-image back to the narrator who, in turn, incorporates it into her dysphoric portrayal of the figure of the prostitute and, obviously, of herself. At another point in the text, the dog metaphor forms part of a depiction of prostitution as an onerous activity that literally wears young women out in the ritual performance of the same gestures. Obliged to repeat the same scenario of seduction and sexual service, day after day, forced to entertain a large number of clients, the narrator turns to rhythm and lexical repetition to convey the slow death which accompanies her work:

> et finalement la mort, la sensation d'avoir tout vu, tout entendu, d'être allée où il ne fallait pas, si loin qu'il faut continuer, l'impression d'avoir épuisé toutes les combinaisons, et puis la lourdeur des gestes qui se répètent, qui engendrent les mêmes réactions, les mêmes couinements de chiens contents, de chiens baveux, de chiens de Pavlov, la queue automatique (151).

> [and finally death, the feeling of having seen everything, of having heard everything, to have gone where one shouldn't have gone, so far that I must continue, the impression of having exhausted all possibilities, and then the heaviness of gestures which repeat themselves, which provoke the same reactions, the same whimpering of contented dogs, slobbering dogs, Pavlov's dogs, the automatic dick, (up like a tail)].

In this excerpt, the narrator reiterates the metaphor of the dog, used earlier in the text to characterize herself, but in a striking linguistic pirouette she reverses the referent, simultaneously repeating and varying her own discourse. While she is forced to perpetually reproduce the same, stereotypical behaviour, it is the men, the satisfied customers, who are contented, Pavlovian dogs responding mechanically on cue. The narrator's agency in such passages consequently manifests itself on a plurality of levels, as the metaphor of the dog is first applied to the figure of the prostitute, expressing individual self-denigration,[33] but subsequently its referential scope is widened to encompass the male participants in the prostitute's sphere of activity, who are equally meritous of the narrator's disdain.[34]

Beauty and the Burnout: A Repetitive Cycle

The narrator's claim to agency, tenuous though it may be, is also evident in her acerbic critique of the eternal quest for beauty and youth, obsessively pursued by Western society and crucial to her profession. But once again, her critical insight notwithstanding, the narrator fully participates in this endless war waged on aging, in this dogged insistence on surface appearances, while simultaneously recognizing and exposing its superficial, empty nature. She admits, for example, to having learned "qu'il ne faut pas vieillir, surtout pas, qu'il faut rester coquine et sans enfant pour exciter les hommes entre deux rendez-vous d'affaires, maman, papa, dites-moi qui est la plus belle" [one must not age, certainly not, one must remain seductive and childless to excite men between two business appointments, Mother, Father, tell me who is the most beautiful] (2001, 35). Only in her early twenties, the narrator confides that she has nonetheless already been treated by a plastic surgeon at several intervals, since the writing of the many signs of age and "ugliness" must be erased from the body: "la laideur, c'est exactement ça, le décompte, la liste de ce qui est à supprimer" [ugliness, it's exactly that, the list of what must be removed] (41). And this ongoing search for youth and beauty, as "Cynthia" discovers, is exhausting, endless, and demanding, as expressed in the following list of activities, in which the large number of verbs in the infinitive aptly render the considerable time and energy that the narrator must necessarily devote to her appearance, if one is "necessarily whore," to borrow Théoret's expression:

> et puis la jeunesse demande tellement de temps, toute une vie à s'hydrater la peau et à se maquiller, à se faire grossir les seins et les lèvres et encore les seins parce qu'ils n'étaient pas encore assez gros, à surveiller son tour de taille et à teindre ses cheveux blancs en blond, à se faire brûler le visage pour effacer les rides, se brûler les jambes pour que disparaissent les varices, enfin se brûler toute entière pour que ne se voient plus les marques de la vie, pour vivre hors du temps et du monde (102).

> [and then youth requires so much time, a whole life of moisturizing one's skin and making oneself up, having one's breasts and lips enlarged and then the breasts again because they still weren't large enough, watching one's waistline and dying one's hair blond, having one's face burned to remove wrinkles, having one's legs burned to make varicose veins disappear, finally burning oneself entirely so that the traces of life can no longer be seen, to live out of time and the world.]

What is noteworthy in this citation is the lack of an acting, animate subject: there is but a lengthy series of verbs in the infinitive, often pronominal verbs that reflect back upon an unspecified, unnamed subject, depicting aethestic procedures performed on the female subject's body. Once again, the focus is on body parts, particularly those which attract the male gaze, and those which will most likely fail in this endeavour if they are marred by the traces of aging. Just as she speaks of having her legs and face burned for aesthetic purposes, the narrator remains imprisoned within the frenetic life which is literally burning her out, a life populated by an endless stream of clients attracted precisely by the seductive results of the burning laser treatments. In this repetitive list, where the personal and collective spheres are closely entwined, there exists both a critical self-examination and an air of resignation, for the narrator finds herself trapped within this "éternel retour du même, de la baise et du culte du beau, le culte de faire durer la jeunesse pendant la vieillesse..., comme Madonna" [eternal return of the same, of sex and the cult of beauty, the cult of making youth last into old age..., like Madonna] (91). To express one's awareness of this repetitive cycle, to be conscious of the emptiness of this relentless pursuit of physical perfection, is already to act critically, to perform a repetition, but with a variation. Nonetheless, the narrator of *Putain* remains tied up in her own knot, a dilemma reflected discursively in the list cited above, as she is unable to break out of the vicious cycle in which she is entangled.

Writing the Knot

As the above analysis demonstrates, the writing of the autofictive narrative enables the narrator to intervene critically in her own life, to accentuate the numerous aspects of the servile condition of female objectification. In a manner which recalls Théoret's valorization of the act of writing as a possible means of gaining agency, Arcan recycles the metaphor of the knot to convey her own, tortured state:

> Ce dont je devais venir à bout n'a fait que prendre plus de force à mesure que j'écrivais, ce qui devait se dénouer s'est resserré toujours plus jusqu'à ce que le noeud prenne toute la place, noeud duquel a émergé la matière première de mon écriture, inépuisable et aliénée, ma lutte pour survivre entre une mère qui dort et un père qui attend la fin du monde (17).

> [What I was supposed to overcome has only become a larger burden as I have been writing, that which was supposed to untie itself has become even tighter until there was only the knot and nothing else, the knot from which the raw material of my writing has emerged, my inexhaustible and alienated

writing, my struggle to survive between a mother who sleeps and a father who waits for the end of the world.]

If this knot aptly represents the narrator's predicament of entanglement in the ever-tightening stranglehold of a repetitive, degrading lifestyle with a difficult access to agency, a critical awareness is nonetheless evident, and the knot of her existence is named as the raw material of her repetitive writing, which, in its tortuous twistings and turnings of multiple threads, itself resembles a knot. In addition, this description of the knot clearly illustrates the burden of being tied too tightly to her parents. In this sense, the knot is a discursive companion piece to the image of the mirror, which reflects and repeats the dreaded images of her mother and father, conjuring the eventuality of being forever bound to these representations of passivity, oppression, and death. As the chiasm in the following excerpt indicates: "mon père est comme mes clients et mes clients comme mon père, ma mère est comme moi et je suis comme ma mère…, je finis par me perdre dans tous ces jeux de miroir" [my father is like my clients and my clients like my father, my mother is like me and I am like my mother…, I end up losing myself in all of these mirror games] (97–98). The lexical repetition and chiasmic specularity in this passage aptly communicate the return of the same, those unwanted family resemblances that haunt her daily life. Like her mother, the narrator is often prostrated—on the bed with her customers, or on her analyst's couch—using the money earned in the former activity to pay the fees of the latter. And those men with whom she lies in bed incessantly recall her own father, a client of prostitutes such as herself, who is frequently substituted for her clients in her imaginary: "je ne sais que serrer les dents toujours plus sur l'insistance des queues dans ma bouche, sur la queue de mon père qui commerce avec des putains" [I only know how to clench my teeth ever more tightly on the repeated series of dicks in my mouth, on my father's dick, he who does business with whores] (85). Caught in this knot of kinship where family ties have led to a living death, the narrator reenacts the Oedipal drama in the feminine, fearing the possible incestuous union with her father—represented by each of her clients—and repeatedly reviling her mother in a verbal murder that reeks of hatred and disgust.

In both Théoret's and Arcan's autobiographical texts, the polysemic figure of the knot simultaneously represents the intricate embedding of the subject in various discursive fields, be they cultural, psychic, or social, which act to constrain her; the difficulty of her access to subjectivity and agency; and the act of writing itself, used as a means of what Sidonie Smith and Julia Watson have termed "writing back," "a strategy for gaining agency" (2001, 176).

Théoret and Arcan both employ particular forms of discursive repetition in tandem with other textual devices, such as rhetorical figures and metatextual discourse, in an effort to review and reshape the cultural scripts into which they have been written, eloquently demonstrating how "autobiographical practices become occasions for restaging subjectivity, and autobiographical strategies become occasions for the staging of resistance" (Smith 1993, 156–57). In Théoret's *Journal pour mémoire*, the narrator's knot of patriarchy is more closely entwined with specific historical and political realities of Québécois society, and its gradual emergence from an oppressive past. The narrator in *Journal pour mémoire* is already an agentified subject, who retrospectively recounts and re-examines the process by which she has claimed and gained agency; she describes the progressive untying of the knot from a position temporally posterior to it. If the narrator of *Putain* recycles and literally becomes the prostitute figure as a form of protest and resistance against the imposition of her father's conservative values and her mother's state of passive subjection, she uses a highly coded cultural scenario of female subjection in order to do so. While giving a voice to prostitutes, perhaps the most silenced of all women, "Cynthia" remains, as she herself admits, entangled in the very knot of writing intended to release her from the grip of the psychic paralysis of a dysfunctional family. The narrator of *Putain* is best characterized as a "critically aware subject in process" (Smith and Watson 2001, 146), extremely conscious of the ties that bind her but unable to extricate herself from them, even at the end of the narrative. Her poetic, self-conscious lament of emotional scars, her candid critique of her own subjugated state as a prostitute, and her repeated address to the pronoun *vous* [you] in the desperate quest for a listener, however, constitute significant attempts to claim agency. In the text's concluding passage, the narrator makes a final gesture of interpellation of the other, calling to life from death ["lorsqu'on interpelle la vie du côté de la mort"] (2001, 187), investing the reader with the responsibility of response.

Notes

1 This essay forms part of the research project entitled *Subjectivity and Agency in Contemporary Women's Autofiction*, funded by the Social Sciences and Humanities Research Council of Canada, whom I thank for their financial support.

2 For an extensive inventory of writings of all autobiographical genres in Quebec since 1860, see Yvan Lamonde (1983; 2000) and Françoise Van Roey-Roux (1983).

3 A number of contemporary Québécois women's autobiographical texts are examined in a special issue of the journal *Voix et images* devoted to this subject (see Havercroft and LeBlanc 1996).

4 Several of Théoret's fictional texts feature this exodus from the rural to the urban setting, the latter of which provides women with a degree of freedom from familial and ide-

ological obstacles blocking the path to self-realization. See the prose poem entitled "La marche" ["The Walk"] in *Nécessairement putain* [*Necessarily Whore*] (1980), the autobiographical novel *Nous parlerons comme on écrit* [*We Will Speak As We Write*] (1982), and the novel *Laurence* (1996), to cite but a few examples.

5 Interviewed on a number of Québécois and French television shows dealing with literature and culture, Arcan was also featured on the cover of Air Canada's *EnRoute* magazine, as part of an article on celebrities and the media (see Baillargeon 2002). Her autofiction, while the subject of much controversy for its "scandalous" content, was also highly praised by the critics and was nominated for two of France's most valued literary prizes, the Médicis and the Femina.

6 Feminist theoreticians of agency include Rita Felski (1989), Judith Butler (1990, 1993, 1997a, 1997b, 2000), Judith Kegan Gardiner (1995), Susan Hekman (1995), and Helga Druxes (1996). For a more detailed discussion of feminist theories of agency and their bearing on the interpretation of contemporary women's life writing, see Havercroft (2001a).

7 It is precisely on this point of "enabling" and non-hegemonic discourses available for reconfiguration that Hekman's and Butler's theories appear to diverge. Hekman cites the discourses of maternity, liberalism, and Marxism (of which the latter two neglect women but harbour "implicit" agency) as enabling, whereas Butler specifies "disabling" discourses of explicit subjugation (such as hate discourse) as potential sites of agentified reiteration (see Butler 1997a).

8 All English translations from literary and theoretical texts originally written in French are my own.

9 The denigrated figure of the patriarchal mother is common to much contemporary Québécois feminist writing, especially since the publication of Nicole Brossard's *L'Amèr ou le chapitre effrité* (1977, 24). According to Louise Dupré, the patriarchal mother occupies one of the two poles accorded to female characters in Théoret's texts. Contrary to the female subject "qui tend à un idéal personnel et collectif" [who strives towards a personal and collective ideal], the patriarchal mother is a character who is "soumis à sa triste condition, à son triste conditionnement" [submitted to her lamentable condition, to her lamentable conditioning] (Dupré 1989, 34). On the patriarchal mother, see also Santoro (2002, 166–68) and Saint-Martin (1999, 77–88).

10 On the autobiographical nature of Théoret's writing, see Dupré (1988, 24–30), Gould (1990; 1993, 83–93), Green (1993, 119–30), and Smart (1988a, 11–23; 1988b, 307–25).

11 This referential and onomastic identity forms part of Philippe Lejeune's well-known definition of autobiography (1975, 14); it also characterizes other subgenres of life writing, such as diaries and memoirs.

12 The canonical characteristics of the *journal intime* are outlined by Béatrice Didier (1976), Pierre Hébert (1983), Françoise Van Roey-Roux (1983), and Françoise Simonet-Tenant (2001).

13 Joëlle Vitiello characterizes Théoret's journal as "une écriture réflexive sur le féminisme" [a reflexive writing on feminism], noting the fragmentary nature of Théoret's entire *oeuvre*, which is "peut-être une tentative postmoderne de documentation historique" [perhaps a postmodern attempt at historical documentation] (1999, 326).

14 Examples of such textile metaphors in the French literary tradition include Madame de Lafayette's *La Princesse de Clèves* (1678), in which the eponymous heroine decorates her beloved's cane with knots and bows, but refuses to "tie the knot," and Françoise de Graffigny's *Lettres d'une Péruvienne*, in which the kidnapped Peruvian princess Zilia uses the Incan knotting system of quipus to convey her love and life events to her absent fiancé Aza (see Miller 1988). On textile metaphors and women's writing, see Gilbert and Gubar

(1979), Joplin (1984, 25–53), Miller (1986, 270–95; 1988, 125–61), Showalter (1986, 222–47), and Woolf (1929). See Havercroft (2001b) for an analysis of intertextual memory in Théoret's journal, and its relationship to weaving and theories of memory.

15 As Suzanne Lamy explains, the phonic affinities between *noeud* and the negative particle *ne* signify the void, the aporia of the female narrator's negative state in *Nous parlerons comme on écrit*, which reflects the image that her society constructs of women (Lamy 1983, 142). A similar semantic and phonic grouping of knots and negation carries over into the English translation of these terms, as "knot" and "not" are homonyms. Furthermore, as Louise Dupré points out, the text entitled "Noeud" aptly expresses "l'exil de la femme, sa souffrance, son mal à vivre" [the exile of woman, her suffering, her difficulty in living] (1989, 50).

16 Butler's position is neither that of fatalism, nor that of naive "political optimism" (1997b, 17). As she explains, the very subjugating power which initiates the subject may actually shift in status from a "condition of agency to the subject's 'own' agency," through a "significant and potentially enabling reversal" (1997b, 12).

17 Drawing upon Judith Butler's work, Sidonie Smith has investigated the relationship between autobiography and performativity, conceiving the act of autobiographical narration in its entirety as an example of the performativity of identity, a history of the re-citation of the self, during which "the power of discourse produce[s] effects through reiteration" (1995, 31).

18 Antoine Compagnon proposes this image of the citation as a foreign body, as "la greffe d'un organe [qui] comporte ... un risque de rejet" [the graft of an organ [which] harbours ... the risk of rejection] (1979, 31).

19 While these intertextual reformulations of the Antigone figure are not explicitly mentioned in Théoret's journal, George Steiner's *Antigones* (1984) provides an informative survey of many of them.

20 Theoret's treatment of the Antigone figure is similar to that of Luce Irigaray, who considers the tragic heroine as a model of the audacious contestation of social laws, downplaying characterizations of Antigone as anarchistic or suicidal (1989, 79–100; see also 1974, 266–81). Helga Druxes also adheres to this portrayal of Antigone as a positive example of contemporary relevance: "[she is] one of the earliest archetypes of female agency and civil disobedience in a hierarchical society" (1996, 35). Although she acknowledges Antigone's subversive potential, noting her speech in a borrowed language, "the language of entitlement from which she is excluded" (2000, 82), Judith Butler focuses primarily on Antigone's trespassing of the norms and configurations of kinship and gender, with a view to relating the psychoanalytic dimension of her fate and actions to the social.

21 Consider Richard Lanham's definition of this rhetorical figure: "An example cited, true or feigned, [an] illustrative story" (1968, 139). Lanham uses the term *paradigma* as a synonym of *exemplum*, explaining that *paradigma* is derived from the Greek word for "model, example, lesson" (70).

22 Interestingly, Judith Butler notes that one of the etymologies of Antigone's name yields the meaning "anti-generation" (2000, 87–88). Given Antigone's heritage of incestuous, confused, and difficult kinship relations, her name thus connotes a possible opposition to, or at least a distancing from, previous generations. This connotation also brings to mind Théoret's efforts to free herself from the loathsome legacy of her predecessors, the "knot of generations."

23 Metatextual commentary is also used to clarify Théoret's objectives in writing the journal (1993, 22); to describe its atypical character (11–12); to highlight the critical dimension of her language and the distance she now possesses in relation to the past events

recounted (21, 96); and to comment specifically upon the journal's fragmentary form and its consequent reflection of women's time and interrupted lives (29, 110, 224).

24 Théoret was writing a volume of literary essays, L'homme qui peignait Staline [The Man Who Painted Stalin] (1989) concurrently with Journal pour mémoire, and discusses this writing project in the journal.

25 Constantly interrogating the rapport between writing and life, Théoret uses metatextual discourse to describe and explore the knotting together of the two: "Écrire pour lutter, sinon cela n'a aucun sens" [Writing in order to resist and fight, otherwise it has no meaning] (56); "Il y a un rapport en droite ligne. Vivre et écrire" [There is a direct relationship. Living and writing] (59).

26 First proposed by Serge Doubrovsky on the cover of Fils (1977), the autofictional text has two main criteria: the same onomastic identity as in the canonical autobiography (author, narrator, and principal protagonist, all of whom share the same name), and the generic marker "novel" (Lecarme 1993, 237).

27 See, for example, Chartrand (2001), Kéchichian (2001), and Tremblay (2001), all of whom contend that Arcan unquestionably was a prostitute. Loret (2001) insists that what is important is the reader's belief that this is the case. Extratextual links are more readily made with specific locations in Montreal, such as the easily identified campus of the Université du Québec à Montréal. Arcan's description of the university she attends shows how its location, architectural design, and geographical proximity to the sex trade district are emblematic of three major elements of the narrator's existence: education, prostitution, and the rejection of religion (Arcan 2001, 14).

28 In his discussion of the truth value of autobiography versus that of the novel, Philippe Lejeune uses the term "espace autobiographique" [autobiographical space] to refer to "l'espace dans lequel s'inscrit les deux catégories de textes, et qui n'est réductible à aucune des deux" [the space to which the two categories of texts belong, and which cannot be reduced to either of the two] (1975, 42). The expression "espace autofictif" [autofictive space], which I have proposed elsewhere (Havercroft 2002), denotes a similar generic territory, but accentuates the text's precarious inscription within the confines of autofiction.

29 As Karen Gould observes in her analysis of Théoret's Nécessairement putain, the prostitute is the "most silenced woman of all. She is the woman about whom society does not speak, the woman with whom men sleep but do not speak, [and] the woman who is forbidden to speak for 'other' women" (1990, 221).

30 Arcan's tale of attending a strict Catholic school run by nuns may seem rather anachronistic, given the largely secular nature of the contemporary Quebec education system. Indeed, her depiction of these self-sacrificing nuns, "ces modèles de dévotes réduites à un nom de remplacement" [those exemplary, devoted women reduced to a substitute name] (9), harks back to the period during which Théoret attended primary and secondary schools (the 1950s and 1960s), when public education was controlled by the Catholic church. Today, however, Catholic schools for girls still exist, but they are private and small in number.

31 In this passage, Arcan playfully exploits the polysemy of the French adjective "propre," which translates as "own" when preceding a noun, and as "clean" when following a noun. This pun produces comical effects through its use of the clean/dirty opposition to qualify the narrator's profession, which is commonly deemed to be "dirty."

32 In Nécessairement putain, Théoret's narrator strikes a similar chord: "Je ne suis pas humaine et je saccage vos tombes" [I am not human and I devastate your graves] (1980, 21), thereby testifying to the prostitute's (woman's) status of inhumanity and her desire for revolt.

33 The critique of the self and other prostitutes is also evident in the title of this autofiction—
Putain [Whore]—an insult used by the narrator to disparage herself and her colleagues.

34 Another recurrent metaphor woven into Arcan's textual web, the worm [*la larve*] is subject to a referential multiplicity similar to that of the dog image. Reactivating the servile register of subjugation, the narrator uses the figure of the lowly worm alternatively to refer to herself (as a prostitute), to the general female population, and also to her own mother, a depressing figure of passivity and submission whose enunciative capacities are limited to moans and tears. Moreover, both the canine and vermicular metaphors denote two different referents—mother and daughter—suggesting not merely a resemblance between the two, simple family ties that bind, but also the possible substitution of the mother's fate for the daughter's: the frightening prospect of the repetition, without variation, of the maternal destiny of silence, solitude, and sadness, a fear which becomes the daughter's obsession.

References

Arcan, Nelly. 2001. *Putain*. Paris: Éditions du Seuil.

Baillargeon, Stéphane. 2002. Bawdy talk/À corps perdu. *EnRoute* 5:037–044.

Brossard, Nicole. 1977. *L'amèr ou le chapitre effrité*. Montreal: Quinze.

Butler, Judith. 1990. *Gender trouble: Feminism and the subversion of identity*. London and New York: Routledge.

———. 1993. *Bodies that matter: On the discursive limits of "sex."* London and New York: Routledge.

———. 1997a. *Excitable speech: A politics of the performative*. London and New York: Routledge.

———. 1997b. *The psychic life of power: Theories in subjection*. Stanford: Stanford Univ. Press.

———. 2000. *Antigone's claim: Kinship between life and death*. New York: Columbia Univ. Press.

Chartrand, Robert. 2001. La solitude natale des sexes. *Le Devoir*, 15 September, D3.

Compagnon, Antoine. 1979. *La seconde main ou le travail de la citation*. Paris: Éditions du Seuil.

Didier, Béatrice. 1976. *Le journal intime*. Paris: Presses Universitaires de France.

Doubrovsky, Serge. 1977. *Fils*. Paris: Galilée.

Druxes, Helga. 1996. *Resisting bodies: The negotiation of female agency in twentieth-century women's fiction*. Detroit: Wayne State Univ. Press.

Dupré, Louise. 1988. Une poésie de l'effraction. *Voix et images* 40 (Fall): 24–30.

———. 1989. *Stratégies du vertige*. Montreal: Les Éditions du remue-ménage.

Felski, Rita. 1989. *Beyond feminist aesthetics: Feminist literature and social change*. Cambridge, MA: Harvard Univ. Press.

Gardiner, Judith Kegan, ed. 1995. *Provoking agents: Gender and agency in theory and practice*. Urbana: Univ. of Illinois Press.

Gilbert, Sandra M., and Susan Gubar. 1979. *The madwoman in the attic: The woman writer and the nineteenth-century literary imagination*. New Haven, CT: Yale Univ. Press.

Gould, Karen. 1990. *Writing in the feminine: Feminism and experimental writing in Quebec*. Carbondale: Southern Illinois Univ. Press.

———. 1993. Autobiographical history and the lure of the recent past: France Théoret's *L'homme qui peignait Staline*. *L'esprit créateur* 33 (Summer): 83–93.

Green, Mary Jean. 1983. Structures of liberation: Female experience and autobiographical form in Quebec. *Yale French Studies* 65:124–36.

———. 1993. Private life and collective experience in Quebec: The autobiographical project of France Théoret. *Studies in Twentieth-Century Literature* 17 (Winter): 119–30.

Gusdorf, Georges. 1956. Conditions et limites de l'autobiographie. In *Formen der Selbstdarstellung: Analekten zu einer Geschichte des literarischen Selbstporträts*, ed. Günter Reichenkron and Erich Haase, 105–23. Berlin: Duncker and Humblot.

Havercroft, Barbara. 2001a. Auto/biographie et agentivité au féminin dans "*Je ne suis pas sortie de ma nuit*" d'Annie Ernaux. In *La francophonie sans frontière: Une nouvelle cartographie de l'imaginaire au féminin*, ed. Lucie Lequin and Catherine Mavrikakis, 517–35. Paris: L'Harmattan.

———. 2001b. Fragments d'un parcours remémoré: *Journal pour mémoire* de France Théoret. *Quebec Studies* 31 (Spring/Summer): 36–49.

———. 2002. Espace autofictif, sexuation et deuil chez Denise Desautels et Paul Chanel Malenfant. In *Sexuation, espace, écriture: La littérature québécoise en transformation*, ed. Louise Dupré, Jaap Lintvelt, and Janet Paterson, 43–66. Quebec City: Éditions Nota bene.

Havercroft, Barbara, and Julie LeBlanc, eds. 1996. *Effets autobiographiques au féminin*. Special issue of *Voix et images* 64 (Fall).

Hébert, Pierre. 1983. *Le journal intime au Quebec: Structure, évolution, réception*. Montreal: Fides.

Hekman, Susan. 1995. Subjects and agents: The question for feminism. In *Provoking agents: Gender and agency in theory and practice*, ed. Judith Kegan Gardiner, 194–207. Urbana: Univ. of Illinois Press.

Irigaray, Luce. 1974. *Speculum: de l'autre femme*. Paris: Éditions de Minuit.

———. 1989. *Le temps de la différence: Pour une révolution pacifique*. Paris: Librairie Générale Française.

Joplin, Patricia Klindienst. 1984. The voice of the shuttle is ours. *Stanford Literature Review* 1(1):25–53.

Kappeler, Suzanne. 1986. *The pornography of representation*. Minneapolis: Univ. of Minnesota Press.

Kéchichian, Patrick. 2001. Rose ou morose. *Le Monde*, 24 August, Section "Le Monde des livres," 3.

Lamonde, Yvan. 1983. *Je me souviens: La littérature personnelle au Quebec (1860–1980)*. Quebec: Institut québécois de recherche sur la culture.

———. 2000. *La littérature personnelle au Quebec (1980–2000)*. Montreal: Bibliothèque nationale du Quebec.

Lamy, Suzanne. 1983. Des résonances de la petite phrase: "Je suis un noeud" de France Théoret. In *Féminité, subversion, écriture*, ed. Suzanne Lamy and Irène Pagès, 139–49. Montreal: Éditions du remue-ménage.

Lanham, Richard. 1968. *A handlist of rhetorical terms*. Berkeley and Los Angeles: Univ. of California Press.

Lecarme, Jacques. 1993. Autofiction: un mauvais genre? In *Autofictions et cie*, ed. Serge Doubrovsky, Jacques Lecarme, and Philippe Lejeune, 227–49. Paris: Centre de recherches interdisciplinaires sur les textes modernes, Université de Paris X.

Lejeune, Philippe. 1975. *Le pacte autobiographique*. Paris: Éditions du Seuil.

Loret, Éric. 2001. Le fruit de ses entrailles. *Libération*, 23 August, Section "Livres," 5.

Miller, Nancy. 1986. Arachnologies: The woman, the text, and the critic. In *The poetics of gender*, ed. Nancy Miller, 270–95. New York: Columbia Univ. Press.

———. 1988. The knot, the letter, and the book: Graffigny's *Peruvian Letters*. In *Subject to change: Reading feminist writings*, 125–61. New York: Columbia Univ. Press.

Neuman, Shirley. 1993. ReImagining women: An introduction. In *ReImagining women: Representations of women in culture*, ed. Shirley Neuman and Glennis Stephenson, 3–18. Toronto: Univ. of Toronto Press.

Saint-Martin, Lori. 1999. *Le nom de la mère: Mères, filles et écriture dans la littérature québécoise au féminin*. Quebec City: Editions Nota bene.

Santoro, Miléna. 2002. *Mothers of invention: Feminist authors and experimental fiction in France and Quebec*. Montreal and Kingston: McGill-Queen's Univ. Press.

Showalter, Elaine. 1986. Piecing and writing. In *The poetics of gender*, ed. Nancy Miller, 222–47. New York: Columbia Univ. Press.

Simonet-Tenant, Françoise. 2001. *Le journal intime*. Paris: Nathan.

Smart, Patricia. 1988a. Entrevue avec France Théoret. *Voix et images* 40 (Fall): 11–23.

———. 1988b. *Écrire dans la maison du père: L'émergence du féminin dans la tradition littéraire du Quebec*. Montreal: Québec/Amérique.

Smith, Sidonie. 1993. *Subjectivity, identity and the body: Women's autobiographical practices in the twentieth century*. Bloomington: Indiana Univ. Press.

———. 1995. Performativity, autobiographical practice, resistance. *a/b: Auto/Biography Studies* 10 (Spring): 17–33.

Smith, Sidonie, and Julia Watson. 2001. *Reading autobiography: A guide for interpreting life narratives*. Minneapolis: Univ. of Minnesota Press.

Steiner, George. 1984. *Antigones*. New Haven, CT: Yale Univ. Press.

Théoret, France. 1980. *Nécessairement putain*. Montreal: Les Herbes Rouges.

———. 1982. *Nous parlerons comme on écrit*. Montreal: Les Herbes Rouges.

———. 1987. *Entre raison et déraison*. Montreal: Les Herbes Rouges.

———. 1988. Éloge de la mémoire des femmes. In *La théorie, un dimanche*, Louky Bersianik, Nicole Brossard, et al., 175–91. Montreal: Les Éditions du remue-ménage.

———. 1989. *L'homme qui peignait Staline*. Montreal: Les Herbes Rouges.

———. 1993. *Journal pour mémoire*. Montreal: Éditions de l'Hexagone.

———. 1996. *Laurence*. Montreal: Les Herbes Rouges.

Tremblay, Odile. 2001. Le vertige du nombre. *Le Devoir*, 6 October, C9.

Van Roey-Roux, Françoise. 1983. *La littérature intime au Quebec*. Montreal: Boréal Express.

Vitiello, Joëlle. 1999. Par-delà les frontières: éthique et épistémologie féministes chez les auteures francophones. In *Pluralité et convergence: La recherche féministe dans la francophonie*, ed. Huguette Dagenais, 311–34. Montreal: Les Éditions du remue-ménage.

Woolf, Virginia. 1929. *A room of one's own*. London: Grafton, 1990.

YUKO YAMADE 🦋

Auto/Bio/Fiction in Migrant Women's Writings in Quebec: Régine Robin's La Québécoite and L'immense fatigue des pierres

IN THE 1980S AND 1990S, THE WRITING OF migrant women living in Quebec began to draw attention in that province because of the growing numbers of immigrants in Québecois society. Often autobiographical, these women have tended to write of their immigration experiences, contrasting the cultural differences between their homelands and their new countries, and these experiences of cultural in-betweenness are what they have contributed to the development of contemporary Québécois literature. Mostly political, their autobiographical writings reflect and share important characteristics of recent postmodernist and postcolonial literary trends. For example, these writers are conscious of their self-reflexivity, which is an important characteristic of postmodernism. Their writings also express their sense of hybridity in their new countries' cultures; recent postcolonial theorists, such as Homi Bhabha, have discussed these characteristics in a post-colonial context, saying hybridity "demands you translate your principles in new situations" (1990, 216).

Autobiography itself has expanded as a literary genre, especially since in the last two decades of the twentieth century, when many migrant Québécois women authors were beginning to question both their ethnicity and the status of women in their writings. One such migrant author is Régine Robin, who emigrated from France to Quebec in 1977, and whose autobiographical writings transcend traditional categorization. She has created a new writing style, somewhere between autobiography and fictional stories, which she calls "bio-fiction." In this analysis, I will demonstrate that migrant women's autobiographical writings, and those of Québécoise women in particular, are not just minority writings but are also leading the literature of their "new" countries in new directions.

Autobiography and Feminist Writings in Quebec

As I mentioned previously, writers are expanding the definition terms of autobiography, and there are diverse new ways to write autobiography in Quebec. For example, Québécois women have often questioned the terms of women's identity in their autobiographical writings, particularly during the 1980s. Feminist writers in Quebec often share characteristics with the American radical women's movements that emerged in the 1970s, taking to heart the slogan of second-wave feminism in the United States, "The Personal is Political." As Micheline Dumont-Johnson explains, that radical feminism "was the initial driving force behind feminism in Quebec" (Dumont-Johnson et al. 1992, 357). Karen Gould further defines the characteristics of Québécois feminism as a "cultural triangle," that "Québec feminism and feminist modes of textual inscription can be attributed at least in part to the unusual cross-fertilization of three distinct cultural perspectives—Québécois, French, American" (1990, xiv). Thus, Quebec feminism also has the hybrid quality that characterizes its literature and society.

In the 1980s, Québécois women used autobiographical writings as a medium to convey ideas in their literature and society, and developed various autobiographical writing styles. In France Théoret's *Nous parlons comme on écrit*, for example, Théoret created the style of "poème en prose," and described her childhood memories in a poetic style. In the 1980s and 1990s, some Québécois women writers also began to reuse what is called *journal intime* [diary writings], as when Nicole Brossard published her diary, *Journal Intime: ou voilà donc un manuscript*, in 1984. In addition, many feminist writers and scholars in Quebec discussed autobiographical writings at the 14th meeting of the "Communication de la rencontre québécoise internationale des écrivains tenus à Québéc conference." There, feminist writer and journalist Madeleine Ouellette-Michalaska, during the panel "La tentation autobiographique," emphasized the multiple roles that autobiography can play in inscribing or recording women's memories, a characteristic of autobiography that had been eagerly discussed in the United States throughout the 1980s. Before then, Ouellette-Michalaska had published a diary, *La tentation de dire: Journal*, in which she implied that this style can be used to question and construct women's identity, and that her claim reflects the idea of *écriture feminine* in France, which also questioned women's identity through writings.

I hope to show that a migrant interdisciplinary writer, Régine Robin, has invented another role for autobiography in Quebec literature in her search for new space between autobiographical and fictional stories, and between cultures and/or societies.

Régine Robin's Writings and Auto/bio/fiction

Régine Robin analyzes the in-between spaces of literature in a Québécois context. As a sociologist as well as a writer of fiction, she has searched for the relationship between society and literature throughout her career.[1] In *La sociologie de la littérature: Un historique* she says that the two are connected because "Literary texts have the possibility to be 'others'... it is because they have the ability to repeat and to illustrate ... social reproduction (Robin and Angenot 1991, 39). Robin's literary texts often reflect a multiethnic Québécois society, which is rooted in its bilingual culture. Robin describes this society's main characteristic as "la société cosmopolite" [cosmopolitan society], although her description is not new: this is a concept has already been coined and explained by Québécois literary critics. Simon Harel, for example, who is also a Québécois author, claims that "the cosmopolitanism exists only between "enracinement (implantation)" and "déracinement (displacement)." (1992, 391).

In Robin's literary works, this cosmopolitan social condition is represented by the complexity of literary genres in her writings. By combining autobiography and fiction, biography and her experiences, she invents a new genre in Québécois literature: "biofiction," as she describes her second literary work, *L'immense fatigue des pierres*. To help explain this new genre, it would be useful first to define the term "autofiction." Lecarme defines this genre by saying: "Autofiction is not opposite to autobiography.... Autofiction can become an unleashed autobiography" (Lecarme and Lecarme-Tabone 1997, 268). Robin develops this idea of autofiction in her critical work, *Le Golem de l'écriture*: "Autofiction is a sort of reconfiguration of the self, and it dismantles as well as constructs itself" (1997a, 24). Within her new invention, which she calls biofiction, she combines these characteristics of autofiction as a narrative of self identification and as a biography as a narrative of reality; that is, in her writings, subjectivity and otherness always coexist. Also, her biofiction has complex characteristics, not only within its genre but also in its multidimensional narratives, which travel between New York, Israel, France, and Montreal. Thus, Robin's fictional writing underlines the complexity of society in Montreal. This particular "hybridity" is also characteristic of her protagonist's identity, which is constructed through her relationship with the idea of motherhood as it represents Robin's consciousness of postfeminism.

I would argue that such characteristics of her writing must be based on her experiences being between languages (French and the other languages that she speaks) and cultures (North American and European). However, she does not try to find out her place; rather, she stays *hors-lieu* [outside].

This is the space where her protagonist in *L'immense fatigue des pierres* situates herself. Robin explains this concept by saying: "She (her protagonist) is looking for a place not for *enracinement*, but for *déracinement*.... She searches for another place, her utopia to live and to re-live" (1989c, 179–80). In the same way, Robin herself is looking for a genre to express herself between autobiography and fiction, or between fiction and biography; that is, something outside of fixed genres. She wrote her first fictional work, *La Québécoite*, as a novel, but explains her intention in using this category in the afterword of the English translation of *The Wanderer*:

> In search of a new meaning in the past, I use false biography, false autobiography: "autofiction," the novel in the true sense. Autobiographical elements are inscribed in the narrative and transformed into fiction. Thus The Wanderer is not autobiographical in the customary sense.... While the novel does contain autobiographical elements.... So, if *The Wanderer* is autobiography, it is intellectual or spiritual, not factual, autobiography. (1997b, 179–80)

Robin wrote these two works both as a way to express herself about the place she found, and the way she lived in Quebec, through her ambivalence about language. Having finished two literary works,[2] she explained the reason why she wrote them, in addition to her non-fictional works, especially *La Québécoite*:

> After writing this book [*La Québécoite*] I understood that becoming Québécois was no longer of any importance to me. *The Wanderer* deals with the problem of finding a place for oneself ... once the book was finished, I felt that this was possible through writing ... through friendships and other relationships—and so I turned a page. (1997b, 174)

By admitting to the ambiguous space inside of the self, Robin, a migrant writer, begins to construct the identity and understand the relationship between her self and her host country.

Robin also expresses her identity as a *Cybersoi*, which does not belong either inside or outside of Quebec, a concept obviously influenced by Donna Haraway's feminist theories of the "Cyborg." Robin defines this concept as "a hybrid myself, Cyborg ... one chooses his/her sex, personality, last and first name, and shape" (Robin 1997a, 284). Thus, she began to think of another self within modern "cyberspace" society, and her writings represent her ideas. The following section will examine her ideas on identity in contemporary society, and in Montreal's "cosmopolitan" culture, through her literary works, *La Québécoite* and *L'immense fatigue des pierres*.

Migrancy and Montreal's Cosmopolitanism in Régine Robin's Writings

As a migrant woman writer, Robin inscribes her ethnicity in her writings, and, in them, searches for the place to stand on so as to identify herself as migrant in Montreal. However, she does not intend to be a Montrealer, but deliberately stays a "wanderer" in its culture. As such, her writings can be considered another style of new ethnography, as she examines a foreign culture at the same time that she is a member of its culture. I understand Robin's identity formation to be a cultural wanderer as she stays in *hors-lieu* through her linguistic in-betweenness, as well as her pluriethnicity and feminist ideas. I would like to demonstrate that Robin has contributed enormously to the development of migrant women's writing in Quebec.

Alhough Régine Robin's mother tongue is Yiddish, she never writes in her works in it. In her writings, she often refers to Franz Kafka, who was also a Jewish writer who never wrote in his native tongue. Robin characterizes her first language by using Kafka's discourse on "l'impossible identité": "They have lived among three possibilities ... a possibility of not writing, a possibility of writing in German, a possibility of writing in another way" (1989, 27). Developing Kafka's ideas further, Robin characterizes her mother tongue as "Le Yiddish, c'est le tabou [Yiddish, it's a taboo]" and she continues: "The real loss will redouble the fantastic loss.... I write this loss, in this gap. It must be done in another language" (1991, 9–10). Robin writes to compensate for, or to inscribe, what she and her ethnic identity lost throughout its history, because language plays an important role in ethnic identity formation. Thus, when one constructs one's identity through non-native languages, one's discourse tends to be what she describes as "nomad speech" (48). Robin often uses this concept, and she names herself as "une écrivain nomade" [a nomad writer] in cosmopolitan Montreal. "The cosmopolitanism. The holes among other holes, the immigrants among other immigrants, a possible, improbable place. And a nomad writing" (1989c, 180). This idea of nomad is reflected in her protagonists' characteristics. In *L'immense fatigue des pierres*, her protagonist, "la fille," and her mother, "la mere," are both Jewish French women. After getting divorced, "la mère" moves from Paris to New York and becomes a best-selling author. On the other hand, "la fille" gets married in Jerusalem and owns a gallery. After her husband passes away, she closes her gallery. The two intend to meet at Roissy Airport in Paris to move together to another city. "La mère," who lives in New York, surrounded by non-native languages, sees herself as a nomad: "We are wanderers, shooting stars. We always live by the side of our vanities, our places and languages. You work in Hebrew and I write in English"

(Robin 2000, 11). Observing her daughter's life in Jerusalem, she finds that her daughter, who learned Hebrew, also felt the same foreignness through languages:

> After all these efforts to learn the language, to adapt yourself, to make your hole, to feel at ease ...
> To invent its own language
> To coil yourself up in Hebrew like you
> Or in English like me
> To live with French or to the contrary
> To be a wanderer of Multilingualism (28, 34-35)

Even after experiencing various languages (English, German, French, Polish, and Hebrew), they cannot feel at ease ["sentir chez soi"] anywhere, and they intend to move to Montreal, as they hope to form their identity in their new multilingual city: "In Montreal, one feels fine. Do you really believe it? Of Course! One speaks French there, and one does not feel like being forced to speak the language of strangers" (Robin 2000, 47).

This is also a city where their "lost" language, Yiddish, still exists: "In Montreal, there is a fragility of language, of their language like a tissue, and it reminds one of the aged who speak Yiddish ... one must be Jewish to understand how one feels if one does not have one's own language" (47-48).

They try to find out their identities in this multilingual culture, not as Québécois or Jews, but as migrants: "In Montreal, one would be fine, just because one will not be completely at ease ... a space to be able to easily breathe, a place in the midway between inside and outside" (48).

This is a culture characterized by pluriethnicity, where foreigners are allowed to construct their identities as migrants in the space of *hors-lieu*. This is fundamentally different from Canadian "multi-culturalism," which intends to form a unique identity combining various ethnic characteristics.

Robin uses several characteristics of pluriethnicity and cosmopolitanism to characterize Montreal culture. Her construction of migrant identity through her experiences are reflected in her protagonist's discourses in La Québécoite, as she claims that this is her "autofiction in intellectual meaning." There are roughly four steps in the development of her relationship with Montreal culture: non-coincidence, a recognition of nomad identity, a discovery of *hors-lieu*, and an identification of foreignness (*devenir étranger*).

First, Robin's identity formation begins with her recognition of Montreal culture, which is often characterized by multiethnicity or hybridity. Robin's protagonist in La Québécoite is Jewish and emigrated from France. Her impression of the cosmopolitan Montreal culture is of: "The cosmopolitan city where one hears all sorts of languages, where smells of all markets in the world will assail you ... hybridity of forms, of sounds, a richness of differences" (Robin 1993a: 208–209). In this culture, she identifies herself by *non-coïncidence*. This term is explained by Robin as "non-coïncidence qui permettrait peut-être l'emergence d'un espace nomade" (non-coincidence which will make the nomad space exist) (1992, 25). Her protagonist is a French woman, but in Quebec, the language is different than in France. In describing her discovery of the differences between French and Québécois, she describes Québécois as "the language which is not completely yours." (1993a, 52). As her mother tongue is Yiddish, she finds a double *non-coïncidence* through her immigration to Montreal. From this experience, she finds that she has a nomadic characteristic in her identity, which ties her to those people who belong nowhere and continue to live in the space between cultures and national boundaries. Robin defines nomadism as "a space of migrant writing which marks outside" (1992, 25). As her protagonist does not understand the "sense" of languages in Quebec, she begins to see the gaps between languages, and these gaps are what migrant Québécois writers describe in their writings. As her protagonist says:

> There is no messiah.
> There is no story
> Just a voice of plurality
> a voice of crossroad. (2000, 90)

As Robin's protagonist in La Québécoite finds her *hors-lieu* (not-place, place outside established categories), she begins to form her identity as a migrant in that space. Simon Hamel calls this process *devenir-étranger*. This concept does not refer to those who wander between cultures and languages, or who try to deny the categories of immigrants, that is, those who stay in *hors-lieu* [not-place] and who inscribe their discoveries and inventions in their writings. Robin explains it in *L'immense fatigue des pierres* as "These writers who come from outside inspire something new in [its] language and new styles in [its] literature (2000, 218). In Quebec, these migrant writers are not categorized as minority or immigrant, but they lead their cosmopolitan culture and literature in new directions. Rather, they define themselves as "Néo-Québécois" (1997b, 175), who identify themselves by not being Québécois and who address readers both inside and outside of Quebec. Furthermore, the doubleness and ambivalence of the Néo-Québécois, Robin says, some toether so that "their imagination will create another intertextuality... another kind of hybridity" (1989c, 181). Thus, Néo-Québécois create new values in Québécois culture and literature and thanks to the dynamics of

her work, Régine Robin is one of the most salient Néo-Québécois intellectuals.

Régine Robin's Biofiction and Feminist Translation

Robin's biofiction, *L'immense fatigue des pierres*, is composed of multiple narratives dictated by a mother and her daughter. However, there is no narrative by a male protagonist, as the mother's divorced husband, Jean-Claude,
has already passed away and her daughter's husband, Simon, also has suddenly passed away because of cancer. Thus, a mother and her daughter
intend to restart their lives as "nomads" without men. This narrative technique, which is constructed only through the mother-daughter relation, is
one of the important feminist literary techniques and Robin explains, "I can
easily make disappear men in my writings" (1989c, 179) as a way to explain
this plot decision. That is, her protagonists now have no restriction and
obstacle in their lives; they can choose a place to live and a language to speak.
Intriguingly, two of the male characters have names, and never appear in
their narrative. On the other hand, the two female protagonists do not have
specific names throughout the narrative. Thus, characters seem to occupy
the position of the "cybersoi," described by Robin as a self who chooses its
sex, name, and identity.

This narrative also resembles a computer-generated hypertext, which
Robin defines as the epitome of an age of complexity: "Hypertext inscribes
that the complexity, the multiplicity, the heterogeneity, the confusion, the
uncertainty, the instability and the fragmentation are the redefinition of...
our identities" (1997a, 278). Robin's text is also composed of fragmented
pieces and complex narratives. The two protagonists' biographies are composed of their stories in the past, present, and future. Furthermore, the
daughter is an artist of collage, an art that is made by fragmented pieces.
The mother, who is a writer, describes "the passages on TV, in *New York Times*,
in *New York Review of Books*, in *Village Voice*" (2000, 12), that is, her writing
career is fragmented and unstable.

This fragmentation is one of the central characteristics in both postmodernist and feminist studies. Magali Cornier Michael notes this characteristic of the feminist postmodern novel, when he says, "[The feminist]
novel uses its fragmented narratives to communicate forcefully to its reader
the ways in which male-centred Western discourses are implicated in the
violence and misogyny" (1996, 41). Both postmodernism and feminism aim
to create something new through reconstruction after deconstruction. Magali Cornier Michael goes on to underline the new possibilities of feminism

through the act of reconstruction as "the goal of feminism is ... to offer possibilities for a reconstructing of social and thought systems" (1996, 38). This idea shares characteristics with Robin's techniques in her biofiction, possibly because Robin's multiple and fragmented narratives appeared after the deconstruction of male-centred conventions, discourses, and practices. By combining these pieces like a collage, she reconstructs new possibilities in Québécois literature. That is, Robin's fictional work points not only to a new direction of Québécois literature, but also that of feminism which is accomplished by staying in the space of *hors-lieu*, or the not-place outside established categories of identity and cultural designation.

Throughout her writings, Robin demonstrates her consciousness of women's language and feminist translation. Pamela Banting explains the characteristics of feminist writing when she says "Women's language is simultaneous translation between language and the body, between the already spoken and the unspeakable, between the familiar and the un- and/ or de-familiarized" (Banting 1994, 175). In *L'immense fatigue des pierres*, Robin's protagonist, "une fille," traces her childhood memories through her bodily senses. "I dream of these landscapes, these stones, these monuments, these pieces of fixed history which are your smell, your aura" (2000, 13).

Régine Robin proposes a powerful cultural critique from the perspective of a singular otherness. The cultural translations and creations in the "third space" of migant authors cannot be described as marginal writings, but must be placed at the very centre of contemporary Québécois culture and society as they are leading Québécois literature to new directions.

Conclusion

As I have demonstrated throughout this essay, Robin's migrant writings describe her experiences of marginalization as a migrant in her new society. Her autobiographical writings, in which she inscribes ethnicity and ambivalent positioning between cultures, explore a third space in literature. Thus, by writing migrant woman's lived experiences, Robin is expanding the genre of autobiography, and in reworking this specific genre, she is constructing new autobiographical writing in Quebec. Robin uses such techniques to create new spaces, as Elizabeth Grosz explains in *Architecture from Outside*. Grosz explains the in-between space of subject and object or the subversive space of binary: "The space in between things is the space in which things are undone, the space to the side and around, which is the space of subversion and fraying, the edge of any identity's limits. In short, it is the space of the bounding and undoing of the identities, which constitute it" (2000, 92).

This is what Robin described in her new autobiographical writings: she deconstructs the boundaries between autobiography and fictional stories, and between inside and outside to construct hybrid identities. By so doing, she invents a new possible space in this genre. Furthermore, her in-between writings go beyond the boundaries between fictional stories and cultural critiques. Thus, Régine Robin's autobiographical writings create a new space in Québécois society and culture.

Notes

All translations, except for that of Régine Robin's *The Wanderer* are by this paper's author.

1 For example, Régine Robin edited two issues of *Cahiers de recherché sociologique*: 13 (1989), "L'Énigme du texte littéraire: La sociologie et l'apport des réflexions," and 26 (1996), "La sociologie saisie par la literature."

2 The original versions of *L'immense fatigue des pierres* were published in *Parole métèque* 2 and 3 (1987), and *Vice Versa* 24 (1988). However, she did not call them "biofiction" at the time.

References

Bhabha, Homi K. 1990. The Third Space. In *Identity: Community, culture, difference,* ed. Jonathan Rutherford, 207–21. London: Lawrence and Wishart.

Brossard, Nicole. 1984. *Journal intime ou voilà donc un manuscrit.* Montreal: Les Herbes Rouges.

Dumont-Johnson, Micheline, et al., eds. 1992. *L'histoire des femmes au Québec depuis quatre siècles.* Montreal: Le Jour.

Godard, Barbara, ed. 1994. *Collaboration in the Feminine: Writing on Women and Culture from Tessera.* Toronto: Second Story.

Gould, Karen. 1990. *Writing in the feminine: Feminism and experimental writing in Quebec.* Carbondale: Southern Illinois Univ. Press.

Grosz, Elizabeth. 2000. *Architecture from the outside: Essays on virtual and real space.* Cambridge, MA: MIT Press.

Harel, Simon. 1992. La parole orpheline de l'écrivain migrant. In *Montréal imaginaire: Ville et littérature,* ed. Pierre Nepveu and Gilles Marcotte. Montreal: Fides.

Kogawa, Joy. 1981. *Obasan.* Toronto: Penguin.

Lecarme, Jacques, and Elaine Lecarme-Tabone. 1997. *L'autobiographie.* Paris: Armand Colin.

Michael, Magali Cornier. 1996. *Feminism and the postmodern impulse.* New York: State Univ. of New York Press.

Michalska, Madeleine-Ouellette. 1985. *Tentation de dire: journal.* Montreal: Québec/ Amérique.

Robin, Régine. 1987a. L'Amnésie parfois. *La parole métèque: Le magazine du renouveau féministe* 3 (automne): 22–23.

———. 1987b. L'immense fatigue des pierres. *La parole métèque: Le magazine du renouveau féministe* 2 (été): 10–11.

———. 1988. Ce serait un roman ... ou Montréal comme hors-lieu. *Vice Versa* 24: 23–24.

———. 1989a. *Kafka.* Paris: Pierre Belfond.

———. 1989b. Présentation: L'Énigme de teste littéraire. *Cahiers de recherche sociologique* 12: 5–20.

———. 1989c. *Le roman mémoriel: De l'histoire à l'écriture du hors-lieu.* Montreal: Préambule.

———. 1991. Entre l'enfermement communautaire et le désastre individualiste: une voix pour l'écriture juive. In *Montréal: l'invention juive; Actes du colloque tenu le 2 mars 1990 à l'Université de Montréal,* ed. Groupe de recherche Montréal Imaginaire. Montreal: Département d'études françaises, Université de Montréal.

———. 1992. Sortir de l'ethnicité. In *Métamorphoses d'une utopie,* ed. Jean-Michel Lacroix and Fulvio Caccia. Paris: Presses de la Sorbonne nouvelle/Triptyque.

———. 1993a. *La Québécoite.* Montreal: TYPO.

———. 1993b. *Le Deuil de l'origine: Une langue en trop, la langue en moins.* Saint-Denis, France: Presses Universitaires de Vincennes.

———. 1997a. *Le Golem de l'écriture: De l'autofiction au Cybersoi.* Montreal: XYZ Éditure.

———. 1997b. The writing of an Allophone from France: Afterward to *The Wanderer* fifteen years later. In *The Wanderer* (*La Québécoite*), trans. Phillis Aronoff. Montreal: Alter Ego.

———. 1999a. L'écriture d'une allophone d'arigine française. *Tangent* 59 (janvier): 26–37.

———. 2000. *L'immense fatigue des pierres.* Montreal: XYZ Éditeur.

Robin, Régine, and Marc Angenot. 1991. *La Sociologie de la littérature: un historique.* Montreal: Ciadest.

Robin, Régine, and Jean-François Côté. 1996. Présentation: La sociologie saisie par la littérature. *Cahiers de recherche sociologique* 26: 5–14.

Théoret, France. 1982. *Nous parlelons comme on écrit.* Montreal: Les Herbes Rouges.

WENDY ROY 🍁

"The ensign of the mop and the dustbin": The Maternal and the Material in Autobiographical Writings by Laura Goodman Salverson and Nellie McClung

LAURA GOODMAN SALVERSON'S *Confessions of an Immigrant's Daughter* appears to be a natural candidate for studies of feminist and working-class life writing in Canada. A first-person account of the life of a woman who was born of Icelandic immigrant parents in the latter part of the nineteenth century, the book won a Governor-General's Literary Award in 1939. After the announcement of the award, *Confessions* was touted in *Canadian Author and Bookman* as an important Canadian cultural document that revealed "the resolution, persistence, devotion, loyalty, and capacity for endurance of the immigrant class" and described the "slow birth and development of the spirit of a nation" (Morgan-Powell 1940, 13). More than thirty-five years later, Salverson's autobiography was still appreciated as a fine example of a traditional autobiography; in the 1976 *Literary History of Canada*, Jay Macpherson described it as "one of the most rounded, intelligent, and attractive of Canadian life-stories" (1976, 131).

But as Daisy Neijmann demonstrates in "Fighting with Blunt Swords," neither Salverson's autobiography nor her novels have subsequently been adopted into the Canadian literary canon (1999, 138). Nor, I would argue, has her autobiography been wholeheartedly identified as representative of either feminist or class resistance by the few critics who have engaged with it over the past twenty years. Helen Buss exemplifies this ambivalence when she states in *Mapping Our Selves* that Salverson's experience "does not radicalize her politically or philosophically, giving her a facilitating feminist stance," and that she is never converted from seeing "femaleness as at fault to finding the conditions of female life in patriarchy at fault" (1993, 176, 177). Barbara Powell makes a parallel judgement when she asserts that Salverson "never did learn an authentic woman's tongue to tell her own story," and that her goal in writing "was to write like a man; to be her cultured literate father's 'own true son'" (1992, 78). Kristjana Gunnars precedes Buss and Powell in tacitly criticizing Salverson for her perceived rejection of the maternal and domestic, in an otherwise sympathetic discussion of *Confessions* as an exemplification of a self divided by ethnicity and gender (1986). Terrence Craig's even earlier discussion of culture and ethnicity in *Confessions*, meanwhile, identifies Salverson's resentment of the fact that Icelanders, like other immigrants, were slotted into the working class on their arrival in North America, but then suggests that despite this consciousness of class position, "Her democratic principles were not very socialist." He concludes, in fact, that Salverson wrote out of "a sense of ethnic and cultural superiority," and claimed "kinship" with the English-Canadian elite (1985, 85, 86).

In contrast to these criticisms, I contend that Salverson's autobiography resists strictures of gender and class, as well as those of minority ethnicity, by testifying to the material conditions of life for a child of immigrants to Canada, who lived in urban poverty most of their lives. Details of these life circumstances are abundant in her text, from the sweatshop conditions of the Winnipeg saddlery in which her father worked; to the flies, dirty drinking water, and contaminated milk that killed her infant brothers and sisters; to the lack of medical care and proper nutrition during pregnancy that resulted in the deaths of women who gave birth in her aunt's maternity hospital in Duluth, Minnesota; and to the sexual harassment that she experienced in her own low-paying and back-breaking work as a domestic servant and seamstress in Duluth and Winnipeg. Salverson's narrative is not just that of a woman, not just that of a child of Icelandic immigrants, but that of a person who lived in poverty in North America at the turn of the twentieth century. She points to the combined effects of ethnicity, gender, and class when she asserts that "For girls like us the dice were loaded from the start. The ensign of the mop and the dustbin hung over our cradles" (1939, 323). Her inscription of her life experiences and those of people around her in her autobiography (and to some extent in her works of fiction) represents her resistance to the limited life choices assigned women in her social and cultural position. Although Salverson follows conventional autobiographical practice by structuring her book as a *Künstlerroman*, and by curtailing discussion of her own bodily experience, at the same time she resists in part the traditional autobiographical silence about experiences of the body, by providing details of the material conditions of the lives of poor urban women that led to their deaths in childbirth, and their children's deaths during infancy. The reproductive suffering that helped to define working-class women thus becomes an integral part of Salverson's narrative, as she discusses women's "labour" in terms both of maternity and of paid and unpaid work.

Critical comment on Salverson's autobiography can be contrasted with analyses of two contemporaneous Canadian autobiographical narratives (one published four years before *Confessions* and the other six years after), both written by her friend and mentor Nellie McClung. All three books are about the development of an author, and about what McClung explicitly represents as the birth of a political consciousness. McClung and Salverson directly credit one another's influence on their books. Salverson writes that she sent a few chapters of her first novel, *The Viking Heart* (1923), to McClung, whom she had met when McClung was on a lecture tour, and was influenced by her new friend's suggestion that "a more colourful opening would enhance the story" (1939, 407). McClung, meanwhile, credits the increased introspection of her own second autobiographical work, *The Stream Runs Fast* (1945), in contrast to her more fact-based first autobiography *Clearing in the West* (1935), to criticism from Salverson that she had not revealed enough in her first narrative. She quotes Salverson as writing to her, "Be more personal in your new book.... Break down and tell all! We want to see you and know how your mind was working" (1945, 145).

Neither Salverson nor McClung "tell all," however, especially in their abbreviated descriptions of childbirth and mothering. Yet while feminist critics of McClung often valorize the one passage in which she complains about pregnancy-related nausea, those who tackle Salverson's *Confessions* almost universally critique her personal resistance to the pain and danger of childbirth, and the drudgery of maternity. Writers such as Buss (1993), Misao Dean (1998), and Janice Fiamengo (2000) interpret McClung's comment that if such nausea were a man's ailment a cure would have long since been found, as evidence of a burgeoning feminist consciousness. They point in particular to her judgement that the lack of a cure is a "black conspiracy against women," and her assertion that "Women should change conditions, not merely endure them" (1945, 16). Buss quotes McClung's characterization of this scene as a "climacteric," and suggests that it demonstrates her "desire to make common cause with other women" (129), while Dean calls it her "'conversion' to a life of political activism on behalf of other women" (91). Only Fiamengo notes the apparently contradictory denouement to this scene, in which McClung's male doctor helps her come to grips with her suffering by reinforcing for her the importance of motherhood. Fiamengo interprets this passage as an example of the way that McClung "mobiliz[es] the ethical power of motherhood" in a strategic essentialism that allows her to appropriate conservative ideologies, and revise them for her own feminist discursive purposes (2000, 76).

In contrast, Buss, Powell, and Gunnars find no evidence of the development of a feminist consciousness in Salverson's single, astonishing comment on the birth of her son: "There is nothing to say of my baby, except that the prospect bored me, and to give it an enterprising turn, I decided to travel fifteen hundred miles two weeks before he was born, to test the twilight sleep" (1939, 375). "Twilight sleep" was the name given to a procedure introduced in Austria in 1902 in which doctors administered scopolamine and morphine to labouring women to produce a semi-conscious state and memory loss (Baird 1916; Boyd nd: 2). The Twilight Sleep Association in North America identified as its aim the promotion of "painless childbirth" (Boyd 19). However, as a result of Salverson's decision to seek out these drugs, Gunnars concludes that, for Salverson, "Women's fate is an unwanted fate" and the experience of childbirth "a nuisance" (152). Powell suggests that while Salverson wrote in part to "champion the cause of women and rail against their domestic enslavement," her narrative demonstrates a "distaste and horror for the sorrows and dangers of motherhood" (79, 82). And Buss even more explicitly asserts that Salverson's decision to undergo twilight sleep is an "effort to avoid the worst thing she can imagine, consciousness during the embodied experience of labouring" (179).

An implied critique of the rejection of "embodied experience" is also evident in Buss's discussion of a resolution Salverson makes as a child, recorded near the beginning of *Confessions*: "I WON'T eat an EGG!" (1939, 12). Buss interprets this assertion as a refusal not only of the nourishment offered by the mother, but also of women's reproductive role: what Buss calls "the 'egg' of womanhood" (173). This refusal is further exemplified for Buss in the words Salverson uses to describe the experiences of childbirth she later overhears in her aunt's midwifery hospital in Duluth, and the "shock of horror" she feels when she realizes the significance of "these ghastly cries":

> Everything in me revolted, every quivering sense rebelling hotly against this obscene anguish at the roots of life. Yes, now I understood what was going on up there. What, my terrified mind told me, was going on and on and on all over the whole wide world. A shambles of suffering, senseless and cruel. And, I thought with fierce loathing, no life was worth such a trial of suffering.
>
> I wanted to run, to hide for ever from such hideous reality. (259)[1]

Buss characterizes the use of these powerful words—horror, ghastly, obscene, senseless, cruel, loathing, hideous—as "disgust with birthing." But she adds a comment that I interpret as key to Salverson's decision to include this passage—that it "coincidentally gives us an unusually detailed picture of a bodily activity and its social context" (1993, 177). Salverson's goal, I suggest, is not to demonize childbirth, but instead to attempt to provide readers of her autobiography with a realistic description of the experience for poor and immigrant women, and she does so not only in her autobiography, but also in *The Viking Heart*. In that novel, Salverson devotes six pages to describing the difficult birth of her protagonists' third child, comparing it to "a battle where the valor displayed might have honored any military battlefield" (53). The woman suffers such pain that her husband thinks it "monstrous! Indecent!" (54), and she and her child are saved only when a midwife turns two old soup spoons into improvised forceps.[2]

Discussions of Salverson's dismissive words in *Confessions* about child-birth and mothering often fail to adequately acknowledge what Shirley Neu-man has identified as the autobiographical genre's traditional silence about experience of the body (1989, 1–2). Salverson, like McClung, was ostensibly writing an autobiographical account of the development of a literary and political consciousness. This intellectual focus means that McClung is as silent about personal experiences of the body as Salverson's twilight-sleep-induced memory loss has apparently made her. Thus during McClung's description of the birth of her first son, she provides details about the weather, the scent of roses and wet earth outside, and her child's appearance, but never the labour itself (1945, 25). Similarly, both McClung and Salver-son omit descriptions of any romantic or sexual attraction for their hus-bands. Salverson notes that economic circumstances, including her inability to find anything but the most menial of work, led to her marriage to George Salverson, which she calls a good way to "assume a time-honoured business of commonplace existence" (374). But she hints at previous sexual experi-ence when she writes that he had agreed to marry her despite her "confes-sion" about an earlier Irish sweetheart, "the only man I have ever loved as every good novelist would have his heroines love" (374, 366). In contrast, as Misao Dean points out, McClung never mentions other possible roman-tic interests (1998, 92). She presents her courtship in almost as abrupt and matter-of-fact a manner as does Salverson, claiming that she decided when she met Mrs. McClung Senior, before she had even seen Wes McClung, that she wanted her for a mother-in-law (1935, 269).

Salverson's meagre descriptions of her own bodily experience thus have much in common with those of another woman autobiographer of her era. What is unusual in *Confessions* is the sustained critique of other women's enforced maternity. At first, Salverson represents pregnancy as a force of nature. She writes that her mother's "woman's body, like a creature apart, was pursuing its own creative mysteries" (1939, 206), and later, ironically, that repeated pregnancies were "nature, and the will of God and had to be endured" (289). But by age ten, Salverson is aware that her mother is "oppressed" by unwanted pregnancy (211), and when she and her friends become young women, they are politicized by witnessing the reproductive experiences of their mothers. Salverson puts it this way: "Nature be damned, said we, fierce as fishwives. If other laws of nature were circumvented and controlled, why should generation be the one exception? Why indeed, thought we, glaring at each other helplessly" (289). In raising the desire and the need for contraception, Salverson voices a resistance to enforced childbirth. She also notes the societal double standard that makes abortions available and even condoned for those who can afford them, such as the friend of the wealthy family for whom she works as a domestic servant (333). Given the lack of access to contraception and the dangers of childbirth, Salverson's assessment, after her brief apprenticeship with her midwife aunt, that childbirth is "a messy business at best," thus can be reinterpreted not as personal disgust but as an expression of feminist and class politics.

In *Confessions*, Salverson outlines the dangers of maternity for all women, but especially for poor women. Her autobiography presents sexuality, in the words of Regenia Gagnier, "in material as well as ideological terms—in terms of reproduction as well as discourse and eroticism" (1991, 58). Gagnier argues in *Subjectivities: A History of Self-Representation in Britain, 1832–1920* that a consideration of material conditions is crucial to any study of first-person accounts of pregnancy and childbirth up to the 1920s. She points out that letters from Victorian women "suggest that reproductive suffering was an essential component of the subjectivity in question: that is what it was like to be a working-class woman" (60). During their often continuous pregnancies, working-class women of this era, in contrast to their middle-class counterparts, were deprived of adequate nutrition and medical care, and often had to do arduous work at home as well as continue their labour in the paid workforce (59). McClung's description of her own prenatal and postnatal care in a small Manitoba town exemplifies this class discrepancy. In McClung's experience, which she represents as typical of small-town, middle-class Canadian women in 1897, she paid a doctor $25 for prenatal care and home delivery, and a practical nurse $1 a day for nine days of round-the-clock care and fourteen more days of daytime care (1945, 20). McClung's account is starkly contradicted by Salverson's description of her poverty-stricken urban mother's contemporaneous experience of childbirth, in which she consulted only her midwife sister-in-law, and only when they lived in the same city, because doctors' bills impoverished the family. While McClung writes that "It was all very simple and satisfactory" (1945, 20), Salverson highlights the dangers for poor immigrant mothers and their babies. She reveals that her own mother almost died giving birth to stillborn twins (1939, 70), and that the woman whose experience of childbirth so disturbed her when she overheard it in her aunt's maternity hospital died two years later during another delivery (262). Her strong words about that scene thus can be seen as evidence not, as Buss argues, of "that which should not be represented in communication, a banned content" (176–77), but of that which Salverson feels it essential to testify. Similarly, her reference to boredom at the prospect of the birth of her own child can be reread as a desire to avoid thinking not only about potential pain, but also about very real risks to health and life, both for herself and her child.

A related part of Salverson's testimony is her repeated description of the births and deaths of her own small brothers and sisters as the family moved first to Canada, then to the United States, then back to again in an unavailing quest for the fulfilment of the immigrant goal of prosperity. She herself stops naming them, and even stops counting, but perhaps a dozen children are born and die. When Salverson writes that she has always had "a horror of new-born babies," it is in a passage in which she describes the birth of yet another unnamed and unwanted brother (1939, 215). Her "horror" thus is not of birth, but of the impending death that may follow. In her married life, Salverson repeats part of her parents' pattern as she and her husband move from city to city and job to job in search of economic security. She makes it clear in her narrative, however, that she is unwilling to completely reproduce the life and limited choices of her mother. She challenges her potential future—"Just to eat and sleep, propagate your misery, and die!" (323)—and she determines that she will not spend her life producing children who, if by chance they live, will only provide cheap labour for the sweatshops. As she asks, "Who could be grateful for bleak existence full of misery and deprivation?" (289).

Once economic necessity forces her into marriage at age twenty-two, Salverson concludes that her attempts "to conform to the time-honoured duties of women" result in "nothing but endless work and disillusionment": she writes, "I had no life of my own, no inner satisfaction, no feeling of justifying my existence" (1939, 395). As she has done throughout her childhood, Salverson turns to literature as the locus of inner satisfaction, the sphere where she can develop an alternate subjectivity to the one mapped out for her by her class position. She describes reading a book propped up against a row of jars while she stones peaches to make jam (378) and writing fiction and poetry as she does housework: "I could carry on pages of conversation as I flew about, dusting, sweeping, ironing, and baking, and never lose a word of it!" (398), she writes, then describes composing poetry "while the bacon frizzled in the pan" (404). The psychological effects of such double-duty are evident in her account of the day her first book appears in the bookstores; she is "busily stoning plums" and decides to her husband's amazement that she must finish making the jam before they can go out to look at the book (412).

While Salverson describes the conflicts between housework and writing, she seldom writes specifically of childcare. Helen Buss suggests that for Salverson, motherhood, "like other nasty aspects of life, such as faulty plumbing or cold winters, can be coped with in a competent, no-nonsense manner" (1993, 178). Indeed, when Salverson does mention her son, she comments on his attractiveness, but also notes that "He was very little trouble, for he had never been fussed over" (1939, 391). In Carolyn Steedman's analysis of her own experiences as a working-class child in the middle of the twentieth century, she quotes her mother as saying, "Never have children dear…, they ruin your life." Women to whom Steedman tells this story are shocked, in much the same way that feminist readers are shocked by Salverson's suggestion that she was bored by the prospect of her own child. Steedman concludes, however, that for working-class women "it is *ordinary* not to want your children" and "normal to find them a nuisance" (1987, 17). The economic bases for this feeling become clear when Steedman writes that, as a child, she was afraid to become ill because her mother would have to stay home from work and the family would lose money (41–42). In *Confessions*, Salverson demonstrates even more clearly the unmanageable economic and social burden of working mothers with children. She records a family crisis before her birth when her father was hospitalized with a serious illness, and her mother was forced to permanently give up for adoption their youngest surviving child, a girl, so that she could go out to work to support the family and pay the medical bills. Each day that Salverson's mother went to work, she left her remaining six-year-old son alone in their rented rooms (1939, 92–93).

Salverson provides what Buss calls a "tidal wave" (1993, 175) of documentation of the conditions of working-class life at the turn of the twentieth century. She repeatedly counts out the pittance sweatshop workers earned and compares it to the high cost of lodging and food, and she lists the usurious rates of the loan-sharks who preyed on poor families (139, 85–87,

327, 347). She describes in especial detail her father's work in a Winnipeg saddlery where, she writes, he "eked out a meagre living under the time-honoured piecework system beloved of all sweatshop autocrats" (39). Her father had come to Canada hoping to make his living as an artisan; instead, he sat fourteen hours a day, six days a week, stitching heavy harnesses by hand (49). The factory in which he worked was an abandoned skating rink with inadequate light and no ventilation, where during the summer "rain leaked down through the rotting roof," and during the winter "frost coated the walls" (85). Salverson points out that because her father was raised as a gentleman farmer in Iceland, "he was not fitted for, nor accustomed to, hard manual labour" (81), and as a result was constantly ill. But her description of his experiences makes it clear that no one should be expected to endure such working conditions. She universalizes her father's suffering by fictionalizing it in The Viking Heart; a character in that book dies after working for a few months in a harness shop, described as "an insufferable hole, cold and unsanitary" that "was once an old skating rink" (1923, 109).

McClung also describes sweatshops in Winnipeg, but her analysis is from a position outside rather than inside the system. She herself never worked in a factory or as a domestic servant. Instead, the more prosperous situation of her rural Irish-Scots family allowed her to live out Salverson's unfulfilled dream of going to Normal School and teaching. While Salverson worked as a maid, McClung employed a series of immigrant "hired girls" so that she could leave her children at home while she conducted her political work. But McClung knew that both domestic service and sweatshops entailed unacceptable working conditions. She justified her employment of young women by advocating recognition that "the maid" was a human being with "ambitions, desires and sensibilities" who "must be allowed a certain amount of liberty" (1945, 258). She recounted an occasion when she and a colleague conducted Conservative Manitoba Premier Rodmond Roblin on a tour of sweatshops that employed women, in an attempt to convince him to appoint female inspectors who might improve working conditions. After describing how they escorted him down "dark, slippery stairs to an airless basement," where the floor was littered with garbage, the noise overwhelming, and the toilet blocked, she quotes Roblin as crying "I never knew such hell holes existed!" (103, 104). Instead of improving the regulation of factory conditions, however, he took the two women to task for ferreting out "such utterly disgusting things" (105). McClung represents this incident, and a subsequent conversation with Roblin about women's suffrage, as crystallizing her resolve to work to defeat his government.

In contrast, Salverson's account of her father's inability to bear sweatshop working conditions is sometimes interpreted as an apologia for his failings (Craig 1985, 88), rather than as a condition of her family's life that led to the growth of her political awareness. A related criticism is sometimes made of her apparent psychic identification with her father. Powell concludes, for example, that Salverson "rejected the female mode of domestic discourse, exemplified by the gossiping conversations of her mother, in favour of the masculine, intellectual world of written ideas inhabited by her father" (1992, 80). In parts of her autobiography, Salverson indeed appears to privilege her romantic father over her practical mother. Early in the narrative, she calls him "impetuous" and "warm-hearted" in the same passage in which she describes her mother as "deeply reserved" and "somewhat cold in deportment" (1939, 69). Later, she asserts that "no matter how gentle and kind mamma might be…, I knew quite well that it was papa who came nearer to understanding me," and declares her mother at fault that "this incipient understanding was not permitted to grow and outlast childhood" (108).

Salverson's conflictual feelings about her mother are not unlike those of McClung, who writes that while her father encouraged her curiosity and self-confidence, her mother consistently criticized those same qualities, calling her forward or conceited or a show-off (1935, 150–51, 205–206, 237). Like McClung, though, Salverson identifies with her mother in powerful ways, which include the literary as well as the domestic and the familial. Salverson points out that before the family left Iceland, her father expected his young wife "to shoulder all responsibility" while he gambled away their farm (1939, 69), and concludes that "in any crucial period it was mamma who saved the situation; mamma who exhibited the virtues she thought it beneath dignity to frame in words" (319–20). And far from dismissing her mother's conversation as gossip, Salverson revels in her female parent's intellectual and literary curiosity, relating incidents in which she recited Icelandic sagas (29) and put aside the housework so that she could read the latest serial (107). When in the final chapter of Confessions Salverson discusses the composition of her own novel, she justifies her literary project in part by pointing to her mother's defense of novels and lifelong interest in "plenty of light, and a good story" (401). Thus the parent to whom Salverson relates herself in her title, Confessions of an Immigrant's Daughter, is not necessarily always or only her father. The patriarchally defined tradition of autobiography, which represents the literate father as a crucial formative influence on the development of the author, is supplemented and sometimes contradicted in Salverson's text by passages that reveal the equally powerful influence of the literate mother.

As I have already suggested, Salverson's political awareness is evident in the way that she witnesses and testifies to her mother's experiences of maternity and her father's experiences of work. Salverson's belief in the value of paid labour develops when she works as a domestic servant in a wealthy household, and clears away leftover food while thinking of hungry children she knows. She writes that she becomes convinced that these "natural resources" are not "solely designed for the enjoyment of the few who invested their money"—money that would have been worthless "without the labour of the disinherited" (1939, 328). When Salverson considers war, she decides that it occurs not to maintain liberty but instead "to advance the trade monopolies of private interests." She goes on to compare workers to unwilling conscripts in war, writing that she suspects that "the millions of workers toiling in factories and mines are nothing but conscripts in a service dedicated to wealth and privilege" (376).

While Salverson provides several brief analyses of the relationship between labour and capital, her discussion of the complex interrelation of gender and labour is less articulate. She notes, but does not analyze, the fact that while some of her male school friends have "run to luck" in finding jobs (1939, 318), she and her female friends can find work only as garment workers, servants, or store clerks. She eloquently describes her own versions of the sweatshop experience, hauling water up several flights of stairs or "sitting still, hour upon hour" sewing (346), but her autobiography only alludes to the additional power imbalances caused by gender inequalities in the workplace. These power imbalances lead both to lower pay and to repeated sexual harassment by employers. When Salverson works at a theatre during high school, the stage manager tells her she can sell her "perfect pair of legs" to a vaudeville house down the street, then reaches down and uncovers them (287). When she works as a domestic servant in a wealthy household, she is propositioned by the son, who bars her way on the stairs (336). Unable to show her resistance through words, she can only give him what she calls "a sturdy, bovine stare." Although she claims that "the incident had no significance," she does recognize its class implications; as she writes, she "chalked up another score against a class which has such scant respect for the sensibilities of those whom ill circumstances confine to humble service" (336). Later still, when she is working as a seamstress, she is propositioned by her employer, who uses her as his dress dummy. Again, her resistance is evident only in her silence; she affects what she calls "a pleasant stupidity," and, when he retaliates by "putting the screws" to her, quits and begins working at home (364). In describing this incident, Salverson is unable to make a definitive connection between gender and power. Instead, she records her shame about what has happened, writing that she "confessed this silly episode" to just one person, a female cousin (365).

Shame is often, understandably, Salverson's response to oppression. Pamela Fox points out in Class Fictions that those most likely to feel shame are members of marginal groups who are "made to feel 'inappropriate' by dominant cultural norms." Examples are often class-based, she suggests, ranging from "table manners to dress to a school child's meager lunch" (1994, 13). Just as Salverson's mother is ashamed to have guests witness the poverty of their home (1939, 50), so Salverson feels shame when she realizes how different she is from her schoolmates. Teased at school about her clothing, she suffers from what she terms "the horrid crime of being different" (244). Her shame is acute when, as a homeless young woman, she must work as a live-in servant. She reports having "pocketed pride" in order to do so (322): "On my day out I felt like a thief, stealing into the street from the narrow back alley" (329).[3] Salverson's revelation of her experience of shame might be interpreted as buying into negative constructions of the poor, but Fox views the revelation of shame instead as a possible avenue of resistance, because, she contends, "in the process of revealing the shame of being shamed, often one is exposing oppressive societal norms and values" (16). Salverson's autobiographical act of speech about her shame indeed exposes the social structures that oppress her. She does not just internalize shame; she depersonalizes it, by testifying to the systemic positioning of the shamed subject.

Giving voice to shame is part of the book's purpose, announced in a title that indicates that the book will consist of "Confessions." Leigh Gilmore suggests that confession is "the form of agency allowed a person who must always speak of transgression, who learns to confess in order to codify sinning and manage its presence" (1994, 58). The "sins" that Salverson confesses are her gender, her class, and her minority ethnicity, and she confesses these life conditions in a way that testifies to the systemic oppression at their roots.[4] Taken out of context, Salverson's representation of her life may not appear to exhibit a resistant female subjectivity, but within the appropriate historical, cultural, and material context, her inscription of the conditions of her young life, and her adult resistance to a replication of those conditions, are expressive of both a feminist and a class politics.

When S. Morgan-Powell commented in 1940 about Salverson's Governor-General's Award, he focused not on the often bleak details of her life history, as outlined in *Confessions*, but on the supposed characteristics of the "immigrant class," and on the role played by that class in the creation of Canada as a nation. By way of contrast, in a much more recent discussion of poverty narratives in Canada, Roxanne Rimstead analyzes *Confessions* for its critique of Canadian nationalist discourses of immigrant success (2001, 246). In another contemporary analysis of Salverson's writings, Daisy Neijmann argues that Salverson was eventually excluded from the Canadian canon because of the way that she was classed, including "her position as 'Other,' as woman and as ethnic" (1999, 138). Neijmann suggests that Salverson's literary works were "incompatible with the ruling Anglo-Canadian ideas of a national literature" because of their contentious focus on Canadian society from the perspective of poor immigrants (162).

These more recent recuperative discussions of Salverson's writings provide much-needed correctives to Craig's earlier assertion that Salverson wrote out of a sense of ethnic superiority that uplifted Icelanders at the expense of other groups (1985, 86). Salverson does make broad generalizations about immigrants, associating their characters and temperaments with their ethnicities, and she does negatively stereotype the Métis families that her own family encounters (156–57). Her generalizations are similar to the racialism evident in McClung's autobiographies and other writings, which Arun Mukherjee (1995) and Janice Fiamengo (2002) have so ably analyzed and contextualized.[5] But Salverson does not make her comments about race and ethnicity from the position of a member of the Anglo-Canadian elite. Instead, her position is very like that of the immigrant women McClung hired to take care of her household. Salverson focuses on ethnicity in her autobiography in order to highlight the downward mobility of immigrants, who may be literate gentlefolk in their old countries but become domestic servants or sweatshop workers in the new. In addition, she makes cultural distinctions so that she can consistently represent Icelanders as literary, and thus establish that her own interest in writing is not just an upstart activity by a Canadian newcomer.

Part of the purpose of the concluding chapter of *Confessions* is to reiterate Salverson's point that her modest success as a writer is paradoxically both expected of an Icelander and against all odds for the female child of poor immigrants to Canada. Her novel is represented as the fulfilment of the impertinent goal announced at the end of the second section of *Confessions*: "I, too, will write a book" (1939, 238). But as an engaged and sympathetic reader, I initially found the conclusions to both Salverson's and McClung's autobiographies disappointing. McClung ends *Clearing in the West* as though it were a romance, with the "Reader, I married him" wrap-up essential to fictional autobiographies such as *Jane Eyre*. She briefly describes her wedding, at age twenty-two, almost forty years earlier and concludes with the hopeful and effusive words from which her title is taken: "It was clearing in the West! Tomorrow would be fine!" (1935, 378). Even the more realistic ending of McClung's second autobiography, which mentions her sorrow at the death of her son, is disappointing in that it does not "tell all" and reveal that he committed suicide. The conclusion to Salverson's *Confessions*, meanwhile, makes use of conventions of the autobiographical genre that celebrate personal individual achievement.[6] As with other stories about the development of an artist, *Confessions* ends with the publication of Salverson's first novel at age thirty-two. After describing harrowing details of lives lived in need, Salverson blithely asserts that the publication of that book proves that "what you want, you can do, no matter what the odds against you!" (1939, 413).

Regenia Gagnier suggests that when working-class writers use literary models developed by middle-class authors, the gap between "ideology and experience" leads to "the disintegration of the narrative the writer hopes to construct" (1991, 46). Salverson's concluding assertion of personal achievement indeed destabilizes the narrative of collective struggle she has to this point constructed. But when she goes on to suggest that she could weep for some other hopeful young writer, some other daughter of immigrants who "longs to justify her race as something more than a hewer of wood" (1939, 414), she again evokes her previous descriptions of sweatshop work and class-marked reproductive labour. The practical details of Salverson's autobiographical narrative thus continue to undermine her purported adherence to literary conventions, and assert instead her awakening to political consciousness.

Notes

1 While Buss implies that Salverson witnessed this birth when she was an apprentice at her aunt's hospital, Salverson in fact indicates that she overheard the event as a child sent on an errand by her mother. Buss also errs when she writes that Salverson declared to her parents, "I WON'T eat an EGG!" As her narrative makes clear, she made this resolution only to herself.

2 Salverson's autobiographical description of her own birth is understated, but similarly related to the domestic. Almost one quarter of the way into *Confessions*, she writes that she had "the bad manners to interrupt my mother in the midst of making headcheese—and for no better reason than to be born" (1939, 93). Although Salverson begins her autobi-

ography with her earliest memories (which she relates in third person), much of the first section describes her parents' difficult lives before her birth, including their decision to immigrate and their hardships once they arrive. McClung, in contrast, begins *Clearing in the West* with a description of her birth, but presents it in the third person ("It was a girl!" [1935, 5]), through the perspective of a disappointed older sibling who wanted a brother. The next passage begins with McClung's first memory, written in first person.

3 In light of Salverson's shame, McClung's assertion of the importance of letting her "girls" use the front door and entertain their friends in the den appears to be more than just a minor concession to salve her conscience (1935, 258).

4 Buss points to a "generic ambivalence" in the book: while the title indicates it will be about "the spiritual development of an individual," the foreword proposes a memoir which "interweaves the 'personal chronicle' with the 'record of an age'" (1993, 172).

5 Fiamengo follows Anthony Appiah in distinguishing between racialism, "the belief that particular races share certain inherited traits and characteristics," and racism, the use of these traits "to create a physical, intellectual, and moral hierarchy" (2002, 86).

6 Neijmann points out that Salverson wrote two versions of a second autobiography that was never published (1999, 141). The manuscripts, written in the late 1950s and early 1960s, are held by the National Library of Canada. Unlike McClung's second autobiography, Salverson's unpublished volumes do not cover the latter half of her life, but instead recount again her childhood and the beginning of her writing career.

References

Baird, O.C. European "twilight sleep" or American, which? *National Eclectic Medical Association Quarterly* 7: 1915–16. Reprinted at http://www.ibiblio.org/herb med/eclectic/journals/nemaq1915/02-twil-sleep.html.

Boyd, Mary. *The story of Dämmerschlaf*. New York: Twilight Sleep Association, n.d.

Buss, Helen. 1993. *Mapping our selves: Canadian women's autobiography in English*. Montreal and Kingston: McGill-Queen's Univ. Press.

Craig, Terrence. 1985. The confessional revisited: Laura Salverson's Canadian work. *Studies in Canadian Literature* 10:81–93.

Dean, Misao. 1998. *Practising femininity: Domestic realism and the performance of gender in early Canadian fiction*. Toronto: Univ. of Toronto Press.

Fiamengo, Janice. 2000. A legacy of ambivalence: Responses to Nellie McClung. *Journal of Canadian Studies* 34 (4):70–87.

———. 2002. Rediscovering our foremothers again: The racial ideas of Canada's early feminists, 1885–1945. *Essays on Canadian Writing* 75:85–117.

Fox, Pamela. 1994. *Class fictions: Shame and resistance in the British working-class novel, 1890–1945*. Durham, NC: Duke Univ. Press.

Gagnier, Regenia. 1991. *Subjectivities: A history of self-representation in Britain, 1832–1920*. New York: Oxford Univ. Press.

Gilmore, Leigh. 1994. Policing truth: Confession, gender, and autobiographical authority. In *Autobiography and postmodernism*, ed. Kathleen Ashley, Leigh Gilmore, and Gerald Peters. 54–78. Boston: Univ. of Massachusetts Press.

Gunnars, Kristjana. 1986. Laura Goodman Salverson's confessions of a divided self. In *A mazing space: Writing Canadian women writing*, ed. Shirley Neuman and Smaro Kamboureli. Edmonton: Longspoon/NeWest, 148–53.

Macpherson, Jay. 1976. Autobiography. In vol. 2 of *Literary history of Canada: Canadian literature in English*, 2nd ed., ed. Alfred G. Bailey et al. 126–33. Toronto: Univ. of Toronto Press.

McClung, Nellie L. 1935. *Clearing in the West: My own story*. Toronto: Thomas Allen, 1964.

———. 1945. *The stream runs fast: My own story*. Toronto: Thomas Allen, 1965.

Morgan-Powell, S. 1940. The Governor-General's awards. *Canadian Author and Bookman* 17 (1):12–13.

Mukherjee, Arun. 1995. In a class of her own. *The Literary Review of Canada*, July–August: 20–23.

Neijmann, Daisy L. 1999. Fighting with blunt swords: Laura Goodman Salverson and the Canadian literary canon. *Essays on Canadian Writing* 67:138–73.

Neuman, Shirley. 1989. "An appearance walking in a forest the sexes burn": Autobiography and the construction of the feminine body. *Signature* 2:1–26.

Powell, Barbara. 1992. Laura Goodman Salverson: Her father's "own true son." *Canadian Literature* 133:78–89.

Rimstead, Roxanne. 2001. *Remnants of nation: On poverty narratives by women*. Toronto: Univ. of Toronto Press.

Salverson, Laura Goodman. 1939. *Confessions of an immigrant's daughter*. Toronto: Univ. of Toronto Press, 1981.

———. *The Viking heart*. 1923. Toronto: McClelland and Stewart, 1947.

Steedman, Carolyn. 1987. *Landscape for a good woman: A story of two lives*. New Brunswick, NJ: Rutgers Univ. Press.

Contributors ❧

ALBERT BRAZ is an assistant professor of comparative literature at the University of Alberta, specializing in Canadian literature in its inter-American contexts. He is the author of *The False Traitor: Louis Riel in Canadian Culture* (2003).

SALLY CHIVERS is an assistant professor of Canadian studies and English at Trent University. She is the author of *From Old Woman to Older Women: Contemporary Culture and Women's Narrative* (2003). Her current research interests include Canadian cultural depictions of aging and disability.

SUSANNA EGAN teaches in the Department of English at UBC, and has written on various aspects of autobiography. Her most recent book is *Mirror Talk: Genres of Crisis in Contemporary Autobiography.*

MICHEL FERRARI, associate professor at the University of Toronto in the Department of Human Development and Applied Psychology, is interested in the relations between moral identity and ethical expertise. More generally, his research explores the relations between personal identity and the development of particular forms of expertise these identities require.

ANN FUDGE SCHORMANS is a doctoral candidate at the Faculty of Social Work, University of Toronto. Ann's involvement with people with intellectual dis/Abilities spans her professional career as a social worker in both the Community Living and Child Welfare sectors, and as a foster and adoptive parent.

BARBARA HAVERCROFT, associate professor of French and Comparative Literature at the University of Toronto, has published extensively on recent French, Québécois, and German autobiographical writings, on feminism and post-modernism, and on literary theory. The author of *Oscillation and Subjectivity: Problems of Enunciation in the Novels of Robbe-Grillet, Sarraute, and Johnson* (forthcoming, University of Toronto Press), she is completing a book on gender and genre in contemporary life writing.

GABRIELE HELMS taught in the Department of English at UBC until her death in December 2004. She has published on auto/biography and Canadian literature; she is the author of *Challenging Canada: Dialogism and Narrative Techniques in Canadian Novels* (2003). The essay collection *Auto/biography in Canada: Critical Directions* is dedicated to her memory.

ANDREW LESK has published on Sinclair Ross, Leonard Cohen, John Glassco, Jack Hodgins, Chinua Achebe, queer theory, and the public function of universities. He has given papers on Todd Haynes, Shyam Selvadurai, Rider Haggard, Willa Cather, gay studies and homophobia, the culture industry, and Hollywood film. He teaches Canadian literature at the University of Toronto.

LAURIE MCNEILL is currently on a SSHRC post-doctoral fellowship at the University of Michigan. She has published on World War II civilian internment diaries from the South Pacific, and on web-diaries as life-writing.

JULIE RAK is an associate professor in the Department of English and Film Studies at the University of Alberta. Her recent publications include essays about auto/biography in Canadian and international journals and book collections, and the book *Negotiated Memory: Doukhobor Autobiographical Discourse* (University of British Columbia Press 2004).

DEENA RYMHS is assistant professor of English at St Francis Xavier University. She has just completed her dissertation on the experience of incarceration in First Nations writing. Her work has appeared in *Canadian Literature, Essays on Canadian Writing, Genre,* and *Studies in American Indian Literatures.*

WENDY ROY is an assistant professor of English at the University of Saskatchewan. Her research is on Canadian women's life writing, especially travel writing, and she has previously published articles on Margaret Laurence, Anna Jameson, and Carol Shields.

SI TRANSKEN has a doctorate in equity studies from the University of Toronto and is now completing an MA in First Nations studies and creative writing at UNBC. She also teaches at the University of Northern British Columbia. Her courses include Women and Social Policy, Family Counseling, and Social Work with Victims of Abuse. She has had work published in books such as *Feminist Utopias, Care and Consequences, Caring Communities,* and *Equity and Justice.* Her poetry has been published in Canadian Women's Studies, *Azure,* and *Reflections on Water.*

LJILJANA VULETIC is a doctoral candidate in applied cognitive science at the University of Toronto. For the past twenty years, she has been involved in working on assessment and interventions with children with autism. Her main research interests are cognitive development and early identification of children with autism.

YUKO YAMADE received a PhD Littérature at L'Université de Montréal. She previously taught at L'Université de Montréal and the University of Florida. She is currently doing postdoctoral research at Meiji University in Tokyo, Japan, and specializes in migrant women's writings in Japan, Germany, France, and Quebec.

Books in the Cultural Studies Series
Published by Wilfrid Laurier University Press

Slippery Pastimes: Reading the Popular in Canadian Culture edited by Joan Nicks and Jeannette Sloniowski
2002 / viii + 347 pp. / ISBN 0-88920-388-1

The Politics of Enchantment: Romanticism, Media and Cultural Studies by J. David Black
2002 / x + 200 pp. / ISBN 0-88920-400-4

Dancing Fear and Desire: Race, Sexuality, and Imperial Politics in Middle Eastern Dance by Stavros Stavrou Karayanni
2004 / xv + 244 pp. / ISBN 0-88920-454-3

Auto/Biography in Canada: Critical Directions edited by Julie Rak
2005 / viii + 280 pp. / ISBN 0-88920-478-0

Books in the Life Writing Series
Published by Wilfrid Laurier University Press

Haven't Any News: Ruby's Letters from the Fifties
edited by Edna Staebler with an Afterword by Marlene Kadar
1995 / x + 165 pp. / ISBN 0-88920-248-6

"I Want to Join Your Club": Letters from Rural Children, 1900-1920
edited by Norah L. Lewis with a Preface by Neil Sutherland
1996 / xii + 250 pp. (30 b&w photos) / ISBN 0-88920-260-5

And Peace Never Came by Elisabeth M. Raab with Historical Notes by Marlene Kadar
1996 / x + 196 pp. (12 b&w photos, map) / ISBN 0-88920-281-8

Dear Editor and Friends: Letters from Rural Women of the North-West, 1900-1920
edited by Norah L. Lewis
1998 / xvi + 166 pp. (20 b&w photos) / ISBN 0-88920-287-7

The Surprise of My Life: An Autobiography by Claire Drainie Taylor
with a Foreword by Marlene Kadar
1998 / xii + 268 pp. (+ 8 colour photos and 92 b&w photos) /ISBN 0-88920-302-4

Memoirs from Away: A New Found Land Girlhood by Helen M. Buss / Margaret Clarke
1998 / xvi + 153 pp. / ISBN 0-88920-350-4

The Life and Letters of Annie Leake Tuttle: Working for the Best
by Marilyn Färdig Whiteley
1999 / xviii + 150 pp. / ISBN 0-88920-330-X

Marian Engel's Notebooks: "Ah, mon cahier, écoute"
edited by Christl Verduyn
1999 / viii + 576 pp. / ISBN 0-88920-333-4 cloth / ISBN 0-88920-349-0 paper

Be Good Sweet Maid: The Trials of Dorothy Joudrie by Audrey Andrews
1999 / vi + 276 pp. / ISBN 0-88920-334-2

Working in Women's Archives: Researching Women's Private Literature
and Archival Documents edited by Helen M. Buss and Marlene Kadar
2001 / vi + 120 pp. / ISBN 0-88920-341-5

Repossessing the World: Reading Memoirs by Contemporary Women
by Helen M. Buss
2002 / xxvi + 206 pp. / ISBN 0-88920-408-X cloth / ISBN 0-88920-410-1 paper

Chasing the Comet: A Scottish-Canadian Life by Patricia Koretchuk
2002 / xx + 244 pp. / ISBN 0-88920-407-1

The Queen of Peace Room by Magie Dominic
2002 / xii + 115 pp. / ISBN 0-88920-417-9

China Diary: The Life of Mary Austin Endicott by Shirley Jane Endicott
2002 / xvi + 251pp. / ISBN 0-88920-412-8

The Curtain: Witness and Memory in Wartime Holland by Henry G. Schogt
2003 / xii + 132pp. / ISBN 0-88920-396-2

Teaching Places by Audrey J. Whitson
2003 / xiii + 178pp. / ISBN 0-88920-425-X

Through the Hitler Line by Laurence F. Wilmot, M.C.
2003 / xvi + 152pp. / ISBN 0-88920-448-9

Where I Come From by Vijay Agnew
2003 / xiv + 298pp. / ISBN 0-88920-414-4

The Water Lily Pond by Han Z. Li
2004 / x +254pp. / ISBN 0-88920-431-4

The Life Writings of Mary Baker McQuesten: Victorian Matriarch edited by Mary J.
Anderson 2004 / xxii + 338 pp. / ISBN 0-88920-437-3

Incorrigible by Velma Demerson
2004 / vi + 178pp. / ISBN 0-88920-444-6

Auto/biography in Canada: Critical Directions edited by Julie Rak
2005 / viii + 264 pp. ISBN 0-88920-478-0

Tracing the Autobiographical edited by Marlene Kadar, Linda Warley, Jeanne Perreault,
and Susanna Egan
2005 / viii + 280 pp. / ISBN 0-88920-476-4